Tips for Successfully Managing Your 401(k)

by Ted Benna
Creator, First 401(k) Savings Plan

*2001 Jefferson Awards National Award Recipient
for Greatest Service by a Private Citizen*

Defined Contribution News 2001 Impact Player of the Year

Library of Congress Cataloging-in-Publication Data:
Benna, Ted.
    Tips for Successfully Managing Your 401(k) / Ted Benna
    p. cm.
    ISBN 0-9713546-0-X
    1.   Finance, personal. 2. Retirement income – Planning
    Printed in the United States of America
    1 2 3 4 5 6 7 8 9 19 / 01

Distributed in the United States by 401(k) Association

Trademarks: All brand names and product names used in this book are trade names, service marks, trademarks or registered trademarks of their respective owners. Ted Benna is a special consultant to Persumma Financial, mPower and Successful Money Manager Seminars.

Edited by Kathryn A. Sollmann

Book and cover design by Linda L. Eberly

Cover photography by Fred Mohr

Printed at Intelligencer Printing Company, Lancaster, Pennsylvania, Lisa K. Foscone, Account Rep.

Dedication

I dedicate this book to Ellie, my first and only wife, who has been my life companion for forty plus years, our four children Debbie, Dave, Steve and Dan, their spouses Drew, Donna and Laura, and our grandchildren Mark, Neil, Matthew, Ryan, Michael, Olivia and Alison. You have all helped to make my life worthwhile.

Acknowledgments

Thanks to the production team that made this book possible. The content has been greatly enhanced by the Editor, Kathryn Sollmann, the Designer, Linda Eberly and the Printing Quarterback, Lisa Foscone from Intelligencer Printing. I also thank Bill Karbon who served as the technical reader and Pete Mock for proofreading.

A separate advertiser sponsored version of this book was distributed during November 2001 to 40,000 senior financial and human resource executives who oversee the 30,000 largest 401(k) plans in the country. This project wouldn't have been possible without the financial support of these advertisers. I am grateful to each of you for this support.

— *Ted Benna*

Advertisers

Table of Contents

Introduction

I was asked many times while I was writing this book about my intended audience. My intention is to provide a useful resource for anyone who is involved with 401(k) plans—employers, participants, professional advisors, those who are employed in the retirement field and members of the press.

During my many years of contact with all these individuals I have discovered that the lines constantly blur. You may have a dual interest in 401(k)s—a personal one related to your own plan participation and your business connection. If you are a participant only, you probably often wonder why your employer makes certain 401(k) decisions. This book explores 401(k)s from every vantage point and clears up many common misconceptions.

I've written the book so that it applies to readers at all life stages. As I am sharing this information with you, I encourage you to in turn pass along any ideas that you get from this book to younger family members and co-workers.

The greatest thrill of my business life has been my creation of 401(k) savings plans. I recently received the 2001 National Jefferson Award for Greatest Public Service by a Private Citizen. I was astounded when I received the notice—particularly when I saw Madeleine Albright, Lance Armstrong and Dr. Dorothy Heicht listed as the other 2001 national winners.

I received the Jefferson Award in recognition of the fact that the 401(k) has helped over 40 million average workers save for retirement. This award was a major affirmation that these plans have greatly benefited our country—helping millions of workers become successful savers.

It may surprise you to learn that the government tried to eliminate these plans in 1985—a time when many policymakers viewed the 401(k) as a big black hole sucking up lost tax revenue. We all survived these battles, and it was encouraging to see a major change in attitude in the 1990s. Retirement saving has become so much a part of our national culture that it is hard to remember how strongly the 401(k) was opposed during its early years.

I'd like to share some of the remarks I made when I received the Jefferson Award at the Supreme Court on June 13, 2001:

I have been greatly blessed by the opportunity to play a role in creating a plan that has enabled millions of average Americans to save for retirement. I have received many letters from 401(k) participants thanking me. I want to share a portion of one of them.

"Without the 401(k), Sue and I would have had to move with Caterpillar to another facility for nine years, away from the kids and the grandkids. Thanks to you we are spending much more time with them than we ever dreamed possible." This one is even more touching to me than the others I have received because it came from my brother-in-law, Rick Hahn.

Forty years ago I left the farming community where I grew up, went to the big city and began a career in retirement planning. I never imagined that this would lead to a day like today. Looking back, I feel like Joseph who was sent by God into Egypt to provide for his people. Family and friends who know me tell me how impressed they are by how humble I am. I assure you this is not my true nature. Pride has been a beast I have had to fight all my adult life. It helps to know all that I have ever accomplished or will ever accomplish is a direct result of the fact that God has had His hand upon me every step of the way.

Years ago Nikita Khrushchev told the U.S. that Russia would bury us. We would be taken over by Communism and all of our factories would be owned by the workers. Khrushchev's boast failed—our capitalistic society is alive and well. But some of what Premier Khrushchev said did come true. Approximately 50% of the total value of the U.S. companies listed on the various stock exchanges is beneficially owned by workers through their pension, 401(k), 403(b), 457 plans and IRAs.

The size of our middle class is the major difference between the U.S. and other countries. The opportunity for the average individual to achieve a reasonable degree of financial security is still greater in the U.S. than any place else in the world. The fact that the 401(k) has and will continue to play an important role in this widespread financial security is a source of blessing to me.

Most people feel that the 401(k) has been a major success, but there is room for improvement. We can learn from the first 20 years of 401(k) experience, and make these plans even better in the coming decades. At this stage of my life I am focused on how to improve the 401(k), and this book shares many of my suggestions.

In Chapter 1 you'll find the history and development of the 401(k) and my view of its future. Other industry leaders share their views of the future in Chapter 2. Chapters 3 through 10 help you manage your own 401(k) more successfully.

Chapter 11 is a guide for small employers that don't have a plan. I have included this chapter because I've discovered that virtually everyone has some close connection to a small business. The spouse or child of a senior executive may own a small business. Executives, professionals, business owners and their spouses often serve on the boards of small employers, such as a church or synagogue, a service club, a country club, hospital, etc. In these instances, you are frequently asked to help structure a retirement program, and this chapter should provide some guidance.

In the 20 years since I created the first 401(k) savings plan, I have been asked literally thousands of questions. Section 2 contains answers to 200 of the questions that I'm most frequently asked. I'm happy to provide this at-your-fingertips resource, and I wish you well along the path to retirement security.

Ted Benna
Jersey Shore, Pennsylvania

PART ONE

The Story of the 401(k):

Past, Present and Future

The Birth of the 401(k)

Since I designed the first 401(k) savings plan, I have been interviewed by more than 100 members of the press—for national, regional and local publications in and outside of the financial services industry. I have no control over what is actually written, and many times the origins and evolution of the 401(k) and the role that I have played have been slightly misconstrued. In this chapter you'll see questions that I am usually asked—and, for the record, the accurate answers.

How did the 401(k) actually begin?

I designed the first 401(k) savings plan in 1980. Technically speaking, I used a section of the Internal Revenue Code that was intended for an entirely different purpose.

Before your eyes start to glaze over at the thought of reading a lot of legal terms, let me assure you that this book is intended to be light reading about a very important subject. Now and then I'll refer to things like the Internal Revenue Code when it's necessary background information.

Section 401 of the IRC (that's short for the voluminous Internal Revenue Code) applies to all tax-qualified retirement plans. You're probably familiar with many of these plans—such as defined benefit pensions, profit-sharing, money purchase, employee stock ownership and 401(k)s.

If a plan is "tax qualified" it means that it has special tax advantages that make saving for retirement easier. Not only do participants defer taxes with these plans, they are also tax-deductible for employers.

Investment income is not taxed until the money is withdrawn, and participants have the freedom to roll their account balances into another tax-qualified plan.

Section 401 of the IRC begins with paragraph (a) and runs to paragraph (k), which was added when Congress enacted the Tax Reform Act of 1978. Like many tax bills, this one was passed during the final hours before a tired Congress adjourned for the legislative session. It's common that in the 11th hour "special interest" paragraphs are added to bills.

See Chapter 3 for more on the special tax benefits of the 401(k).

Paragraph (k) was one of those special interest paragraphs—but it originally had nothing to do with 401(k) savings plans. The original objective of paragraph (k) was to make cash-deferred profit-sharing plans less discriminating.

How did cash bonus plans evolve into 401(k) plans?

In the 1960s and 70s many of the major banks had cash bonus plans. Typically, eligible employees received one to two weeks of base pay as a cash bonus at the end of each year. These bonuses were intended to be performance-based compensation tied to the bank's financial results.

The cash bonuses were paid to employees on a year-by-year basis, and they were told not to consider them annual guarantees. But the fact is that after employees received several bonuses, they did indeed expect them every year. As a result, the intended flexibility and incentive factors disappeared.

Then someone came up with a better idea: a cash-deferred plan. With this plan, half of the annual bonus amount was automatically deposited into a tax-qualified retirement plan. This half was not taxable until the employee left the bank and received a benefit distribution.

The employee could elect to take the other half of the bonus as a taxable cash payment—or also deposit it into the same tax-deferred retirement plan.

So if a teller received a $400 bonus, $200 would automatically be deposited into the tax-qualified retirement plan. The teller could take the remaining $200 as a taxable cash payment or also deposit this half in the retirement plan.

This new arrangement made it possible for employees to receive at least half the bonus amount in cash or to defer the entire amount for retirement—paving the way for 401(k) savings plans.

Higher-paid employees tended to defer the entire cash bonus and avoid all taxes. Most lower-paid employees preferred to take half as a cash payment to cover some immediate needs.

These cash-deferred plans were approved by the Treasury Department, even though there was no official provision for them in the tax laws. When Treasury realized that a disproportionate share of the tax benefits were enjoyed by higher-paid employees, they put the brakes on these plans. In 1972 they prohibited any new cash-deferred plans, but allowed existing plans to continue.

Treasury wanted to think about how to handle these plans, but their ponderings were cut short when Congress passed the Employee Retirement Income Security Act (ERISA) in 1974. Congress didn't know what to do with the cash-deferred plans either—but they didn't want their fate in the hands of Treasury.

The answer came when Congress passed the Tax Revenue Act of 1978. Paragraph (k) was added to Section 401 of the Internal Revenue Code with little fanfare. Congress thought they were simply making more cash-deferred plans available to banks and a few other employers. They had no idea that they were setting the stage for the 401(k) savings plan. As a result, the expected tax revenue loss from this new provision was only a few hundred million dollars per year.

How did Section 401(k) change cash-deferred plans?

There were two major elements to Section 401(k): a new non-discrimination test and restricted access to the money contributed to the plan during active employment. Congress had addressed the fact that early cash-deferred plans favored higher-paid employees.

The non-discrimination test tied the amount that the highest-paid third of employees could contribute to the plan directly to the average percentage of pay that the lowest-paid two-thirds of employees actually contributed.

Without getting too technical, here's an example: if the lower-paid employees contributed an average of 2%, the top third could contribute 4%. This was an incentive for higher-paid employees to get lower-paid employees to contribute as much as possible to the plan.

I realized that replacing a cash bonus plan with a cash-deferred plan would work only if the lower paid two-thirds of employees contributed meaningful amounts to the plan. But a $20 tax break would not necessarily motivate them to put a $200 cash bonus into the plan.

When did I get involved?

There's a myth that one day while I was poring through the Internal Revenue Code I unearthed an obscure and unknown goldmine known as paragraph (k). It sounds good, but it's not true.

For starters, I don't sit around reading the IRC. And everyone who follows tax laws, as I do, was already well aware that paragraph (k) had been added.

You might say that I was not the discoverer, I was the interpreter. When I originally read the new paragraph (k), I didn't expect it to be a big deal because I was focusing solely on its intended purpose like everyone else. There was no indication that we were at the beginning of a major retirement revolution. In fact, the change in the law did not take effect until January 1, 1980, which came and went as a non-event.

It was not until the Fall of 1980 that I thought about paragraph (k) again. At the time I was a benefit consultant and co-owner of The Johnson Companies in suburban Philadelphia. I was helping one of our bank clients, Cheltenham National, redesign its retirement program.

Cheltenham had a traditional defined benefit pension plan. The bank also had a cash bonus plan that the president wanted to eliminate because it was no longer an effective compensation tool. As it happened with other banks, his employees expected the annual bonus, but they overlooked this additional compensation when they compared their weekly pay to what other employers were paying.

Not only did the president feel that his employees misunderstood the value of the cash bonus, he also wanted to put his own bonus in a tax-deferred profit-sharing plan. Like other higher-paid executives, he didn't want to lose more than half his bonus payout to taxes.

The Cheltenham cash bonus plan also put the bank at a competitive disadvantage. They had a hard time recruiting executives from other banks that had both defined benefit pension and cash-deferred profit-sharing plans.

A couple of years earlier I had worked with another bank client in a similar situation. At that time the Treasury-imposed freeze prevented this bank from replacing its cash bonus plan with a cash-deferred plan. So they opted to change to a tax-deferred profit-sharing plan that invested the entire employee "bonus" amount into a retirement account.

Since I remembered that few employees were thrilled to have a cash bonus plan replaced with a mandatory contribution to a retirement plan, I knew that Cheltenham would run into the same problems. That's when I was drawn back to Section 401(k).

I realized that paragraph (k) gave me a new tool that would make all employees happy. I could replace the cash bonus plan with a cash-deferred plan and allow employees to defer as little or as much as they wanted.

Where did the employer match come in?

The cash-deferred plan deal needed to be sweetened, so I thought of adding an employer matching contribution. The specific match that I recommended was 25 cents for every dollar an employee contributed. I thought the tax break plus the employer match would get the attention of lower-paid employees.

At the time there was not a specific provision in the tax code for employer matching contributions. There also was not any provision enabling employees to use a portion of their salary each pay period for pre-tax retirement plan contributions. These contributions are known as salary reductions. When you contribute to a 401(k), technically you're authorizing your employer to reduce your pay in order to make a pre-tax contribution to a retirement plan.

Although the matching contribution and the employee salary reduction contributions were not included in paragraph (k) of Section 401, there was nothing that prohibited them either.

There was, however, precedence for the match idea. At the time most large employers had after-tax savings plans that included matching employer contributions. We had a plan at The Johnson Companies where the matching contribution ranged between 25 and 50 cents on the dollar, depending on an employee's years of service. I contributed 6% of my after-tax pay and received a 3% employer matching contribution.

It seemed logical to turn all these after-tax savings vehicles into pre-tax plans. Certainly, it would be a better deal for employees.

How did the pre-tax contribution benefit employees?

Assume my gross paycheck at the time was $1,000. I was contributing $60 of my after-tax money per paycheck. Originally, the entire $1,000 was subject to income taxes. My $60 contribution to The Johnson Companies savings plan was deducted after taxes were deducted from the $1,000.

In a pre-tax situation, the first deduction from my pay would be my $60 plan contribution. Then income and Social Security taxes would be computed on $940 rather than $1,000. As a result, I would take home more money—$705 vs. $690 in the after-tax situation. I could also increase my contribution from $60 to $80, and, due to the tax savings, still keep the same amount of take-home pay.

Here's an example of the after-tax and pre-tax comparison:

	After-tax Savings	Pre-tax Savings
Gross pay	$1,000	$1,000
Contribution	0	60
Taxable income	1,000	940
Taxes payable	250	235
Contribution	60	0
Net pay	690	705
Increase in take-home-pay		15

When you look at this table, it's easy to see why senior executives were highly motivated to change their company plans to a pre-tax status so that they could benefit from more tax savings. At the time the top tax rate for individuals was about 50%. For executives who had contributed $20,000 to an after-tax savings plan, it was like getting a $20,000 raise. And lower-paid employees had the chance to increase their take-home pay as well.

For those of you who are checking my calculations, it's important to note that initially pre-tax contributions to 401(k)s were not subject to either Federal income or Social Security taxes. The law was changed and you must now pay Social Security taxes on the amount you contribute to a 401(k).

Where was the first 401(k) established?

The 401(k) had humble beginnings: it was not an overnight success. When I brought the idea to The Johnson Companies' Advisory Board, they suggested I sell the idea to a larger financial organization for $1 million. They felt it was too big of an idea for our small company to take to the marketplace. But the two organizations that we approached declined, so we eventually decided to go solo.

The Cheltenham Bank did not actually have the first 401(k) savings plan. Their attorney got cold feet when he realized they would be pioneering a new idea. It was not until three years later that we installed a 401(k) savings plan at the bank.

The first 401(k) savings plan was close to home—established for The Johnson Companies employees. This after-tax plan was designed with all the following features:

- employees could contribute up to 10% of their after-tax income
- the employer match was $.25, $.35 or $.50 per $1.00 of employee contributions, depending upon years of service
- the company matched the first 6% of pay that employees contributed.

The ability to make pre-tax contributions was a big plus for employees, but there was a flip side. The Johnson Companies employees had ready access to the money in their after-tax savings plan. They could withdraw their after-tax contributions for any reason, and they didn't have to pay any taxes to do so. But pre-tax contributions could be withdrawn only in the case of financial hardship. When we changed the plan, the first 10% of pay had to be contributed pre-tax. The matching level remained at 6%.

Did the early 401(k) plan interest only higher-paid employees?

We didn't have any idea how our 75 employees would react to the restrictive withdrawal provisions for pre-tax contributions.

Personally, I thought that being able to make at least half of my contributions from pre-tax income was better than contributions that came 100% from my after-tax income.

Our employees were given information on the pros and cons of pre-tax contributions, but we did not give them a hard sell. When all the enrollment forms came in, we were surprised to see that employees at the bottom two-thirds of the pay scale actually contributed a slightly higher percentage of pay than the top third.

We saw that many of these lower-paid employees were females from two-income households. Some of these women were in their 50s and they had spouses with decent incomes and grown children.

Many of the employees in the top third were males who were sole wage earners. Ironically, these higher-paid employees were the ones who did not contribute the maximum amount to the plan. They were generally younger and unable to save as much due to mortgage and tuition payments.

With this pilot program our own employees showed us that both high and low-paid employees would participate. And we learned that some lower-paid employees were willing to maximize their participation.

Were you concerned about how Treasury would react to your new idea?

Ed Johnson, my senior partner, had much more concern than I did. Drew Lewis, who became Secretary of Transportation in 1981, was a friend of Ed's. Ed arranged a meeting with Drew. Drew quickly got the big picture and asked what we wanted. We asked him to introduce us to the top people at Treasury, because we knew that was where the fate of the 401(k) would ultimately be determined.

This resulted in several conversations with Mike Melton, who was the person at Treasury drafting the proposed 401(k) regulations. Mike didn't give me any insight to the proposed regulations prior to their release, but I was comforted by the fact that he realized that we could achieve similar results even if contributions via salary reductions were not permitted. This was of much more concern to me than the employer matching contributions because most large companies already had plans with matching contributions.

I had a bit of anxiety until the proposed regulations were issued in November, 1981, supporting both the matching contributions and employee pre-tax contributions via salary reduction.

What were some of the early barriers to the 401(k)?

The biggest challenge we had was getting media attention for this new idea. But once we did get the 401(k) in the press, initial reactions were that I was doing something illegal.

That was the case after the first newspaper stories appeared in the *Philadelphia Inquirer* and *The New York Times*. Both of these stories were picked up by the wire services resulting in national exposure.

The Philadelphia Inquirer writer received several hundred calls from tax attorneys and human resources executives challenging the legality of the 401(k). Next there was skepticism that lower-paid employees would ever contribute a significant amount.

It may be hard to imagine that today's popular 401(k) took a lot of hard work to gain acceptance.

The concept of employees saving for their own retirement was strange. Up until that point in corporate history, "career" employees expected that employers would take care of them for life. That was the initial attitude at Bethlehem Steel, one of the first large employers to establish a 401(k), and at many other companies nationwide. Little did anyone know that there was about to be a major shift from government/employer to employee retirement responsibility.

What role did prayer have in the birth of the 401(k)?

Before I created the first 401(k) savings plan, I primarily helped professionals and small business owners establish retirement plans. In most cases the primary objective was to get as big a tax break as possible for the owners with little regard for the other employees. At age 39 I no longer wanted to be involved with work that helped those who needed help the least.

I was prayerfully considering alternative careers, including becoming involved in some kind of full-time ministry. It was during this period of searching that the 401(k) ideas came to me. I am convinced that these ideas were an answer to prayer regarding how I should spend the next years of my life.

The 401(k) has restored my enthusiasm for the retirement business because it is a plan that primarily benefits middle class workers earning between $20,000 and $100,000. Our strong middle class makes the U.S. unique. Creating a plan that helps this group has been much more satisfying than my earlier work.

Do I receive a royalty for the 401(k)?

When I first came up with the 401(k) plan idea, we looked into whether The Johnson Companies could obtain a patent. At the time we were told that it wasn't possible. The answer might be different today because the laws protecting intellectual content are much stronger.

Craig Stock, the *Philadelphia Inquirer* writer who did the first story on the 401(k), later wrote an article when the amount of money invested in these plans had reached $440 billion. He determined that if I received an annual royalty of one-tenth of one percent, I would receive $44 million per year.

During an interview with NPR I was asked the same royalty question. After I explained why I don't, I jokingly suggested that it would be okay if each of the 45 plus million participants sent me 25 cents. Not too long after that I received three quarters and a check for 25 cents in the mail.

The 401(k) Grows to Adolescence

A few large companies adopted 401(k) plans in 1981. Soon after that the 401(k) gained momentum—growing to 30,000 plans with 10.3 million participants and $145 billion in assets by 1985.

How were the first 401(k) plans structured?

It depends on whether the company had an after-tax savings plan. If so, many of these companies were unwilling to drop the after-tax contribution feature when they modified their plans. Many of their employees used these plans for short-term savings or glorified Christmas clubs.

At one large company over 90% of the employees withdrew all their contributions at the end of each year. I helped to change this employer's plan by adding a pre-tax employee contribution. This company, like many others, was also not willing to limit employees to just pre-tax contributions that could be withdrawn during active employment only for IRS approved hardship withdrawals.

Companies that didn't have an existing after-tax savings plan usually permitted only pre-tax contributions because they didn't have to over-come a short-term savings mentality. Employees of these companies were typically permitted to contribute between 10% and 15% of pre-tax pay, and they received a matching employer contribution.

In the early days of the 401(k), investments were usually limited to a guaranteed fund and either company stock or a growth fund. It was a period when fixed returns were in the 9 to 10% range and stock returns were less than stellar. With so few choices, it took about five minutes to explain the investment options to employees.

I remember telling employees that they would get all their money back plus interest if they invested $1,000 in the guaranteed fund, and they could get more or less than their money back if they invested $1,000 in the growth fund. We didn't tell participants they were crazy if they didn't invest a large portion of their money in the growth fund because a 9% guaranteed return was very attractive compared to the returns the stock market had been producing.

The primary concern was not investment selection, it was getting employees to contribute. Investing your own money for retirement was a new concept for employees. Most employees also had never invested any money in stocks. They were influenced by parents and older co-workers who had anti-stock investment philosophies formed during the Depression. A favorite investment among the older generation was the Certificate of Deposit or CD. Of course, the general investment outlook during the early 1980s was very different than it is today.

Who were the early 401(k) service providers?

The early 401(k) plans were designed by benefit consulting firms because they had the technical expertise to get the plans up and running. Most early plans operated in an unbundled environment. Banks commonly served as the trustee, but they did not have investment responsibility. The employer picked an insurance company for the guaranteed investment and a growth fund, typically with help from a consultant. The employer sent contributions to the trustee. The trustee sent the applicable money to the insurance company and the mutual fund.

Participant recordkeeping was frequently handled by either the benefit consulting firm or by a third-party administrator (TPA). All activity was paper-based, labor intensive and slow. Recordkeeping was performed on balance-forward systems where participant accounts were updated on specific valuation dates—generally annually or semi-annually. The really advanced plans updated participant accounts quarterly. Transactions such as investment changes or benefit distributions could occur only on these valuation dates. Participants had to wait six to eight weeks after the valuation date before these transactions could be completed.

The recordkeeper had to wait for weeks to get the payroll data from the employer or payroll service and the financial information from the trustee. The financial and payroll data had to be reconciled, entered into the recordkeeping system and processed.

By the time this work was completed, the investment transfer was based on outdated information. As a result, an April 10th request to change your investments would not have occurred until after the work for the June 30th valuation was completed—probably not before the end of July. And participants who requested benefit payments received checks based upon the value six or eight weeks earlier.

The fact that investment changes could be made only two to four days per year compelled participants to make hasty changes. Those who were uncomfortable about the direction the market was heading did not feel they could wait and see. They made immediate decisions because they knew they would not have another opportunity to make a change for three to six months.

Although this seems restrictive, some feel this structure was better than the one we have today. There's a downside to having the ability to make daily decisions about your investments. We all agree that investing for retirement is a long-term game—and in this game each player should pick and stick with an investment strategy. But if it is not abused, the opportunity to make changes any day the market is open has removed much of the decision-making urgency that existed with the old system.

How much participant education was there in the early days?

The term "participant education" did not exist. In the early days employees joined 401(k) plans via enrollment meetings. Our primary job was to tell employees that they should participate in this unfamiliar plan. There were no glossy brochures—we just used our people skills to convince them that the 401(k) had many long-term benefits.

At the time employee benefit communication consisted of distributing a boring black-and-white Summary Plan Description with a staple in the upper left corner. Just the information employers were required to provide—and nothing more. This was largely the case because there was no need for a lot of sophisticated materials to convince employees to participate in employer-funded retirement, health and insurance plans.

The communications situation changed when 401(k) plans came on the scene. No one at The Johnson Companies had media communications skills, so we retained a consultant who had been head of the benefit communications unit of one of the consulting firms. We also hired a creative educator who developed our first 401(k) communications materials. They were very different than anything we had done in the past—they had some color and they were actually readable by the average employee.

This launched our communications unit, which eventually produced videos, glossy enrollment packets and other colorful material to communicate the benefits of the 401(k). One of the best was a two-page highlights brochure that explained the primary benefits and provisions of the plan in a very reader-friendly format.

How fast did 401(k) plans develop?

Some companies were reluctant to adopt 401(k)s because it wasn't clear whether Treasury would support the direction I had taken. Most large employers waited for a definitive response, but there were very early adopters who were willing to move ahead. Bethlehem Steel, J.C. Penney, Johnson & Johnson and PepsiCo were among the first companies to adopt 401(k) plans.

Treasury issued proposed regulations in November 1981 supporting the matching contribution and employee pre-tax contributions via salary reductions. This removed the uncertainty and opened the door for rapid expansion of 401(k) plans. Most Fortune 500 companies had 401(k) plans by the mid-1980s.

401(k) Plan Growth Trends

	Plans (thousands)	Active Participants (millions)	Assets ($billions)
1985	30	10.3	$145
1990	98	19.5	385
1995	201	28.1	865
2000	355	38.1	1,655
	Plans (thousands)	Active Participants (millions)	Assets ($billions)
Compound Annual growth rates			
1985-2000	17.9%	9.1%	17.7%
1990-2000	13.8%	6.9%	15.7%
1995-2000	12.0%	6.3%	13.9%

SOURCE: Society of Professional Administrators and Recordkeepers staff analysis

The rapid growth of the 401(k) attracted attention in Washington, and there was an attempt to kill them in 1985. This is the year that President Reagan's Tax Reform Act passed. The first version of this bill had a provision that would have eliminated 401(k) plans.

Why would the government want to kill 401(k)s? There were growing Federal budget deficits by the mid-80s. These deficits led to annual battles between Congress and the President over how to shrink the deficit. The Democratic-controlled Congress was unwilling to reduce spending on social programs. The President continued to push for increased defense spending and refused to accept tax increases.

This standoff resulted in annual attempts to increase revenue via what became known as "revenue enhancers" rather than tax increases. Eliminating the tax loss resulting from 401(k) pre-tax contributions was one of the revenue enhancers that the Reagan team attempted to include in the Tax Reform Act. This effort failed because many participants protested to their congressmen. Some significant changes were made, including reducing the maximum contribution from $30,000 to $7,500, but the 401(k) survived this direct attack.

How has the 401(k) changed?

Not too long ago, many people would ask, "What the heck is a 401(k)?" Today the 401(k) is as well known as name-brand powerhouses such as Coke, Pepsi and Nike. These once obscure plans are now in the nationwide press every single day.

The most significant change is the current focus on investing. This is the dominant issue because 401(k) balances are the largest single investment for most workers. The average account balance for many of the earlier 401(k) plans now exceeds $100,000. Investing $100,000+ is a much bigger deal than investing $10,000. A 20% drop in account value is a lot more dramatic with a high balance. It's also a lot more dramatic when you're nearing retirement age.

As a result, there is not only an emphasis on investment education, there's also a great movement toward investment advice. Although participants generally have become more informed investors, and there's been a substantial shift from fixed-income to equity investments, there is general agreement that education alone is not enough. We will never teach over 45 million employees to become highly skilled investors.

Participants have always wanted and needed more investment assistance than we have been willing and able to provide. At the end of my first enrollment meetings there were always employees who asked how they should invest their money. Now that is an even more frequent and complex question: we have moved from two investment options to an average of 10 to 12. Some plans offer many more. Explaining the differences among various investment alternatives has become exceedingly challenging. The bottom line is that participants want and need professional help from advisors they can trust.

From an administrative standpoint, the general structure of 401(k)s has moved from cumbersome paper-based processing to electronic processing. System advances have enabled participants to obtain information about their accounts and investments all day every day from anywhere in the world. Participants are also able to initiate transactions such as investment changes, hardship withdrawals and contribution changes just as easily. Gone are the days of waiting weeks for requests to be complete: transactions now occur at current rather than outdated values.

Why has the 401(k) been so successful?

Did I ever think that 401(k) plans would hold $2 trillion of assets? I'm often asked that question and the answer is no. I expected the 401(k) to be big—but not this big.

The 401(k) has given employers a more efficient way to provide an adequate level of retirement benefits. Once employers changed their short-term savings plans to pre-tax plans, the 401(k) combined with Social Security and the company-funded pension increased opportunities for retirement security.

Previously, most small employers did not offer any retirement plan because they could not afford to do so. Employers that did have the resources preferred profit-sharing plans because the employer contribution was discretionary. (Of course, I'm not mentioning retirement plans that were maintained by professionals and highly paid business owners because these plans most often provided a tax break for the owners rather than real retirement benefits for employees.)

The 401(k) really took hold when small and mid-size employers realized that their contributions could not fund an employee's entire retirement. Today this would require contributions equal to at least 10% of pay over an employee's entire career (even with Social Security as a base!).

The 401(k) has provided a more reasonable alternative. A matching employer contribution equal to $.25 of each $1.00 an employee contributes costs only about 1% of pay (if the match is limited to the first 6% of pay an employee contributes).

The 401(k) has also been successful because more and more employees have acknowledged that with today's longer lifespans, they are not saving enough to meet all their retirement needs. The 401(k) has given employees an easy way to supplement their pension and Social Security with additional retirement savings. I remember telling employees that Social Security, their company pension and even profit-sharing plans would likely provide only a survivable level of retirement income. In contrast, the additional income from a 401(k) can bring you a comfortable level of retirement income.

The U.S. private retirement system has always been a three-tiered structure. Social Security provides a base, the employer provides a portion and employee savings is the third source of retirement income. Prior to the 401(k), the employee portion had to be created through after-tax vehicles for most workers. IRAs were available for those who were not covered by an employer plan, and employees of certain tax-exempt organizations could save pre-tax through 403(b) tax-sheltered annuities. The rest of us had to save on our own without a lot of tax help.

Employees have always known that they should save for retirement, but they needed the vehicle to do so. The 401(k) came along at a time when employee confidence in Social Security and employer-funded pensions was about to take a major dip.

Talking to participants over the years has convinced me that the semi-forced payroll deduction savings is the most valuable benefit of 401(k) plans. The tax break and the employer matching contribution are nice, but the payroll deduction has the power to convert spenders into savers. Most of us are unable to save over a long period of time if we have to do it on our own each pay period. Saving becomes the last, not the first, priority. Many participants have told me that the 401(k) has helped them save thousands of dollars that they otherwise would have spent carelessly. The major reason that the 401(k) has been so successful is that it has met a real need—helping employees truly save for retirement.

The 401(k) in Adulthood: What the Future Holds

Now that 401(k) plans hold $2 trillion in assets, some people wonder how much more growth is possible. The 401(k) will continue to grow—but it will probably take on different characteristics. I'm often asked to give my predictions for the 401(k) market, and these are the questions that usually arise.

What are the factors that shape the current 401(k) market?

The 401(k) products and services available today have evolved during the last 20 years largely through market pressure from participants—not government regulation. About 10 years ago I began advising 401(k) providers to shift their marketing focus from the employer to the participant. Although employers are still the gatekeepers, participants strongly influence employer buying decisions.

For example, the average number of investment options is in the 10 to 12 range, compared to only three that are necessary to comply with the Department of Labor's Section 404(c) regulations. Participant demands have also led to increased access to information, the ability to conduct transactions 24/7/365 and greater investment support. The latest major product enhancement is the addition of actual investment advice. Virtually all participants will have access to investment advice within the next couple of years because participants want more than just educational material.

The fact that change has largely been driven by participants shouldn't be surprising since they contribute most of the money to 401(k) plans. I believe that the pace of participant-influenced change will not slow. Some disagree with me on this point and say that most participants are content with the way that 401(k) plans are currently structured. I agree that at least 80% of participants are either content or indifferent—but that's only part of the story. Change has historically been driven by the 20% of the participant population who are more knowledgeable and proactive.

What participant demands are coming down the pike?

The two big words are *choice* and *control*. Participants who have access to unlimited investment alternatives through IRAs and other personal investments want the same flexibility with the 401(k). When participants can select from thousands of alternatives to invest only a couple of thousand dollars in an IRA, they have difficulty understanding why a much larger 401(k) balance is limited to only 10 alternatives. Today's participants have been told investing for retirement is their responsibility, but these investment barriers seem contradictory.

Several months ago I was asked a question that typifies the frustration that participants feel. This employee works for a Fortune 500 company that has 16 Fidelity funds and company stock. She asked why ex-employees (who can select from thousands of funds via an IRA rollover) are treated better than active employees. As 401(k) account balances continue to grow, more participants will ask similar questions and push for greater flexibility.

The second issue is control. Again, it's important to note that employers, service providers and the media have told employees that it is their responsibility to not only plan for retirement—but also invest their 401(k) dollars. Most employees have taken this message to heart. But when these same employees receive a notice from their employers telling them that their money is being moved from one set of funds to another, they become frustrated and annoyed.

Employees who receive these notifications frequently ask me if their employers can legally force them to change funds. The answer is yes—but doing so is inconsistent with the employee responsibility message. This inconsistency is becoming increasingly uncomfortable for both employers and employees. When employees are forced to move their money, they ultimately do not have control.

What will the employer's role likely be in the future?

Today employers are in a high-risk 401(k) game—one that is difficult to win and easy to lose. Despite how carefully or skillfully 401(k) plans are designed, there will always be unhappy participants. Employers are most at risk when they select plan investment options, because by doing so they assume the responsibility and liability for participant investments.

Should employers continue to hold this major responsibility and liability?

I don't think so. I feel this way because I have come to the conclusion that ERISA's fiduciary standard is unworkable. ERISA requires employers to act solely in the best interest of their employees—and I don't believe that this is possible.

Back in 1974 when ERISA was enacted this was a workable standard. At the time the dominant defined benefit plans were employer-funded. The employer decided what was in the best interest of employees as a group and assumed the investment risk. Now retirement plans are primarily employee-funded and employees assume the investment risk. But how could employers possibly know what is in the best interest of each and every employee?

This sole benefit fiduciary standard is also routinely violated when participants are forced to move their money from one set of investments to another. This situation is not uncommon during an M&A or a change in service provider.

The main objective in most mergers, for example, is to get all employees into the same benefit programs. Typically, the 401(k) balances of employees at the acquired company are transferred into the buyer's plan. The major factor driving this decision is administrative simplicity—not what is in the sole best interest of participants.

The problem is that there is a strong possibility that one or more of the new funds will not perform as well as the participant's previous funds. This opens the door for a lawsuit where the employer has to prove that the change was made for the sole benefit of participants. Administrative reasons do not hold a lot of weight. And the fact is that even when employers win these lawsuits, they lose overall participant confidence.

Selecting investment options, monitoring performance and replacing managers is time consuming and rather expensive for employers. Some of the Fortune 500 companies have highly skilled professionals whose sole responsibility is to oversee retirement plan investments. But this is uncommon: roughly 90% of 401(k) plans cover less than 100 employees. The vast majority of employers do not have dedicated or skilled 401(k) staff. As a result, investment selection is too often based on decisions that have no real connection to what is in the best interest of participants.

In my opinion, the employer's role should change. Simply stated, employers should stop being investment gatekeepers. Choice and control should truly be passed to participants. Employees should have the same flexibility when they are investing their 401(k) money that they have when they invest any other money. They should never be forced to move their money from one set of investments to another. Participants should also be able to establish lifetime investment relationships regardless of whether and where they are employed.

How will participants who are used to a limited number of options cope?

Five years ago a major concern was that participants were investing too conservatively. That led to a lot of educational effort to convince participants to increase their stock investments. This education was beneficial because current studies show general participant stock ownership to be in the 60 to 70% range.

But the expanding number of investment options is stretching many participants far beyond their comfort zones. The 401(k) market seems to be heading to an open environment that gives participants an unlimited number of alternatives. This is not what most participants want—it reflects the demands of the vocal minority that wants more choice. Now more than ever the needs of all participants must be considered.

It would be a huge mistake if next Monday morning all participants suddenly had to sort through thousands of investment alternatives. Most would be totally lost. In fact, the existing investment structures are already too complex for many participants.

Some employers and service providers have attempted to make the investment process easier for participants by offering lifestyle or other pre-mixed allocation models. Although their intentions were good, these pre-mixed choices have failed their objectives. The idea is to choose the one lifestyle fund that best fits your needs. You then invest your entire 401(k) balance in this fund. Unfortunately, many participants have mistakenly considered lifestyle funds just another fund offering. As a result, it's common for participants to split their 401(k) money among three lifestyle funds and several other funds—totally negating the value of the pre-mixed option. These funds were typically introduced as suitable funds for only novice investors—a major marketing mistake.

Employers and service providers have few other ideas to make participant investing easier. Frankly, I would like to blow up most of the existing investment arrangements and start over. I suggest only two investment alternatives: pre-mixed, fund of funds and open fund options.

The fund of funds would be structured around investment time horizons with three alternatives for each slot. For example, the 2020 fund would be geared to those who expect to retire at that time. There would be a conservative, moderate and aggressive 2020 fund to address individual risk tolerances. The goal would be to help participants make an easy choice, pick an appropriate portfolio and then do nothing more until they retire. Unlike most structured fund portfolios, stock holdings and risk exposure would be reduced automatically as the participant ages. Education could be limited to helping participants choose only one appropriate portfolio.

The other investment alternative would be an open fund option that would give participants access to the entire universe of managed funds. This would include indexed and institutionally priced alternatives that have substantially lower fees than traditional retail funds. Participants choosing this option could build their own investment portfolio or use an investment advisor, financial planner or any other professional.

In an ideal world, the pre-mixed portfolios would be mixed and managed by independent investment advisors such as mPower, Morningstar and Financial Engines. These advisors would build the portfolios by selecting funds in each category from the entire universe. Fund choices would not be limited to a specific fund family and they would have to meet performance standards. The funds in the pre-mixed portfolios would be monitored and replaced, as needed, by the independent advisor. The investment advisor would receive a flat fee per participant, which would not be related to the amount or the allocation of the investments. The advisor would also assume fiduciary responsibility.

Currently, ERISA does not allow the financial organizations that manage 401(k)s to give investment advice. It's considered a conflict of interest because the firm's revenue is impacted by participant fund choices. If independent advisors were to choose the funds, this conflict of interest would be eliminated. But then you'd have an equally problematic situation: a lot of power would be in the hands of a small number of investment advisors.

As a result, fund managers have been pushing Congress to amend ERISA so that they can provide investment advice. Enactment of this change is likely at some point. I can personally live with this change if there are appropriate controls to protect participants, such as:

1. *Independent, annual audits.* This is especially important if the investment advisor's revenue is influenced by participant fund selection.
2. *A limit on participant fees.* I recommend a maximum of 1% per portfolio, including all participant charges except transactional fees (such as for loans).
3. *Funds that meet performance standards in all categories.* If a provider's offerings do not include a fund that meets the performance standards in a specific category, a non-proprietary fund would be required.
4. *Fiduciary responsibility that is assumed by the organization choosing the funds.*

You may have noticed that I have not mentioned investing in individual stocks. This is because I don't favor giving the average participant the opportunity to do their own stock picking. The vast majority are not qualified to do so—and I put myself in that category. I am far from the most knowledgeable investor in the country, but I probably know as much or more than most plan participants. But I prefer to own only a few stocks and invest all my retirement savings in mutual funds. I don't want to be responsible for the specific stock selections.

How will the new 401(k) structure I'm proposing affect the employer's liability?

In my opinion, moving to this type of structure will substantially reduce an employer's liability, particularly if participants have access to an independent investment advisor who can help them make their investment selections. I strongly believe that the highest risk an employer can take is to force employees to change their investments—particularly when the change is not due to poor investment performance. Modifications to ERISA and/or a regulatory change relieving employers from the investment-related fiduciary liability exposure they now bear is desirable. But employers don't have to wait for the government to move in this direction. Historically, change has been driven by market pressures, and the government has acted to bring the law and/or regulations up to date with what is already happening. This is likely to be the case in this situation.

What will the 401(k) look like in 2010?

Here's a snapshot of what the 401(k) will look like by the next decade:

- Participants will decide where their money is invested and select the organization where their contributions will be deposited.
- Participants will choose among service providers that offer a wide variety of alternatives. One provider may be a fund company that offers only its own funds. Another may offer access to a wide range of retail mutual funds and individual stocks. Still another provider would enable participants to access any retail mutual fund, institutionally priced alternatives and individual stocks. The economics will vary among these providers—ranging from traditional retail funds to low-cost, institutionally priced investment options. Some providers will receive a fee for service and will be financially independent. Others will continue to receive compensation that is asset based.
- 401(k) contributions will be deposited directly into participant accounts the same day that payroll is run—similar to the way that net pay is direct deposited into a bank. This will eliminate the payroll reconciliation process.
- Participants will deal directly with the financial organizations they select. Statements will no longer be sent by mail—all account information will be readily available online. Separate 401(k) recordkeeping systems will disappear.
- Participants will be able to establish long-term relationships with their financial organizations. Life events such as job changes, unemployment or retirement will not require major 401(k) decision-making. Participants will retain their investments throughout these events.
- Employers will never be able to force participants to change their investments. Only participants will wield the power to change.
- Plan loans will be repaid electronically via participant bank accounts rather than through payroll deductions. Participants will be able to continue repaying their loans when they leave their employers. This will avoid having to repay the loan immediately or pay tax on the unpaid balance.
- Participants will have unlimited investment alternatives similar to what is now available outside the 401(k). They will be able to invest in a structured fund portfolio managed by an investment advisor if they do not want to do their own fund picking—or they will be able to build their own portfolios using whatever tools they wish.

As I look toward the next generation of 401(k)s, I recall a lot of interesting 401(k) related experiences. Many of these were casual conversations about the 401(k) in restaurants, on airplanes or at various gatherings. I've even had several humorous conversations with representatives of large financial institutions who attempt to tell me how the 401(k) works without knowing who I am.

The best experiences, however, are when I meet with average workers who tell me how thankful they are for the 401(k). My greatest reward for creating the 401(k) is that the plan will continue to give millions of workers the discipline to save and the very real chance for a comfortable retirement.

Notes

The Future of the 401(k):

Industry Perspectives

Chapter One gives you my perspectives on the history of the 401(k) and where I think the industry is heading. Obviously, there are others who are equally qualified to comment on the future direction of the 401(k).

In this chapter, you'll read insights from 11 prominent individuals in the retirement field. I hope all of our comments help you maximize the 401(k) today and in many years to come.

Your 401(k), Your Choice: How 401(k)s are Evolving to Give You The Help You Really Need

By Tom Johnson, Senior Vice President, Marketing
MassMutual Financial Group

If you were a teacher and your 401(k) retirement plan were a student in your class, you'd probably be writing a note to its parents. And the note would read something like this:

401(k) has a lot to offer, but is an average to poor communicator. Tends to rely on pat answers and doesn't respond well to new problems, despite having the right ideas. Needs to be a more proactive contributor to group; right now seen as just average. Class is unaware of how much 401(k) can do for them.

It may seem to be a strong rebuke, but it's on the mark. The note fairly sums up what 401(k) plan participants say when asked about how well their retirement plan is meeting their expectations. Plan sponsors, who generally approve of their 401(k) service providers' work, are often surprised to learn of their participants' overall opinion. And it's surprising news as well to the companies that make and sell the nation's 401(k) plans and spend hundreds of millions of dollars in a seemingly futile effort to educate participants about the intricacies of investment management.

The reason behind this latent dissatisfaction? We believe that participants, each of whom have unique circumstances, goals and dreams, are frustrated and poorly served by one-size-fits-all 401(k) products.

To meet this evolving need, we think providers must pay closer attention to participants, enabling greater customizing of plans so that participants can get what they need when and how they want it.

"Tell Me What to Do"

Why has it taken so long to come to this realization that participants need more personalized help?

In reality, the 401(k) industry has been struggling for years to offer participants the help they need. However, the industry has faced a number of thorny issues concerning what kind of help to provide, how it can be delivered, and where legal liability rests once the help is provided.

But even as the industry grapples with such complex issues, most participants continue to simply want advice from someone who is trustworthy and reputable. "Tell me what I should do" is the most common participant request. It is too often met with silence.

The result? According to a 2001 study by the Profit-sharing/401(k) Council of America, the average number of options in a plan has risen from about 4 in 1993 to nearly 14 today, yet participants are on average invested in only three of those options. And the average participant has about 62% of his/her investments in some equity holding, with another 19% on average in company stock. That's more than 80% in total in equity—a very aggressive profile for the average investor who would not likely intend to be that aggressive.

Recently some of the industry's largest 401(k) providers commissioned an independent study of participants to learn whether their expectations are being met. The bad news: the entire industry got a "C" to a "C-". My son's high school defines a "C" as "satisfactory" and a "C-" as "below average". With the retirement futures of 42 million 401(k) participants at stake, I am sure we can agree that "below average" is unacceptable. We should settle for nothing less than excellence.

An Intimate Understanding

How do you move to excellent from average? A number of studies indicate that many companies with extremely satisfied clients share, among other things, intimate understanding of their customers. Knowing what customers want, when they want it and how they want it, are key.

Yet it appears most plan providers don't yet

have that intimate understanding of participants, and some seem to have a very poor understanding.

For example, much of the investment education offered to participants is sophisticated and usually includes abstract concepts like risk/return analysis, diversification and the variety of investment classes. Those are complex subjects with which even investment experts have difficulty.

For the most part, however, participants don't see themselves as investment experts. In July 2000, MassMutual sponsored research that surveyed some 2,000 U.S. 401(k) participants who held blue- and white-collar jobs in a variety of industries. Of those surveyed, only 3% identified themselves as investment "experts", and only 11% ranked themselves as "experienced". Of the remaining 86%, 41% said they were "intermediate" and 45%—nearly half of all the participants surveyed—called themselves "beginner".

That's a significant percentage of participants who likely could use more help in managing their investments—and whose needs are evidently not being met by the investment education they currently receive. Participants have made it clear: they want help in deciding what they should do with their money. Answering that need can only help sponsors build participant appreciation for their 401(k) plan.

To Each His Own

Our study also indicates that only individual participants can say what type of investment approach is right for them. And few providers today can offer a 401(k) plan that is flexible enough to meet this demand.

Plan sponsors who seek to offer a 401(k) that's a good fit for their participants face an enormous, if somewhat obvious, difficulty: not all participants are alike. Nor do they fit into neat subcategories. Through research, we understand that, regardless of job title, rank, tenure, or any number of demographic segments, virtually every participant has an individual preference about

how to invest their 401(k) money.

For example, in our study:

- One third of participants indicated they would prefer to choose from six model managed portfolios, using a quiz to choose an appropriate style and letting the portfolio do all the rest—allocate, diversify, rebalance and replace options if necessary
- One third would prefer to choose their investment options from about 10 funds selected for the plan (how a typical 401(k) works), but about half of this group would prefer advice in making these selections
- One third would prefer to choose from a universe of about 1,000 mutual funds and would like to have independent advice available to assist in their selections.

These groupings are a reflection of individual preferences unrelated to job category or worker type. To respond to this variety of needs, it is becoming increasingly important for sponsors to offer 401(k) plans that let participants invest their money according to their individual preferences. Doing so not only enables participants to make choices that are right for them, but also ensures that plan sponsors are maximizing their investment in this important benefit by offering 401(k) plans that participants fully appreciate.

A Flexible Solution

The disappointing grades that participants give their 401(k) plans is likely a result of several factors: education programs that don't address their needs, a lack of meaningful guidance and advice and an inability to manage their investments according to their individual preferences.

We believe these trends, combined with new types of 401(k) plans that allow participants to address their individual investment needs, are beginning to move sponsors away from one-size-fits-all 401(k)s to custom fit plans. And as they do, we expect participants to begin rewarding their 401(k) plans with higher marks.

The 401(k) Market:
Today vs. Tomorrow

By Trisha Brambley, President
Resources for Retirement Plans, Inc. and
Al Otto, Director Retirement Services, Hobbs Group

In recent years, 401(k) plans have seen tremendous improvements and increases in areas as wide-ranging as volume of assets, funds offered, plan flexibility and back office efficiency. These improvements, including the availability of on-demand information and immediate opinions, gave every participant the possibility of feeling like a certified financial analyst during the bull market of the late 1990s. The result has been a false sense of security on the part of 401(k) investors and sponsors.

So even at this point, when the industry is relatively mature, well oiled and operationally sound, there is room for further improvement. The most dramatic changes in retirement planning services involve investor education, fiduciary responsibility and the legislative environment.

The Current State of Affairs

Three notable areas within 401(k) plans need attention and improvement:

Participant investment education — More material doesn't mean better education. Note the three basic rules for education: the message must be repeated, the media must be varied and the lesson must be personal. While these concepts seem simple, accomplishing them requires planning and perseverance from both the plan sponsor and vendor.

Understanding of fiduciary responsibility — Most plan sponsor executives do not understand their fiduciary duty nor the liability associated with it. Process is the key to minimizing fiduciary liability and ensuring a smooth-running plan.

Confinements of ERISA — Many agree with Mr. Benna's assessment of ERISA. However, ERISA is a statutory law and changing it will literally require an act of Congress — not likely to occur quickly. For the foreseeable future, we may have to work better within the confines of what we have.

Five Ways to Make Your Plan Cutting Edge

To satisfy the needs of the most sophisticated participants as well as the needs of the average investor, we recommend a custom-built platform that contains fund flexibility with multiple education and advice channels.

1. Create more fund flexibility.

Self-directed brokerage (SDB) accounts are relatively new to the 401(k) plan offering, but more plan sponsors offer them every year. With this tool, participants can choose from virtually any fund, stock or bond. They are popular with the minority of participants who want to do it themselves and are sophisticated enough to do so.

Just under 10% of 401(k) plans currently offer the SDB option. Of SDB participants, 75% have account balances over $75,000, with the majority invested in mutual funds. Generally, 5% of plan assets are directed into the brokerage account and this number is growing.

2. Build a better investment array.

Today, most plans offer 10 to 12 funds. Our experience has been that the plan sponsor's investment company takes the responsibility of selection and monitoring seriously. One or two funds should be offered in each asset class.

3. Create improved lifestyle funds.

The lifestyle funds suggested by Mr. Benna

in Chapter 1 are already available or could be created through several top 401(k) vendors. Mid to large-size plans can create a matrix of lifestyle choices to fit the needs of the participant base. However, some questions remain:

- When do the participants move to the next category?

- Do they automatically move to the same risk tolerance level in the next age group? Or do they choose a tolerance level where the asset mix changes automatically throughout their career?

- Who decides on the above?

4. Offer expanded educational opportunities.

Advice online … Many Internet advice providers have already priced their services below the $50 per year mark. Most 401(k) vendors have aligned themselves with one or more of these companies — amazing since the market did not even exist five years ago.

Participants will eventually choose among advice providers, and we expect this to become a standard "no extra charge" service in the next few years. These advice providers are now used mainly by the highest wage earners — earning an average $80,000 per year — who already make 8% average contributions.

Of these, less than 50% actually implement the advice they receive! Why? Because technology cannot substitute for human interaction. We see financial planning groups emerging to supplement education and advice needs. According to our client surveys, most employees want seminars and one-on-one sessions. Most plan sponsors need outside help to understand the unique needs of their participant base, and create workable, practical strategies to help employees.

Financial planners … Advice from professional financial planners will become inte-

grated into plan offerings as participant balances increase. But not for free. Participants can expect to pay between 0.25% and 2% of their plan balances for the advice they seek, which will range from basic "hand holding" to full discretionary investment management.

Planners will have to be selected and monitored by a third party to protect plan sponsors from liability and participants from unnecessary losses. New benchmarks and monitoring services will facilitate this new market.

Data aggregation … Technology provides the ability to aggregate information from many sources into one. This is an emerging trend and it is a requirement for truly integrating financial planners into the education and advice offering. Many top vendors are preparing to provide total financial services for their clients.

5. Make more use of retirement plan negotiators.

Plan negotiators offer a better due diligence process, provide a framework for evaluating vendors and ultimately help select a vendor that matches the unique characteristics of every plan. Documentation to support the ultimate vendor selection is another important service that is typically provided. Plan negotiators can also use their knowledge of the marketplace and clout to help plan sponsors and participants obtain better pricing.

Typically, large consulting firms can obtain better pricing than participants can on their own. In addition, the unique characteristics of every plan dictate an absolute need for experience and marketplace knowledge.

Conclusion

Implementing these tactics with the help of a quality consultant will ensure that your plan is a five star program for your employees.

The Complete Retirement Plan

by Robert Leeper, Managing Director
CharonECA

The Need For Supplemental Non-Qualified Deferred Compensation

In Chapter One Ted speaks about the employer's role in addressing the need for adequate retirement income and the success and popularity of 401(k) plans as a partial solution. As Ted has stated, 401(k)s are great for the average worker, but the 401(k) contribution restrictions and the basic design of Social Security combine to make it mathematically impossible for highly compensated employees (HCEs) to develop an adequate level of retirement income through those programs.

Social Security provides a benefit that represents less than 20% of a highly compensated employee's final pay. By comparison, the average employee will receive a benefit equal to about 40% of final pay. For the highly compensated employee, this means that they will need other retirement benefits representing 50% of final pay or more, if they are to reach the traditionally recommended level of retirement income.

Although the 401(k) has become the plan of choice for the average employee, they are of limited value for HCEs because of the special non-discrimination rules found in the IRC. These rules frequently limit contributions for executives to between 4 and 8% of pay, much less than what is needed to build an adequate retirement nest egg. HCEs may be able to save larger amounts outside their employers' plans, but doing so without any tax breaks is very painful and unlikely to occur.

The Supplemental Solution

In order to achieve attractive retirement plan results for their most valued employees, employers can supplement their tax-qualified plans with programs that are designed to "not qualify" for the favorable treatment found in IRC Section 401. By not qualifying, a plan can provide an employer with tremendous flexibility, generally unrestricted by the law. These supplemental "Non-Qualified" plans provide:

- Unlimited contributions (both by the employer and the employee)
- Flexible criteria—benefits can be tied to productivity or a contribution level can be tailored to an individual or groups of individuals
- Benefits with creative vesting formulae.

The most common form of non-qualified plan in use today is designed as a "supplement" to a 401(k) plan. In much the same way as Ted designed the first 401(k) plan to respond to an specific employer's perceived need to provide a benefit to specific employees, non-qualified plans have evolved to respond to the special retirement needs of HCEs. The distinction between qualified and non-qualified plans has little to do with the need of the participants. Most employers and HCEs think of the combination of these two plan types as elements of a "complete" retirement program.

Distinctive Characteristics of Non-Qualified Programs

Most Supplemental 401(k) plans have seen the same evolution that Ted described in Chapter One. Fifteen years ago they were 1) uncommon, 2) had very limited if any investment choices, 3) were designed to provide benefits at termination of service only, and 4) administrative support was manual, slow and very limited. Early versions of these types of plans tended to be poorly documented and poorly understood by many employers and participants. When planning a supplemental program, a number of important characteristics and consequences will apply:

No Delayed Tax Deduction. From the employer's point of view, the most important difference between qualified and non-qualified plans is that the employer is not allowed to take a tax deduction for non-qualified contributions. Instead, the employer can deduct the actual benefit payments. Although it would be preferable to deduct contributions instead of benefit payments, employers often opt for the latter deductibility so that they can achieve acceptable outcomes for their most valued (in terms of compensation) employees. While the tax efficiency is not as great as a qualified plan, a non-qualified plan can be very efficient overall because the employer can pinpoint its contributions to the employees it wants to receive them. An analogy that I use with employers is to contrast shooting a rifle bullet as compared to throwing a hand grenade.

ERISA Compliance. It is often mistakenly assumed that a non-qualified plan is also not covered by ERISA. Not true. Any employer-sponsored program that delays compensation for significant periods of time is subject to the ERISA statute. ERISA includes language that permits an employer to exempt a plan from all but the basic legislative requirements if that plan is:

- Un-funded and
- Maintained for a select group of management or highly compensated employees.

ERISA can come into play in a much more significant way if either of these concepts is violated. In my practice experience, the more troublesome of the two is the select group issue because the ERISA statute provides no clear definitions for terms like "management" or "highly compensated". Often, employers can unwittingly cross the invisible line on the issue. A worst-case scenario penalty is to turn a non-qualified plan into a qualified program after the fact. (It should also be noted that the definition of HCE found in the IRC is not an acceptable definition per the Department of Labor when looking at the ERISA statute.)

More Options. Today, non-qualified plans are characterized by more creative and flexible plan options than their tax-qualified counterparts. It is common to see non-qualified account balances that dwarf the participant's balance in their tax-qualified plans, and the demands for investment choices and plan features are correspondingly greater. Just as Ted has described the movement toward more investment alternatives within 401(k) plans, we have seen an even greater demand in the non-qualified arena.

Administrative Complexity. As a result of the number of options, a complete array of administrative capabilities is needed for these plans. Today, almost all have the same level of administrative services and support that you would find in a qualified plan.

Early Distribution of Benefits. One of the most attractive features of non-qualified plans relates back to the savings plans at banks that Ted describes as the precursors to 401(k). Non-qualified plans may permit participants to receive benefit payments while still actively at work. Employers can adopt a comprehensive saving system that allows participants to address a variety of savings objectives in addition to retirement (e.g., college, purchase of a home, travel).

Conclusion. Many HCEs celebrated when they first read that the 401(k) contribution limit will increase to $15,000 by year 2006. Whatever enthusiasm was initially generated quickly disappeared when it was revealed that the non-discrimination tests would continue to severely restrict how much the HCEs can contribute. Without question the need for non-qualified plans will continue unabated.

The Growing Importance of Financial Education

by John H.P. Wheat
President and CEO
SMMS, Inc.

The creation of the first 401(k) plan in 1981 shifted the responsibility for employer-sponsored retirement savings from the employer to the employee. In contrast to the traditional company-pension model, the 401(k) obliges employees to decide whether to participate, how much to contribute, how to allocate their investments, and how to effectively distribute their assets upon termination or retirement. Furthermore, the recent development of employers tying their matching contributions to corporate profitability or earnings targets adds another level of uncertainty to the employee's retirement security.

Until recently, the downside risks associated with the 401(k) employee-directed retirement model lay hidden. Since the introduction of 401(k)s, the stock market has been on a nearly uninterrupted rise. This unprecedented market performance, coupled with the continued overlapping availability of traditional company pensions, fostered a false sense of security for employer and employee alike.

However, as the number of guaranteed company pensions dwindles, and as employees are forced to grapple with increased market volatility—not to mention inevitable market downturns—the risks to retirement security become evident. The uncertainty posed by this new retirement-funding landscape raises questions for both 401(k) participants and sponsors, such as:

- Are plan participants adequately prepared to manage their own accounts?

- Do participants understand the importance that account management has in their overall retirement planning?

- Do participants have ready access to appropriate education and advice?

- Do plan sponsors have any fiduciary responsibility to help plan participants make informed investment decisions?

- How well are employees adapting to the challenges and responsibilities of the 401(k) model? Current research suggests that ample room for improvement exists:

  - Twenty-five percent of all employees eligible to participate in 401(k) plans elect not to do so.[1]

  - Fifty percent of employees in their 20s are not participating.[2]

  - Most employees would make the wrong decision in the event of a market downturn.[3]

  - A majority of employees have never assessed their future retirement income needs.[4]

  - Few employees invest according to a pre-established asset-allocation plan.[5]

- Employees between the ages of 35 and 50 are saving only 60% of what they will need for retirement.[6]

If employees are to be self-reliant for the adequacy of their retirement income, three facets of the 401(k) plan become critical to their success: plan communication, financial education, and financial advice.

Historically, plan communication was little more than a photocopied technical summary of the corporation's 401(k) plan, otherwise known as the Summary Plan Description (SPD). Today, many creative and innovative communication materials and delivery media make it easier for employers to increase participation.

Financial education services for employees have been—and remain—very loosely defined. The most common form of financial education is a workshop on asset allocation during the annual 401(k) enrollment meeting.

The relative newcomer is online financial advice. The use of online services benefits only the 20% of "knowledgeable and proactive" employees, whom Mr. Benna contends are the ones largely responsible for new services. Unfortunately, there is a "missing link" for the other 80% of employees who would benefit most from financial advice.

Isn't education a prerequisite to making informed decisions and heeding good advice? Based on 15 years of experience in delivering financial education, SMMS, Inc., can answer "yes" to this question.

The diversity of workplace demographics requires educational programs that are comprehensive in their content and use a greater number of media to reach individual employees. Reaching a larger percentage of employees with relevant financial education and advice can be an effective solution for 401(k) providers, employers, and employees alike.

The changes that Mr. Benna is prescribing would foster individual choice. However, if only 20% of employees are "knowledgeable and proactive" enough to make informed decisions, significant efforts aimed at delivering financial education and advice will be necessary to provide equality among all employees. Empowering individual employees to make informed retirement planning choices is not optional. It is essential.

[1,2,6] Fidelity, Building Futures: Opportunities and Challenges for Workplace Savings in America, 2001

[3,5] Reuters, Workers Waver on 401(k), May 2001

[4] Employee Benefit Research Institute (EBRI), Retirement Confidence Survey, 2001

One Future, Many Opportunities

by Mark A. Trieb, FSA
Principal,
Milliman USA

Since Ted Benna found the key to 401(k), we have seen 20 years of retirement legislation, product evolution and change in buyer behavior. For many American workers, 401(k) balances represent their primary financial asset. As a people, our expectations have largely moved from entitlement to empowerment. Competitive forces, business realities and technology innovation are all driving key industry trends.

Competition

Just as no one really planned for the industry we have today, many service providers find themselves in a competitive and unforgiving market without a clear strategy or vision that takes new market realities into consideration. Such legacy thinking can be deadly.

Demand for services by plans and participants is increasing in breadth, depth and richness. Consumers at all levels seek more and better support. Service pricing is under pressure through increased disclosure of soft revenue sources to vendors and buyer preference for sound economic relationships with their vendors. This trend has been supported and accelerated through the efforts of the US Department of Labor.

Employers are asking suppliers for more efficient pricing, resulting in greater value for plans and their participants. Revenue sharing, expense subsidies and rebates are all on the table as employers seek to discharge their fiduciary obligation to act in the best interests of their employee/investors.

Consolidation

The investment required to be a viable provider in the universe of defined contribution service providers is substantial. Further, vendors must commit investment capital to pay for new services and to offer pricing that keeps them competitive with other providers. At some point, such capital investments must have a return.

The 401(k) market has matured and few large employers are creating new 401(k) plans. Unlike the early days of 401(k), there are not many conversions of existing profit-sharing and money purchase plans. As a result, relatively few new asset sources are available to 401(k) providers.

The 401(k) industry has experienced classic business phases that can be seen as:

1. *Start-up* (1980 to 1990) – From the establishment of the Johnson Company's first 401(k) through the end of that decade when daily-valuation plans became common and expected by participants.

2. *Growth* (1990 to 2000) – The 401(k) became the retirement vehicle of choice for over 40 million American workers with many plans using mutual funds combined with expanded participant direction of their investments. Broad adoption, increased employee participation and market appreciation combined to create 401(k) assets of some $2 trillion, with corresponding vendor revenues.

3. *Maturity* (Today) – The 401(k) industry faces marginal growth and the "commoditization" of its products and services as customers find fewer differences between offerings. This leads some buyers to view offerings as more or less comparable in features, value and therefore, price. Low revenue growth, constrained margins and scarce capital for investment in systems and staff are all characteristics of a mature industry.

Departures from the full service, in-house providers include nationally known insurance, brokerage, bank and mutual fund companies. It is not surprising that some vendors are considering an end to their offer of in-house retirement services in favor of working alliances with partner firms that fulfill client needs for operational support. Participant accounting, plan administration, trading and customer service processes are the very components that offer efficiencies of scale and process automation, given adequate levels of investment capital—both financial and human.

As vendors leave the marketplace, there will likely be fewer but larger service platforms offering a broad and adaptable range of solutions for clients. Remaining vendors will be more efficient and profitable, with improved customer service and pricing.

Identifying vendors that are likely to survive provides an interesting exercise for industry observers. The advantage will be held by firms that are not overly dependent upon asset-based revenues, but provide reasonably priced services with flexible, efficient and effective systems through the efforts of motivated, professional staff.

Convergence

The near future provides technology and business solutions that bode well for higher levels of choice, control and confidence in the delivery of services:

Employer/Plan Level – Decision-makers will acquire services from new vendors in new ways. Research suggests that corporate decision-makers are not only willing, but eager, to realign their service purchasing decisions if tangible benefits can be realized. Examples include integrated service offerings from administration platforms for 401(k), defined benefit and deferred compensation plans on a common platform. Flexible and durable technologies will better coordinate and integrate services such as retirement administration, other employee benefits, payroll, human resources management systems and enterprise planning tools such as financial software. This will improve operational efficiency and service delivery to human resources, finance and general management executives of corporate employers.

Employee/Participant Level – Today employee/investors are demanding more and better services, including comprehensive data aggregation (investment account data and supporting content), objective advice and efficient implementation of their decisions. At the same time, research shows that, given a choice, 401(k) participants prefer to have lower fees rather than more services. This apparent contradiction is one that can be managed at the individual level, through efficient, personalized services providing investment and advice services. The service platform of the future will also support other elements of the employee/investor's lifestyle needs, including cash flow and debt management, together with college, retirement and estate planning activities.

"Co-opetition"

In this view of the future, new relationship models will be forged, not only between corporate client and vendor, but also between competitors that would previously not have teamed up to meet client needs. Through conditional and situational "co-opetition", vendors will find new and better ways to meet their business objectives. This must happen if we are to realize all available efficiencies from enabling technologies.

Collaboration

The next phase of the 401(k) phenomenon will offer significant benefits for employers, employees and the American people. The key to this reality will be equitable, working partnerships between cooperating competitors, the employers they serve and their employee/investors.

Making Twenty Years of Saving Last Thirty Years

By Julia R. Vander Els
Vice President, Retirement Education
Delaware Investments

Twenty years of saving in defined contribution 401(k) retirement plans shifted the financial accountability for retirement security to the wage earner. Employers facilitated the savings process by offering 401(k) programs, without bias, to all eligible employees. They assumed the fiduciary responsibilities associated with the offering, and in many cases chipped in via company matches and, in certain cases, profit-sharing contributions.

But what does the retirement planning landscape look like for those who mature out of the system and retire?

The Accumulation Years

During the past 20 accumulation years, employers and their providers of choice have focused on helping employees determine how much they need to retire. They have also attempted to train employees on how to save from current income and how to invest those savings appropriately to meet their retirement savings goals.

How well we have, as an industry, done with this task remains to be seen. What is clear, however, is that employees and future retirees will ultimately need help in making their savings, whatever the amount, last as long as their financial needs do.

First, we need to understand the basic factors that will influence a retiree's decision.

How long . . . Not only do workers want to start their retirement earlier than prior generations, chances are they will live longer, too.

According to statistics published in the 2000 Social Security Trustees' Report, 65-year-old males and females can expect to live an additional 16.4 years and 19.6 years respectively. This forces future retirees into making budget and asset management decisions that will support their needs well into their 80s.

With medical advances focusing on managing disease diagnoses and treatment, and the health-conscious nature of many future retirees, living well into their 90s is not that unreasonable to expect. It is certainly something to factor into the planning equation.

These projected time horizons will prove unsettling to the generations of 401(k) plan participants who have been told that they are responsible for paying for their future. Most will not have guaranteed pension payments in the form of periodic defined benefit distributions. Employer-sponsored retiree health care benefits will also be rare.

. . . and how much matters. There has been a great deal of speculation on how to make the money last. A study was conducted by Cooley, Hubbard, and Waltz (1998) to determine, based on the current accessible asset classes, what percentage of savings could be spent annually to support various projected life expectancy assumptions.

Based on a diversified portfolio of stocks, bonds and cash, a 3% annual withdrawal rate was determined to last a projected 30 years. That factor held an 80% probability of having the savings pool – no specific amount identified – last 30 years. Assuming a more aggressive asset allocation predominately in stocks, the withdrawal rate increased to 4%, again supporting a high probability of the savings pool lasting 30 years.

It's key that future retirees assume nothing will mirror the retirement years their parents enjoyed. And, it's important that those future retirees start early by making a list of their future needs and the representative cost. This eye-opening exercise puts the retiree's future challenges into perspective.

This list should include, but not be limited to: long term health care providers, assisted living communities, nursing or terminal care facilities, and legal and trustee services to manage your affairs and financial commitments when they no longer can. Whether it makes sense to contract some of these services with financial advisers should also be considered. How these service areas can help, and the costs associated with the services, will determine how well retirees can best manage their financial resources.

Helping People Spend Their Savings

How will the upcoming self-sufficient generations manage? The employers did their part during the accumulation years. Assuming that future retirees will have to rely on the securities markets for their income and as a defense against inflation, chances are the 401(k) plan providers and financial services industry will step up and help.

Multi-manager investment solutions will extend from the accumulation years into retirement. The investment basics of diversification among asset classes, style and management remain prudent guidelines for retirees. Accessibility and the ability to analyze investment alternatives in parity are also 401(k) plan holdover principles.

401(k) accounts will turn into Individual Retirement Accounts (IRAs) in record numbers. Providers of both programs will need to facilitate this process by adding services to help retirees determine the best way to draw down their savings. Tax management will become paramount. Seamless account look-up, access and transaction processes will become service differentiators.

Alternative investment vehicles will surface to address a retiree's comfort in counting on some form of regular income. This could come in the form of reasonably priced annuity programs or alternative individual managed account programs. Mutual funds and individual stock and bond investments will still be valid. However, alternative income-producing mechanisms will be sought to support 30 years of spending.

Retirees will want advice – investment, tax management and estate planning. They will start with web-based services and other services sponsored through their 401(k) plans. And they will want to stay with those services in retirement. However, future retirees will also seek out accessible advisers to help them through the maze of decision-making initially, and throughout the next 30 years.

The pre-retiree population will also seek help and planning guidance **before** they pick their retirement date. That request will fall on the employers and they should be able to rely on their service providers for help.

Conclusion

Before 401(k) plans and the popularity of participant investment direction, the retirement services industry was very different. Retirement programs were actuarially managed in the back rooms of consulting firms without ever having to meet the people they were intended to benefit. 401(k) plan sponsors and the partnerships formed with their service providers have created a model of mutual benefit that will extend into those retirement years.

Thirty years is a long time. Those fortunate enough to manage those years financially sound and reasonably healthy, will do so with the help of others. And the 401(k) provider industry will extend its accountability to serve that market as well. Although their service status has changed, the point remains the same – to help people save and manage their savings for a financially secure retirement.

Statistical data cited in this article is from Employee Benefit Research Institute (EBRI) Issue Brief Number 232, dated April 2001. The study reviewed: *The Changing Face of Private Retirement Plans*, by Jack VanDerhei, Temple University and EBRI Fellow and Craig Copeland, EBRI.

Key Issues Facing the 401(k) Industry Today

An Interview with Douglas L. DuMond,
President of CDC IXIS Intermediary Services

Q. *What are some of the key issues facing the 401(k) industry today?*

A. First, employees should have the choice of best-in-class investments, from a style, performance and pricing standpoint, regardless of the recordkeeper. Participants should not be restricted to the fund company that's sponsoring the plan. Too often, employers, particularly small and mid-sized employers, don't demand enough investment choices.

Second, plan sponsors should hire managers based on closer scrutiny of fees and more thorough style and performance attribution analysis versus the peer group. Plan sponsors should exercise due diligence over investment choices, making sure that options are monitored and evaluated periodically. Too often, employees end up in plans that have wrap fees or expense ratios that are out of line or unnecessary.

Last is the issue of employer advice. I believe that there has to be some regulatory relief for non-partial advice, helping employees access their future obligations, income needs and risk profile to come up with an overall plan. The current law is restrictive. Presumably, the employer could negotiate a better program of advice and service for their employees than the employees could do on their own.

Congressman John Boehner (R-Ohio) recently unveiled the Retirement Security Advice Act, which would shield plan sponsors from liability relating to advice given by financial advisors to employees, but would keep them responsible, as an ERISA fiduciary, for the prudent selection and review of advisors. Support for the bill has come from TIAA-CREF, the National Association of Manufacturers and the American Benefits Council.

Q. *Beyond giving access to advice and making matching contributions, what should the employer's role be?*

A. My feeling is that there's a valuable role for employers beyond contributing to their employee's own retirement savings through matching or profit-sharing contributions. When choosing pension fund managers, most companies have an intensive process to make sure they have the best fund in its category. There is a very thorough evaluation process in terms of peer group performance, investment process and appropriate fees. The same should be the case for employee retirement plans.

Finance, treasury and leading-edge pension consultants are finally playing a more significant role in 401(k) fund selection. These decision-makers do not succumb as easily to the marketing machines that have spent millions of dollars branding their funds. What is becoming more important is the quality of the firm, the investment process, and the performance compared to its peer group. Is that performance sustainable? Would it stand the same intensive scrutiny that a pension consultant would insist upon when choosing managers for a corporate plan? That's where the market is going, and I think that's healthy. While brand has a role, the investment process and discipline are more important than just name recognition.

Ultimately, the market is moving in an institutional direction. From the employee perspective, that should be very comforting. Otherwise, it's buyer beware. Even in companies with very sophisticated employees, you may find that they are poor at manager selection or fund evaluation or they'll wind up buying load funds, doing too much trading and not diversifying properly.

Q. *What impact does the new tax law have on retirement accounts?*

A. The maximum IRA contribution, which has been $2,000 for about 20 years, rises to $5,000 (plus applicable catch-up contributions) by 2008. Some people may be concerned that the new law favors IRAs since the percentage expansion in contributions is greater.

Still, 401(k) plans are superior to IRAs in several ways. First, employers can match part or all of their employees' contributions, resulting in a substantially greater build-up in savings. Second, participants in 401(k) plans can often obtain tax-free loans, a feature not available with IRAs. Third, employers typically have access to higher quality investment advisors who can offer services at lower fees. True, the Roth IRA, in which contributions are not tax deductible, grows on a tax-free rather than tax-deferred basis. However, as of 2006, the new law allows employers to create a type of Roth 401(k) and encourages employers to establish or maintain qualified retirement plans through more flexible nondiscrimination rules.

I am a believer in the employer-sponsored plan concept. On the whole, employees have been well served by these plans as opposed to going independently through their own IRA savings. There is an even greater benefit gained when an employer uses their scale and buying power to achieve lower fees on the custodial, recordkeeping and management functions. The due diligence role that companies play because of ERISA and the prudent man rule works to the participant's advantage.

Q. *With the increased limits, do you think that companies will continue to match the contributions?*

A. Yes I do. By and large, corporate America and public employers very much supported the increased limits. Whether they match it dollar-for-dollar or they match 25 to 50 cents on the dollar,

they'll match some of it – and I think that trend must continue. The 401(k) plan, although it may be one of the least costly benefits, is the most popular. From a recruiting and retention standpoint, companies will actively make matching contributions and even discretionary profit-sharing contributions through the 401(k) vehicle. Those that do offer attractive 401(k) plans will attract long-term contributors, not job hoppers, who are building their wealth through the 401(k) savings vehicle.

If you look at retirement savings as a three-legged stool, you have Social Security, traditional pension plans and 401(k) savings plans (or your own personal savings). Today, most companies have either never established a traditional DB pension plan, or have eliminated it – so one leg of the stool is missing. So this expansion is very important, because 401(k)s have become the primary retirement savings vehicle and many people have under-funded their retirement because of the maximums imposed. In some cases, it doesn't make up for the third leg of the stool. Employees can help themselves by making the maximum contributions so that they can receive the maximum match.

Q. *How has the recent market volatility affected the 401(k) industry?*

A. Investors remain committed and flows have remained consistent. If anything, this market has prompted people to think more about whether they are adequately diversified and whether they're balancing value and growth appropriately. There was an overweighting in the technology sector and the growth style, and many suffered significant depreciation in terms of their overall account balances, so they are currently looking more closely at asset allocation. Employees are taking a closer look at their plans, making adjustments to their portfolios or seeking out asset allocation advice. They are also looking closely at whether fixed income or yield-oriented equities have a place in their portfolio.

Meeting the Needs of the Financial Procrastinator

By J. Michael Scarborough
President and CEO, Scarborough Group Inc.

A 2001 survey by The Spectrem Group, Chicago, found that of 1,557 DC plan participants, 46% indicated they had not used advice offered by their employers because "I just haven't gotten to it."[1]

In your own office you will find people in the same circumstance – employees who want the benefit of a tax-advantaged retirement savings vehicle, but who do not make the time to effectively manage it on their own. Some lack the interest and others lack the expertise. Ideally, procrastinators prefer the structure of a defined benefit plan, where everything is managed professionally for them. Without professional investment management, procrastinators are not likely to have enough replacement income when they reach retirement.

In most industry and employer discussions about investment advice for plan participants, little attention is given to the large number of employees who make investment planning a low priority. Employers need to better understand employee attitudes and motivations toward financial matters in order to offer advice solutions for all employees.

When it comes to managing their company-sponsored savings plans investments, employees tend to fall into one of four categories:

Financially savvy, informed investors who may read educational materials to augment their knowledge, but whose retirement planning skills need not be a major concern to their employer. They know the right thing to do, and they do it.

Those highly motivated to learn about saving, investing and planning for a secure retirement. Providing education and information, in a variety of formats, is probably sufficient to meet their needs. They are able to understand asset allocation and diversify their 401(k) dollars appropriately. Their motto is, "Teach me how to invest and I will do it."

The do-it-yourselfers who only need instruction. Individuals whose motto is, "Tell me what to do and I'll do it." In general, these individuals are delighted with the onset of investment advice web sites, where they can plug in some personal information and come up with an asset allocation model.

The financial procrastinators. For these employees, investment matters are not a top priority, and are therefore not given the time and effort needed for a secure retirement. Their motto is, "Do it for me." They may understand the benefits of their defined contribution plan, but they prefer the professional management of defined benefit plans. These employees may or may not have adequate financial knowledge or expertise; they lead busy lives and do not have the time or inclination to think about investments. What they have in common is a desire for someone else to plan and manage their retirement security. Unfortunately, the financial procrastinator is often the forgotten employee, since they typically do not vocalize their needs like those who are more self-directed.

There's one thing we know for sure with employees – whether it's financial planning, health insurance, or investment education or advice . . . one size does NOT fit all.

Professional savings plan management is the answer for the financial procrastinator. Investment advice helps them allocate their 401(k) appropriately by diversifying their investment dollars. Research by Ibbotson Associates estimates the asset allocation decision accounts for 91.5% of the variation among returns in different portfolios. However, maintaining an appropriate asset allocation is difficult in today's volatile investment environment.

Savings plan management proactively maintains the strategic asset allocation and tactically reallocates specific investment selections, as market, economic and personal conditions dictate. In this way, employees' asset allocations are continually positioned to potentially receive a healthier return at their specified level of risk. Regular rebalancing and tactical reallocation helps participants sell when investments are up and buy when they are down.

Savings plan management requires a high level of personal contact with a competent professional advisor. The advisor should help the employee understand the rationale behind the strategic asset allocation. The advisor should then further define and qualify the employee's investor profile through ongoing discussions in order to tactically reallocate specific investments. The advisor should regularly and proactively contact the employee to discuss his or her needs, goals and investor profile.

Savings plan management can increase a participant's ability to replace income during retirement. A study by Watson Wyatt Worldwide of 503 companies with both a DB and DC plan found that from 1990 to 1995, DB plans showed an improvement of 10%, net of contributions and fees. DC plans had a net improvement of only 8.1%, showing that professionally managed accounts may perform better. Our experience shows that a personal advisor also:

- Gives participants a higher level of comfort
- Increases the level of plan contributions
- Helps participants understand the plan specifics
- Helps participants set attainable goals and understand market conditions.

Unfortunately, few employees have been offered this type of service. Employers are still concerned about their fiduciary liability, which stops them from implementing personal investment management services, in spite of the increasing use of web-based advisory services and more specific guidance and encouragement from the Department of Labor. Unfortunately, it may take revised legislation before plan sponsors become completely comfortable with this level of service. In the meantime, perhaps the best way for employers to utilize this type of service is to add it to the menu of choices available on a cafeteria benefit plan.

Cafeteria plans are defined under Section 125 of the Internal Revenue Code as plans maintained by an employer that allow each participant to select among cash and a variety of nontaxable "qualified" benefits. While initially the plans covered only a basic core group of benefits – including medical and life insurance, sick leave or disability – today the scope of benefits has become much broader. With recent legislation approving employer-provided retirement advice as a de minimus fringe benefit, the door is open for plan sponsors to consider offering far more to procrastinating employees.

The stakes are high for employers as well as employees. According to research by Virginia Tech's National Institute for Personal Finance Employee Education, approximately 15% of the U.S. workers experience enough stress from their personal financial situation that it reduces their productivity. Within some workplaces the negative impact may even shoot as high as 40 or 50%. Workers may waste as much as 24 hours on the job every month dealing with money issues.

The time has come to offer services that address the needs of all employees, whether the employer pays, the plan plays or employees share in the cost. Someday, savings plan management will be a standard corporate benefit. But for now, it is the rare employer who is meeting the needs of all employees.

---

[1] Reported in Pensions & Investments, June 25, 2001, page 30.

Socially Responsible Investing: A Growing Investment Trend

by Craig Cloyed, President
Patricia Stewart, Senior Financial Writer
Calvert Distributors, Inc.

Growing numbers of people—over 33 million to date[1]—want to invest in socially conscious companies that reflect their values and concerns for quality-of-life issues like the environment, product safety, and human rights. The market for this investment strategy, generally known as socially responsible investing (SRI), is experiencing explosive growth.

Over $2 trillion, or 13% of the $16 trillion under professional money management in the US—retail and institutional—is invested in a socially responsible manner.[2] The lion's share of institutional business comes from DC plans, like 401(k)s. In 1999, Yankelovich Partners conducted a survey on 401(k) plan participation and SRI for Calvert and found high investor demand for SRI options. "Our 401(k) client base has more than doubled over the past couple years as a result of this increased interest in SRI funds," says Christine Teske, Calvert's VP for Institutional Sales.

In 401(k) plans that offered an SRI option, 70% of investors utilized the SRI fund, the Yankelovich study showed. It also revealed that 69% of employees who do not currently have a SRI option in their employer-sponsored retirement plan want one. Not surprisingly, 81% of the investors surveyed also said that taking a company's business practices into consideration is a good long-term investment strategy. And, more employers are realizing that SRI funds can lead to higher employee participation. "This type of investing also attracts people who otherwise might not be investing," explained Alisa Gravitz, VP of the Social Investment Forum.

There's also been a sharp rise in interest in SRI products in institutional markets, like endowments, foundations and DB plans. According to a recent Dow Jones news article, the state of California is leading the way in implementing SRI DB plans for two of its largest pension plans covering teachers and public employees.[3] These plans are divesting their tobacco holdings or are seeking investments that support environmental and human rights standards.

The Dow Jones article noted there are three main drivers behind the rise in SRI products for retirement plans. First, SRI funds have turned in highly competitive performance over the last several years. A second factor is the 1998 DOL "Calvert letter" that stated SRI funds meet ERISA standards and are prudent investment options for retirement plans. Third, the SRI market has broadened, with about 9,000 to 10,000 companies meeting various SRI criteria. Twenty-five years ago, the selection of companies to choose from was very narrow.

Also fueling the trend toward SRI investments in retirement plans is new pension legislation recently adopted in the UK. The UK law requires pension fund trustees to disclose their SRI policies. Retirement policy analysts in the US believe this law is likely to impact US pension fund SRI practices and policies in the near future, according to Dow Jones.

The SRI Legacy: A Historical Perspective

Although the term "socially responsible investing" may have a contemporary ring to it, the practice of screening investments is hardly new. What is new, however, is the increasing investor demand for mutual fund companies that scrutinize the "total return" of their portfolios— not just in terms of financial performance, but also in terms of societal impact, both globally and locally.

According to the Social Investment Forum, approximately 13% of the $16.3 trillion under professional management in the US – a total of $2.16 trillion – is invested in a socially responsible manner. That's an increase of 82% since 1997, with SRI investments growing at nearly double the pace of the broad market.

Today, there are 155 SRI funds available to investors. This narrows to about 48 socially screened funds with a three-year performance record, according to the Social Investment Forum, a nonprofit group promoting SRI.

According to the Social Investment Forum, for year-end 2000, two-thirds of all SRI funds got top ratings from Lipper, Morningstar and Wiesenberger—outperforming most of their non-screened peers. Top-performing SRI funds crossed all key asset classes, including global, international, domestic equity, balanced and fixed-income categories. In view of these trends, there is every indication that the demand for SRI investments will continue to grow.

The SRI Investment Process

Most managers of SRI funds first analyze the financials of a company they are considering. They apply a disciplined, rigorous analysis of a company's financial fundamentals—such as earnings, balance sheet and management practices—which is the baseline for all portfolio construction. Then they add an extra layer of analysis—evaluating whether the firm meets certain societal and/or environmental criteria. The purpose of societal research is to complement the financial analysis of a company with a full picture of what a company does and what it stands for.

There are basically two approaches to screening companies. The first involves eliminating companies whose corporate practices do not meet certain minimum criteria in specific areas. The second involves applying positive screens and seeking out companies based on their proactive, positive track records. In practice, many SRI fund companies employ a combination of both methods.

The specific screens applied vary from company to company and fund to fund. Different mutual funds have adopted distinctive standards and social missions, reflecting the wide range of investor concerns and the individual philosophies of the company's Board of Directors. The following screens are the most prevalent:

- Environmental track records
- Workplace issues, such as race or gender discrimination
- Safety of products manufactured
- International human rights.

Of course, SRI is a dynamic process that is driven by, and reflects, investor concerns of the day. While apartheid was a dominant issue in the 1980s, areas such as the rights of indigenous peoples, human rights, and environmental issues like global warming are now at the forefront. Certain areas, such as tobacco, alcohol and weapons have long been screened out of portfolios for certain investor groups, particularly religious groups. It's important to keep in mind that selecting companies based on societal criteria has a large philosophical or world-view component that drives investment selection. Companies excluded in one fund family may pass another fund's screens. Therefore, investors need to examine an SRI fund's policies and criteria closely to ensure they match their individual goals and preferences.

Clearly, SRI is making a permanent impression on the investment landscape. This arena offers investors and institutions the opportunity to build sound, dynamic portfolios while making a positive impact on the world. As SRI funds continue to deliver competitive returns, it's likely that increasing numbers of investors will demand investments that address a broad range of societal concerns.

---

[1] Calculation based on ICI 2000 Mutual Fund Fact Book and 1999 Yankelovich Partners, Inc. survey.

[2] Social Investment Forum's 1999 Report on Socially Responsible Investing Trends.

[3] Socially Responsible Investing Gaining Institutional Ground, Dow Jones News Service, April 20, 2001.

Benefits Access: Altogether New Solutions

By Vincent De Palma,
President, ADP Benefit Services

Never before have employers faced such a complex and cost-sensitive benefits landscape. The sharpest employees, counting benefits as a critical part of their compensation, ask questions about their 401(k) participation, such as: Should I participate? How much should I save? Where do I invest my money?

Employees also have questions about Health and Welfare plans, such as: Which benefit program is best for meeting my family's medical needs? How much should I put into my Flexible Spending Account?

Increasingly, employers are balancing the demands of responding to these questions and the demands of the balance sheet through outsourcing. Data tells us that 30% of employers will seek an outsourcing solution that integrates key HR services (such as benefits) by 2003[1]. Clearly, the gauge of effectiveness for the outsourcing business model is changing in the eyes of employers.

Today's message is clear. Employees need easy access to information to make wise choices in managing their portfolio of employer-provided benefits—quickly and efficiently. Employers need cost-effective solutions that enhance their perception as an Employer of Choice. For both employee and employer, integrated HR outsourcing with self-service solutions is the future. Over the next five years, integration needs will touch even employers of several hundred employees.

What has changed? Employees have always needed access to relevant benefits information to make informed decisions about 1) building adequate retirement, and 2) healthcare options for their family medical needs. The difference is that decades ago, benefit options equaled one pension plan and one indemnity plan. Now, adaptability and choice have replaced stability and simplicity.

Adaptability replaced stability, when M&As became common in the '80s. Mergers require some party to adapt—be it a business unit integrating new processes or employees being laid off. Employees responded to this new business environment with less loyalty (holding 7-9 jobs during a career, up from 1-3 jobs in the '70s). More frequent employee turnover demanded a more portable retirement savings vehicle. The old DB pension plan was supplanted by a new DC plan, most often a 401(k).

Choice replaced simplicity with the proliferation of 401(k) plans. Today, even common plan options can be complex: with daily valuation, brokerage accounts and employee capability to redirect their investments 24/7. In the Internet age, consumers expect more choice. Technology has bred opportunity, but at the price of increased complexity. Employees want an instant, personalized presentation of all benefit choices.

Financial repercussions of increased choice and flexibility, in both retirement and healthcare, have fallen on the employee's shoulders. Generally, 401(k) plans require employees to take responsibility for developing their own investment strategy. On the healthcare front, employees began sharing costs when healthcare costs skyrocketed during the '80s. Employers offered a variety of choices (e.g., PPOs, HMOs) to balance plan flexibility with employee out-of-pocket costs. The benefits landscape became even more complex with flexible spending accounts.

Outsourcing responds. In one decade, the benefits world exploded. Outsourcing was first a way for employers to off-load increasingly complex administrative and compliance burdens. Employers found that outsourcers could better answer employee questions and stay current with quickly changing legislation.

The second generation of outsourcing applied technology (i.e., IVR, Internet) to introduce self-service options to plan participants. Self-service flourished for routine inquiries about

401(k) plan balances, plan information and benefit elections. At their convenience, employees enjoyed changing 401(k) asset allocations, enrolling in benefits or updating dependent information. Employers delighted in the 50%-80% transaction cost savings[2].

Today's self-service options include training modules and sophisticated investment decision-making tools that have on-line advice about retirement savings. Healthcare on-line self-service provides side by side plan comparisons and calculators for determining which medical plan option is best. But today's employee must visit separate sites to access such information.

Application integration is the future. The next generation of outsourcing will allow employees to have all of their HR questions answered through a single point of access, 24 hours a day—while still ensuring employer control of data. Ironically, where technology introduced a new level of benefits complexity, it now becomes the simplifying solution. The Internet-enabled organization is fast becoming the Internet-leveraging organization. These organizations are harnessing the power of web-based portals for a broad range of internal business processes. But, the visionary organizations, looking for every way to become an Employer of Choice, tap outsourcers for portals exclusively designed for HR services.

Portals that integrate all HR services through a single access point offer employees the ease of a single information source, 24-hour access and more sophisticated self-service options. Employers benefit from simpler contract administration, process re-engineering, and improved efficiency[3].

All constituencies benefit from an integrated HR outsourcing service model. Our recent survey of 400 companies confirms that nearly 40% of benefits managers expect their companies to use an integrated benefits services outsourcing approach over the next few years. Why?

Single point of access to all HR, Benefits and Payroll applications eliminates problems associated with data housed in different locations, typically with different points of contact. HR professionals are freed to focus on more strategic initiatives, while employees get a personalized view of their benefits from a single Web site. Employees can conduct 401(k), Health and Welfare, and Flexible Spending Account transactions, with the help of decision support tools. And now, employers have the ability to extend this resource to their retirees.

Access 24 hours a day neatly addresses today's busier workstyles. Employee satisfaction increases with accessibility and ease of use. HR Professionals and managers are no longer hampered by time zone differences.

Data control is enhanced, since access to applications and data is granted based on the requestor's role. For example, where a non-supervisory employee has access to only his/her own benefits profile information, an HR professional has broad access to, and transaction capability for, all employee data. By making the location and control of the data transparent, an integrated HR outsourcing solution resolves most companies' biggest objection to outsourcing.

We believe the evolution of employee benefits, and today's employee and employer needs, build a compelling business case for a single source solution for HR, Benefit and Payroll administration. The question is whether employers will deliver these services internally by investing in their own technology, or partner externally. External partners will need to demonstrate an ability to meet isolated requirements, as well as deliver on the integrated service delivery promise. Because, at the end of the day, the value of outsourcing to employers should always be measured by whether they add or detract from the equation of effective benefits, delivered efficiently to employees.

[1 & 3] Gartner Group, 1999, Demand Analysis of Integrated Multi-process HR Outsourcing.
[2] Hunter Group, 2000, Self-Service Survey.

Structuring Investment Menus To Meet Participants' Needs

By James McCarthy
Director of Plan Marketing
Merrill Lynch Benefits and Investment Solutions

One major benefit of defined contribution plans is that plan sponsors can allow participants to make their own investment decisions. To begin, it's safe to assume that most workers who are planning for their financial futures are not expert investors. Accordingly, these plans have to be manageable, while providing smart investment choices. Plan participants should feel empowered to confidently take the reigns of their retirement savings.

It is also important to recognize that a rather diverse group of people may be participating in any given plan; that is, plan sponsors are likely to have both sophisticated and not-so-sophisticated investors in their participant populations. As such, plan sponsors need to consider the needs of both types of investors and design plans for both—robust enough for the sophisticated, but simple enough for the novice. Strategies that sponsors have used to help the less sophisticated investors with their asset allocation needs include the use of products like asset allocation and rebalancing programs, life cycle funds and simple yet diverse core menus. More sophisticated investors are often accommodated by additional menu offerings (often called mutual fund windows) and/or the use of self-directed brokerage accounts.

The Search for Balance

Presently, many plans don't offer a sufficient balance between the different investment styles. The strong performance of growth stocks in the late '90s led many plans to supplement their arsenal of equity funds with more growth-oriented funds. Now, the offerings within these plans remain tilted at a time when balance is critical. The plan sponsor should remember that, in the long term, it may not be appropriate for historical strong performance to outweigh the value of balance.

The Importance of Asset Allocation

Although fund performance is important, it is widely recognized that asset allocation is one of the greatest contributors of portfolio return over time. Consequently, sponsors should periodically audit their investment menus to determine whether they provide enough options for proper asset allocation. If a menu doesn't offer a strong menu of choices (i.e., if it is skewed in one direction), its participants are likely to allocate in one direction, which may hurt them over time.

A robust menu should balance a variety of asset classes and styles. A plan participant should have several growth, value and blend choices; and within the styles, a spectrum of market sizes—large-cap, mid-cap and small. In addition, participants should be presented with foreign investment opportunities and fixed-income securities. Ultimately, plan sponsors should seek a two-pronged approach: 1) creating an investment menu with this sort of variety, and 2) providing education that focuses on asset allocation.

To thoroughly address the needs of plan participants, many well-balanced menus offer the following:

Characteristics of a Sound Investment Menu

- Offers an array of broadly diversified investments, and provides a balance across investment styles, market capitalization and asset classes

- Avoids too many choices within any single asset class or style

- Addresses the needs of both sophisticated and less sophisticated participants (e.g., through the use of asset allocation tools)

- Encourages appropriate asset allocation and diversification, powered by participant education.

The Call for Education

While a solid plan structure sets a strong foundation for success, one shouldn't undervalue the importance of education. Merrill Lynch recently conducted a survey of over 600 affluent plan participants, reflecting the top-third household income levels in the U.S. The survey indicated that over 35% of respondents are using a professional advisor to assist them with their investment decisions for defined contribution plan assets. We might expect that less sophisticated investors readily seek guidance, but our survey indicates that even the affluent investor is looking for additional knowledge and insight.

In another survey, plan sponsors were asked to remark on their levels of confidence regarding their employees' asset allocations. Almost 70% of respondents reported some level of concern.* Many plan sponsors are likely looking to provide their employees with further educational resources. In this time of market volatility, it can be expected that more and more participants would like to increase their knowledge base to be better able to maneuver themselves out of financial storms.

In short, education is paramount. From structuring plans to enable clients to take the wheel to providing superior education to help them steer, the goal is to assist plan participants in their journey toward financial success. In their fiduciary capacity, plan sponsors should think of their participants—choosing from a wealth of investment options, while stressing asset allocation—and provide them with the tools that will help them achieve long-term success.

---

*Source: BARRA RogersCasey/IOMA 2000

©2001 Merrill Lynch, Pierce, Fenner and Smith, Incorporated (08-01). Member, NASD, Securities Investor Protection Corporation (SIPC).

Notes

Why Employees Benefit from the 401(k)

Retirement as we know it is a relatively new phenomenon. The first formal retirement system was established in Germany during the mid-18th century by Bismarck. The normal retirement age for this program was 65. Life expectancy was only age 45. At the time, funding the benefits of those who survived until retirement age wasn't too difficult.

Our Social Security system originated at a time when most workers were males— many of whom were employed in jobs that involved hard labor. Those who survived to retire at age 65 lived an average of about 10 additional years.

Even a few decades ago the biggest retirement-related decision for many workers was whether to take a reduced pension benefit so that payments from the employer-funded plan would continue after death to a surviving spouse. Only a modest amount of personal savings was needed to provide a financially secure retirement. My parents, aunts and uncles were average members of the middle class. The combination of Social Security, an employer-funded pension and personal savings enabled all of them to live into their 90s in reasonable comfort. They didn't have to sit around at family gatherings when they were in their 30s and 40s talking about how much they were saving for retirement and how they were investing their savings.

Fewer workers are expected to spend their careers with one employer in the future—and even if they do, a shrinking number of these employers will offer an employer-funded pension plan that guarantees a lifetime income benefit. Employers will continue to shift to plans such as a cash balance pension and defined contribution plans where the employer contributes only a percentage of pay each year. Approximately 40% of employees work for employers that do not provide any retirement plan at all.

The retirement picture is very different today. Regardless of where you work, the bottom line is that planning for retirement is your responsibility. You can't rely on the government, an employer or anyone else to do it for you.

Many employees retire well before age 65 and a large number survive for an additional 20 to 30 years. These additional years of retirement require much larger retirement nest eggs than were needed a generation or two ago. It's not a simple matter of tripling the amount of money that participants once needed. Inflation has to be factored into the "how much is enough" equation.

At a modest 3% inflation rate, it will take 2.42 times as much income after 30 years to buy what you can buy during your *first year* of retirement. In your 30th year of retirement, you will need $84,700 to buy what $35,000 will buy today. This sobering fact is one of the reasons why I plan to keep working as long as I am able. Continuing to earn an income is the best hedge against inflation.

Financial security during retirement requires income from a variety of sources. I am shocked when I still encounter people who are not aware that Social Security isn't enough to cover your retirement needs. This has little to do with the current Social Security problems—the system was never intended to be the sole source of retirement income. Social Security will provide only about 40% of the average worker's income at a normal retirement age.

The percentage of your pre-retirement income that you will need in retirement depends upon many personal factors. Most professional advisors recommend an annual income equal to 70 to 80% of your pre-retirement income. There is no standard percentage—the right amount is whatever you will need to fund the retirement lifestyle you want.

Your Social Security Resource

You are not entitled to receive any Social Security benefits before you reach age 62. So if you are considering early retirement, you need to make up for this resource. The other problem with Social Security is that an even smaller portion of your pre-retirement income is provided by Social Security as your income increases. For example, the amount payable at your normal retirement age is only 25% or less if your income exceeds $75,000.

Social Security will provide 30 to 40% of your pre-retirement income if you earn $30,000 to $50,000 per year and retire at your Social Security normal retirement age. A defined benefit plan normally provides 20 to 30% of pre-retirement pay for a long-term employee who retires at normal retirement age. This benefit, plus the 30 to 40% provided by Social Security, can provide a survivable level of retirement income.

Personal savings must provide the difference between Social Security and any defined benefit resources. If you earn $75,000 or more, and you're entitled to lower Social Security benefits as a percentage of pay, you have to save even more—enough to replace about 50% of your pre-retirement income. Hopefully, your employer will help you save by providing and contributing to one or more retirement plans. The ideal scenario is to spend most of your career with the same employer. This employer would fund a defined benefit plan that guarantees you an income for

See Chapter 6 for more details on how to determine how much you need to save for retirement and how inflation affects your planning.

life and provide a 401(k) or similar plan for you to make pre-tax contributions.

The Future of Social Security

Each time we have a national election, attention is focused on Social Security. Political debates over what to do with Social Security and Medicare will continue for at least the next three decades. One does not have to possess great intellect to come to this conclusion.

As the Baby Boomers transition to their retirement years, our country will experience great financial strain. The aging of America will continue to be a major focus of the first three decades of the 21st century.

In the early and mid 1990s politicians were split over whether there was actually a Social Security crisis. Democratic candidates contended the system was financially sound, and they assured us there wasn't any reason for concern. Then President Clinton also told us not to worry after the Social Security Summit held during the first year of his presidency.

On the other side, Republican candidates were challenging the financial soundness of the system and proposing changes. By the late 90s, candidates from both parties finally reached agreement that the program is in trouble. The debate shifted at this point to who had the best solution. Nothing was ever resolved, and it is no small wonder that most Americans remain confused.

The real question is how big is the problem and when will it actually become a crisis? I was attending a board meeting of a benefits industry trade group in 1998 shortly after a special commission had submitted its recommendations for preserving the Social Security system.

The commission included highly respected members of both parties and the public and private sector. A Democratic Senator reported the commission's findings and recommendations to our group. The commission's major finding was that the Social Security system would run out of money by 2029 unless drastic changes were made.

After many years of listening to people deny that there is a problem, I was encouraged. I only quarrel with the commission's time estimate: the fact is that cash flows for the Social Security system will become negative around 2014.

Currently, Social Security taxes collected each year exceed benefits that are paid by around $150 billion. Sometime around 2014, annual benefits paid will exceed payroll taxes collected. This is a known fact—not my theory.

Those who contend that we won't have a problem until 2029 say that the extra money needed to cover benefits will be taken from the Social Security trust fund. They ignore the fact that there isn't any money in this fund because the government has already spent it for other purposes.

Suppose that by the time you reach retirement age you have borrowed all the money out of your retirement account and used it for other purposes. Instead of having $100,000 invested in a variety of funds, the only asset your retirement account has is your IOU for $100,000. The loan obviously won't provide retirement income to you.

> *"I'm 26 years old and have been contributing 10% of my salary for three years. In these three years I've managed to save $9,000. My wife has saved $30,000 in her 401(k) account in 9 years. Our goal is to save $1.2 million by the time we retire. Already, the $39,000 we've both saved will be worth almost $800,000 in 35 years (assuming a 9% return). That's without additional contributions—and we plan to keep saving!"*
>
> —Neal Kennedy
> Wyoming, OH

Likewise, the excess Social Security taxes we have been paying should have been retained in the Social Security trust fund, and then invested and preserved to provide retirement benefits to the Baby Boomers. The loans the Social Security trust fund holds can't be converted into retirement benefits either but our elected officials want us to believe they can.

I had planned to keep my mouth shut while the Senator spoke, but I was not successful. During the question and answer session, I told him that although I am not an actuary or economist, I believe that the problem will occur around 2014. He sputtered for a while and finally responded by saying, "We are committed to this system. We will keep our promise to pay benefits even if we have to print money." Needless to say, I was neither impressed nor comforted by this response. By the way, in my opinion both parties are equally guilty of playing political games with the Social Security system.

As a semi-amusing side note, one fairly recent presidential candidate advocated using some of the money in the Social Security trust for other social needs. The money had already been spent for other purposes so either he didn't know better or he wanted to double spend the money that is supposed to be used solely to provide retirement benefits.

Unfortunately, Social Security will continue to be a political football. There will be mounting pressure for candidates to provide supposedly painless solutions. This will be impossible unless we continue to be blessed with strong economic growth that can generate sufficient general budget surpluses to cover the Social Security shortfall. All or most of the budget surpluses we have heard so much about during the last few years are really due to the fact that Social Security taxes collected each year currently exceed benefits that are paid.

Once Social Security becomes a budget deficit around 2014 something has to give. Rather painful changes will eventually be needed unless tax revenue from other sources can make up the difference. Reduced Social Security benefits or increased Social Security taxes—or a combination of the two—is inevitable. The longer we go without facing this very real problem, the more severe the changes will be.

How bad can it get? Again, the facts are quite simple. A dollar in revenue must be collected by the government to pay a dollar of benefits. This is because Social Security is in fact a transfer system rather than an insurance or funded retirement system. The taxes you and I pay are used to pay benefits first and whatever is left is spent on other government programs or used to reduce the national debt.

Many people think they have actual retirement accounts at the Social Security Administration, but there is nothing more than a central computer that keeps records of how much we contribute. These contributions don't grow because they are not invested. As a result, we obviously don't have an option to withdraw our money from this account.

When I begin to collect Social Security benefits, I won't be drawing money out of an account. I will instead be receiving taxes paid by you and other workers. The Social Security taxes that are deducted from each paycheck for your retirement benefits amount to 5.3% of your pay. An equal amount is paid by your employer.

In 1945 there were 41.9 workers for every retiree. The ratio dropped to 3.4 workers for each retiree in 1999. By about 2030 the ratio is expected to drop to two workers for every retiree. The current taxes that two workers pay cannot cover the Social Security benefits for one retiree. In order to provide sufficient future benefits, Social Security taxes must at least double.

It was no problem when the taxes paid by 41.9 workers and their employers covered the benefits for each retiree. But today it's a different story. The average monthly benefit per retired worker was $804 in 2000 or $9,648 annually. Assume the average taxable salary for those who are contributing to Social Security is $35,000. The total taxable income for the 3.4 workers that are supporting each retiree is $119,000. The tax needed to pay each retiree's benefit is 8.1% ($9,648 divided by $119,000). This tax is split between you and your employer and your share is 4.05%.

Now assume that the worker/retiree ratio is 2 to 1 rather than 3.4 to 1. The taxable wage base per retiree would be only $70,000 ($35,000 times 2). The tax required to pay this retiree's benefit would be equal to 13.8% ($9,648 divided by $70,000). This is 70% more in taxes than what is needed today (13.8% divided by 8.1%).

The Medicare Dilemma

Once you start talking about Social Security, you also have to think about Medicare. It's impor-

> "My 401(k) plan has really helped my husband and I save for retirement...and I'm only 36. My husband and I decided we need $3.5 million to maintain our current lifestyle in retirement, and the 401(k)'s automatic saving feature is helping us get there.
>
> When I was 22, my Mom gave me that old chart that shows the benefits of saving early. We're planning to have $100,000 of inflation-adjusted income per year for 40 years. And because we started early, we think we can reach our goal when we're in our 50s."
>
> Beth Prickett
> San Diego, CA

tant to realize that Medicare is in worse financial condition than Social Security. Solutions will be even more difficult to find on the Medicare front.

Most people fail to consider health care a retirement issue, but it is an important one. For starters, if you or a dependent is under age 65 when you retire, access to health care and the related costs is a big problem. This is because Medicare isn't available until age 65.

The future financial demands on Medicare are huge. The greatly expanded number of participants is one reason. Another reason relates to our high expectations. There are many procedures available today to extend life that didn't exist a generation ago. Other procedures can make this extended life more comfortable. It is great that knees and hips can be replaced to relieve the pain of 80-year-olds, but in the next couple of decades we will unfortunately be forced to determine a level of health care the nation can afford.

Medicare doesn't cover all medical expenses, which is why most participants buy supplemental coverage. Prescription drugs and extended care are the other major expenses for many retirees. Many seniors are spending thousands of dollars per year for prescription drugs. The pressure for the government to help will increase. But is it likely that already heavily taxed workers be willing to pay even more taxes to provide further assistance to seniors? I wouldn't count on it.

We all need to realize that the government can't make health care less expensive for some without increasing taxes for others. For example, government subsidized prescription and/or long-term care benefits at less than market rates that I receive will increase the tax burden placed upon my children and grandchildren. But their tax burden is already heavy, and I don't want additional burdens imposed on them for my benefit. Senior members of our society must face the fact that this is what they are doing when they push the government for additional help.

Taxes, Taxes and More Taxes

The fact is that you and other workers are already over-taxed. FICA (Social Security) taxes take a big chunk out of your paycheck. You currently lose a total of 7.65% of your pay to FICA taxes (an acronym for the Federal Insurance Contributions Act). These FICA taxes are paid for various reasons: 5.3% are imposed for your retirement benefits, 1.45% for your Medicare benefits and 0.9% for disability and survivor benefits. The employer pays an equal amount which totals 15.3% of your pay. In 2001 these taxes were paid on the first $80,400 of your income. You and your employer each paid an astounding $6,151 in FICA taxes in 2001 if you earned at least $80,400.

The maximum FICA wage base is increased annually and it has mushroomed since 1977. The maximum FICA wage level was only $16,500 in 1977 and the tax rate was 5.85%. The combined employee/employer FICA maximum has increased from $1,931 to $12,302 since 1977. This is an increase of 637% or an average of 8% per year. If this pace continues, in 2025 the combined employee/employer FICA tax will exceed $78,000 for those who earn the maximum wage base. The 1.45% Medicare portion of this tax applies to all earned income and results in a 2.9% combined employee/employer tax.

To make matters even worse, we must also pay Federal, state and local income/wage taxes on the FICA taxes we pay. This means that we must pay tax on the tax! How painful is this double tax burden? Assume you have a gross income of $60,000 and your combined Federal, state and local income/wage taxes are equal to 20% of your income. The FICA tax you must pay is 7.65% of 60,000 ($4,590), but you have to first pay income tax on the entire $60,000.

Let's do the math so you can grasp the full impact of the double tax. You pay $4,590 of FICA taxes (7.65% of $60,000), but you also pay income/wage taxes on these FICA taxes. This means that you pay a tax on the $4,590 tax! Assuming a 20% tax rate, you will pay an additional $918 of tax. In addition, you must of course pay income/wage taxes on your remaining income of $55,410 ($60,000 minus the FICA tax of $4,590), as well as many other taxes, such as sales taxes, gasoline, real estate, occupational taxes—the list goes on and on.

The tax burden is even worse for those who own small businesses because they personally have to pay both the employee and employer portion of the FICA tax. A small business owner who earns $60,000 of W-2 income must pay the entire 15.3% of FICA taxes ($9,180) plus income and other payroll taxes. I occasionally bump into people who think they want to be independent contractors rather than employees. Any perception that being a contractor is better then being an employee is erased when I explain the situation with Social Security taxes.

With the eventual decline of Social Security, employer-sponsored plans such as the 401(k) that include employee pre-tax contributions will play an increasingly important role in helping workers save for retirement. As I've illustrated above, the taxes we pay are a big financial drain. It's virtually impossible to save for retirement without tax breaks. Contributions you and your employer put into a tax-qualified retirement plan are not taxable until they are withdrawn. All investment income and gains are also sheltered from tax until they are withdrawn. I encourage employees who are entering the work force to save 10% of their incomes for retirement at as early a stage as possible—and the combination of employee and employer contributions make this a realistic goal.

The Positive Side of Taxes

I've talked about the negative side of taxes, but there's also a flip side. Saving for retirement is so important that the government provides big tax breaks to help you achieve your retirement goals. Tax breaks are provided to avoid having a country full of senior citizens who are financially dependent on others.

As you know, the money you contribute to a 401(k) comes from your pre-tax "gross" income. This is a significant point because you pay three different types of income or wage taxes. Federal taxes increase as your income increases. The top tax rate is 38.6%, but the tax rate for most workers is either 15 or 27%. Many states also impose their own income tax and many local and municipal governments have wage taxes. Not all states and local governments follow the Federal tax code.

Some things that are deductible when you pay your Federal income tax are not deductible when you pay your state and local taxes. Employee pre-tax contributions to 401(k) plans are one of these exceptions. You don't have to pay Federal income tax on your 401(k) contributions, but you may have to pay state and local taxes. Your contributions to a 401(k) are also subject to Social Security taxes.

I know this is all very confusing, so let me try to clarify it with an example. Assume the following:

- Your gross pay is $2,000 each pay period.
- You live in a state that has an income tax equal to 2% of your income.
- Your wages are subject to a 1% local wage tax.
- Contributions you make to a 401(k) plan are exempt from state and local tax.

Next assume you do not contribute to a retirement plan. The following illustrates the difference between your gross and net pay:

Gross pay	$2,000
Federal income tax	350
State income tax	40
Local wage tax	20
FICA tax	153
Net pay	**$1,437**

Now assume you contribute 6% or $120 per paycheck to a 401(k) plan. The impact on your net pay is as follows:

Gross pay	$2,000
Federal income tax	329
State income tax	38
Local wage tax	19
FICA tax	153
After tax pay	**$1,461**
Retirement contribution	**120**
Net pay	**$1,341**

The reduction in take-home pay is only $96 but you have invested $120 for your retirement.

Next assume your employer contributes $.25 for each $1.00 you invest. No taxes are paid on the employer contributions at the time they are contributed. This additional $30 ($120 times 25%) increases the amount invested into your retirement account each pay period to $150. This is 56% more than the reduction in your take-home pay.

With a 401(k) plan, you not only reduce your tax bill, you also save faster. Without a 401(k) plan, taxes eat away the money you could save. Assume you work for an employer that doesn't have any retirement plan and your total tax rate is 37.65% (FICA taxes of 7.65% plus 27% Federal income tax plus 2% state and 1% local wage taxes.) It will take almost 16% of your pre-tax income to have 10% left to invest for retirement after paying these taxes.

Assume you earn $50,000 and your goal is to save 10% or $5,000. The results are as follows:

See Chapter 4 for more information on the employer contribution.

Pre-tax earnings required to get $5,000 after paying taxes	
· · · · · · · · · · · · · · · · · **$8,017**	
FICA taxes · · · · · · · · · · · · · ·	613
Federal income tax · · · · · · ·	2,164
State/local wage tax (3%) · ·	240
Amount left · · · · · · · · · ·	**$5,000**

You are able to avoid the $2,164 of Federal income tax and probably the $240 of state and local wage taxes with a 401(k) plan's pre-tax savings. Remember, employee contributions to a 401(k) are subject to FICA taxes. Without a 401(k) plan, it takes you $8,017 in pre-tax income to save $5,000. When you avoid paying $2,164 in Federal, state and local taxes, it only takes $5,613 in pre-tax income to save the same $5,000.

How the Employer Match Reduces Your Tax Bill Even More

Your tax situation gets even better if your 401(k) has a matching employer contribution. Assume all the facts are the same except the employee contributions are also based on your pre-tax income. Also assume that your employer will contribute 3% of your pay via a $.50 per $1.00 match limited to the first 6% of pay you contribute. You need to contribute 7% to achieve your 10% savings goal. There are no taxes on the 3% employer contribution before it is contributed. Your total savings are as follows:

Employer contribution of 3% :	$1,500
Employee contribution of 7%:	3,500
Total contribution	**$5,000**

The first advantage is that the employer contribution makes it possible to save the same

$5,000 through only a $3,500 personal contribution. In order to make that $3,500 contribution, you must earn $3,790 in pre-tax dollars to cover the $290 in FICA taxes. If you were not in the 401(k) plan it would take $8,017 of your gross, pre-tax earnings to save this $5,000. As you can see, the help you get from the 401(k) tax breaks and employer contribution is huge.

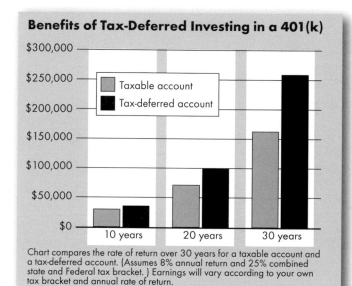

Benefits of Tax-Deferred Investing in a 401(k)

Legend:
- Taxable account
- Tax-deferred account

Chart compares the rate of return over 30 years for a taxable account and a tax-deferred account. (Assumes 8% annual return and 25% combined state and Federal tax bracket.) Earnings will vary according to your own tax bracket and annual rate of return.

I hope these two comparisons really grab your attention if you haven't previously thought about how important it is to work for an employer that offers a 401(k) or similar plan with an employer contribution. The advantage becomes very clear when you consider how much faster tax-sheltered money can grow.

A 401(k) or similar plan offers yet another tax-related advantage. The actual reduction in your take-home pay is less than the amount you put into the plan due to the immediate tax savings. For example, if you contribute $1, your take-home pay is reduced only by about 70 cents.

As you consider the benefits of a 401(k), you may wonder why you need a company plan to invest your money. The first reason is that it's difficult to start investing a small amount of money on your own due to minimum requirements that apply to most investment vehicles. When you contribute to a 401(k), your contributions are combined with those of your fellow employees, giving you access to investments that would not otherwise be available. And in many instances, the fees you pay in a 401(k) are less than those you would pay for the same investments outside the plan. This is particularly true if you have a small amount invested.

See Chapter 7 for more detail on investment risk.

The second major reason that you should think carefully about going solo relates to diversification—the first key investment concept. If your investments are diversified, they are not all invested in the same thing. Spreading your money into a number of different investments reduces risk. It is very difficult to diversify small amounts of money on your own. With a 401(k) your investments are immediately diversified—usually through mutual funds that in turn invest your money in a variety of stocks and/or bonds. It's also no small matter that investing through your 401(k) plan gives you access to investment pros who manage billions of dollars.

It's obvious that I think 401(k)s have many more pros than cons. When I'm asked to name the single most important benefit of the 401(k), my answer is *semi-forced savings*. With a 401(k), savings becomes the first rather than the last priority. Very few employees can achieve long-term saving goals on their own.

Tips on the Benefits of the 401(k)

- *Plan for an annual income equal to 70 to 80% of your pre-retirement income.*
- *Factor inflation into your retirement plan. At a modest 3% inflation rate, you will need 2.42 times as much income after 30 years to buy what you can buy during the first year of your retirement.*
- *Remember that Social Security will provide only a portion of the retirement income you will need.*
- *Factor access to affordable health care into your retirement planning because Medicare is not available to you or your spouse until age 65.*
- *Don't forget that Medicare doesn't cover many medical expenses-including prescription drugs and extended care.*
- *Take advantage of the semi-forced savings accomplished through the 401(k) payroll deduction feature. Make saving your first, rather than your last, priority.*

Notes

What Makes a Good 401(k) Plan?

Are you looking for a new job? If you're deciding among a few opportunities, you may also want to consider the quality of each employer's retirement plans. There is no standard plan—each company creates their own features, and some are better than others.

You may be happy with your current employer and just curious to know if your plan is up to snuff. Or you may be a plan sponsor who wants to know which cutting-edge features to consider for your plan.

Here's a guide to the features of today's best 401(k) plans.

Employer Contribution

An employer contribution is the single most important 401(k) plan feature. To achieve an adequate level of retirement income, you need to save at least 10% of your income each year. The more you get from your employer, the less you have to save.

Any employer contribution needs to be considered—not just a 401(k) match. This includes an employer-funded pension benefit and the many other types of employer contributions. Unfortunately, many different names are used to describe the same type of employer contribution—making comparisons difficult. The following is a brief summary of the different types of employer plans and contributions.

Traditional Defined Benefit (DB) Pension: This is the kind of retirement benefit your grandfather probably received each month of his retirement. There are still some of those critters around, but they're a dying breed. These plans are typically worth less than 1% of your pay in your 20s, about 1% in your 30s, 3% in your 40s and 5% or more in your 50s. These percentages of pay are approximate amounts employers must contribute to this type of plan.

If you leave the company, you receive a frozen benefit based upon your final salary. DB plans aren't very valuable unless participants spend most of their careers with the same employer.

Cash Balance Pension: This is a modified version of the traditional defined benefit plan. In this case, the employer contribution is usually a specific percentage—typically between 3 and 5% of pay. Your current benefit value is equal to the percentage of pay that your employer contributes.

Employer Non-Matching Contribution: There are many different types of defined contribution or "DC" plans. The employer contributes a specific or variable percentage of pay each year. This type of contribution may be included in a 401(k), 403(b), defined contribution/money purchase pension, employee stock ownership, 401(a), Keough, Simplified Employer Plan, profit-sharing or SIMPLE-IRA plan.

The amount of the employer contribution could be as small as 1% of pay or as much as 25%. The one common characteristic among all these plans is that you do not have to contribute to get the employer contribution. And in all cases your benefit value is equal to the employer contribution.

Employer Matching Contribution: This is the most common type of 401(k) employer contribution. But employees get the employer contribution only if they also contribute to the plan. An employer matching contribution may also be part of a 403(b) or SIMPLE plan.

Typically, only a portion of the amount you contribute is matched. The benefit value is equal to the percentage of pay your employer contributes. You maximize the value by contributing the full amount that your employer will match.

The matching contribution may be the only employer contribution, or it may be in addition to an automatic or variable employer profit-sharing contribution. For example, your employer may automatically contribute 3% of each eligible employee's pay plus a 25 or 50 cent matching contribution.

See Chapter 5 for tips on getting the maximum benefit from a 401(k).

Employers are not required to have any retirement plan and they are not required to contribute to a 401(k) plan. Employers that do so are making a financial commitment to help you save for retirement.

The level of the employer's contribution is a strong indication of the company's culture and financial strength. For example, in *Employee Benefits News* I read about the SAS Institute, the largest privately owned software company in the world with 7,700 employees. The company has contributed 15% of each eligible employee's pay to a profit-sharing plan for the past 25 years. You don't have to worry about contributing to a 401(k) plan if your employer already contributes 15% to a plan for you.

When you evaluate your employer's retirement plan, don't just look at the 401(k) company match. If the SAS employees did that, they would think they worked for a lousy company because they don't have a 401(k). Obviously, any plan that includes a 15% employer contribution is a lot better than a 401(k)—even one that has a dollar-for-dollar employer matching contribution.

Employees and writers for financial publications often make the mistake of focusing only on the 401(k)—overlooking the many other types of employer contributions. This prevents "apples to apples" plan comparisons. Don't make the same mistake: look at the total package of employer contributions.

The first step is to compare the amount of the employer contributions. For example, an employer contribution equal to 5% of pay in a cash balance pension is generally better than a 3% employer matching contribution in a 401(k) plan. An employer contribution equal to 10% of pay in a profit-sharing plan is generally better than a 401(k) with an employer matching contribution. If an employer contributes 10% or more of pay to a retirement program, there is no need for comparisons—it's a great place to work.

Level of Employee Contributions

As of January 1, 2002, the maximum amount you can contribute to your 401(k) has increased to $11,000. This limit will continue to increase over several years:

Year	Limit
2002	$11,000
2003	12,000
2004	13,000
2005	14,000
2006	15,000

These limits apply only to your pre-tax contributions. Any employer contributions aren't counted toward this limit.

Additional employee "catch up" contributions are permitted as of the same date for those who are age 50 or over:

Year	Limit
2002	$1,000
2003	2,000
2004	3,000
2005	4,000
2006	5,000

Before this change in the law, the combined employee/employer contributions could not exceed 25% of pay. As a result, it was necessary for employers to limit the percentage of pay you could contribute. For example, you would have been limited to a maximum of 20% if your employer contributed 5%.

The combined employee/employer limit is now 100% of pay with a $40,000 maximum, but your employer must modify the plan so you can contribute this higher percentage. In reality you can't contribute 100%, even if there aren't any employer contributions, because you must pay Social Security taxes and possibly state and local taxes. In addition you may have other pay deductions for medical coverage or contributions to a Section 125 flexible benefits plan.

If you could afford to do so, you could potentially contribute 80 to 90% of your pay. This opportunity will be a real plus for those who get started saving later in life, two income wage earners and those who start second careers after earning a military, police or other pension. For example, if you earn $20,000 working part-time (after retiring from the military), you could contribute $11,000 of this amount to a 401(k).

Push your employer to increase the percentage of pay you are permitted to contribute if they haven't already done so. There isn't any reason for your employer to limit the amount you can contribute, unless you are one of the highly paid employees. But, as you compare employers, remember that working for an employer that makes generous contributions for you is a lot better than an employer who contributes nothing.

Vesting

The fact is that employees will eventually leave their employer and it may be sooner than they expect. Vesting is an important retirement plan issue: if employees are not vested, they will not take their employer contribution with them when they leave. Employer contributions that are deposited into plan accounts don't really belong to employees until one of the following standard conditions gives them ownership rights.

1. Disability—as defined in the plan
2. Attaining normal retirement age, which is usually age 65
3. Death
4. Termination of the plan, or
5. Completing a specific number of years of service.

Once you achieve full vesting, all employer contributions belong to you, regardless of why or when you leave. Of course, if you change jobs, you're not immediately vested in your new employer's plan. This point should be fully factored into any employee's job search once full vesting is achieved in a plan that includes substantial employer contributions.

The maximum number of years of service that may be required before fully vesting matching contributions are legally defined. The two permissible methods are cliff and graduated vesting. With cliff vesting, ownership of the employer contribution goes from zero to 100% as soon as three years of service are completed. Graduated vesting occurs in 20% increments, reaching 100% after six years.

The following is a comparison of the two vesting schedules:

YEARS OF SERVICE	CLIFF	GRADUATED
Less than 2	0%	0%
2 but less than 3	0%	20%
3 but less than 4	100%	40%
4 but less than 5	100%	60%
5 but less than 6	100%	80%
6 or more	100%	100%

An employer may select an alternative that is equal to or better than these schedules. The two most common vesting alternatives for the 401(k) plan are cliff vesting of 100% after three years or graduated vesting of 20% per year for five years.

Eligibility

How long you have to work at a company before you are permitted to join the plan is an issue only when you are changing jobs—but it's a very important one. Until recently it was common to make newly hired employees wait one year before they could join a 401(k) plan. Actual entry into the plan was also commonly tied to quarterly entry dates—typically January 1, April 1, July 1 and October 1.

This delayed plan participation significantly: a new employee hired on January 12, 2001 would not have been able to start contributing to the plan until April 1, 2002, the first entry date after completing one year of service. If you change jobs more than five times, and you have to wait to join each plan for one year (and you wait even more time for entry dates), it could cost you up to 8 years without retirement benefits. A gap of this magnitude can have serious savings consequences.

Plan eligibility periods have been shrinking, however. Newly hired employees are now commonly eligible to join the plan within 90 days or less. Quarterly entry dates are being replaced by immediate or monthly entry.

Access to 401(k) Money

Loans and in-service withdrawals are a mixed blessing because an employee's ultimate goal is to achieve an adequate level of retirement income. But having some access to savings can be an important plan feature, particularly for younger employees who have a long way to go to retirement.

Employees often say, "Why can't I do what I want with my money?" The answer is that employees are given various tax breaks to encourage them to save for retirement. These tax breaks come with a price: restricted access to savings for non-retirement purposes. These restrictions apply during active employment with the employer that holds the retirement account.

There are three situations when money can be accessed from a plan account during active employment. Although each of these alternatives are legal, the employer is not required to make these plan features available.

The first alternative is to allow unrestricted access to plan assets after employees reach age 59-1/2. The withdrawn amount then becomes taxable, however. Next is the option to allow withdrawals for financial hardships (as defined by law and IRS regulations). Hardship withdrawals are also fully taxable and an additional early withdrawal tax penalty is imposed. The third possibility is to allow plan loans, which are also subject to numerous restrictions.

See Chapter 9 for a detailed explanation of loans and hardship withdrawals.

In service withdrawal and loan provisions should only be considered attractive plan features if employees are likely to need access to their money before they reach age 59-1/2.

Investments

The big issue is the quality and the range of a plan's investment options. Ideally, the investments should include at least one fund from each of the major asset classes. It's impossible for employers to pick consistently top-performing fund options in each category. And funds that can boast top performance records may not even be the best choices. But there is no question that employees don't want to be stuck in funds that are at or close to the bottom of their respective categories year after year.

Timely access to investment information is another big issue. It's hard to manage a retirement account in the best of circumstances, but it's almost impossible when important information is unavailable. Frustrated participants often tell me that they're unable to get performance information from both their employers and their service providers.

It's critical that appropriate standards are used to evaluate the quality of the investments in a plan. This comment may seem blatantly obvious, but it still needs to be said. The first step in performance evaluation is to compare a fund's total investment return over a period of time against similar funds.

You can't expect bond or other fixed-income funds to perform like stocks and vice versa. You also can't expect a value-oriented stock fund to perform like an aggressive growth fund. A value-oriented stock fund manager looks for bargain stocks. These may be specific companies or industries that are out of favor among major investors and stock analysts.

On the other hand, an aggressive growth fund manager typically looks for companies that are expected to have above average growth due to innovative products or new technology (Internet companies are a recent example). First understand what type of funds are in the plan, then make accurate comparisons.

Chapter 8 helps you understand and evaluate the different types of funds.

Expenses

Plan expenses are another key factor for comparison. There are four common types of expenses—administrative, investment, transaction-related and wrap fees.

One of the major administrative services involves keeping track of the money you have in your plan account and generating periodic statements. These records are maintained on computer systems that are designed to handle retirement plans like the 401(k). This recordkeeping function can be provided by a single person working on a PC in a home office or a massive financial organization. The employer selects an organization to provide the function or decides to handle it internally. There aren't any standards for this service, which accounts for the wide range of providers.

Other administrative services include determining benefits that are to be paid when employees terminate, issuing checks to participants, withholding and paying taxes, loan and hardship withdrawal processing and plan compliance testing.

The annual cost for administrative services, including the support to participants that is discussed below, are in the range of $100 per participant annually. This is a fixed cost for all participants in a plan, regardless of account size. Administrative costs are also similar among providers because they all must hire people with similar skills, use similar computer systems, and so on. The factor that varies the most is who pays these fees.

Administrative expenses are usually paid by the employer in young plans because this is the only viable alternative. A new plan participant would be reluctant to pay a $100 annual administrative fee. That fee would represent, for example, 5% of your annual contribution of $2,000. If the investments you chose then dropped 10% in value, your account would then be worth only $1,700 (after deducting the administrative fee and the investment loss). This significant drop in value might discourage you from further plan participation.

It's a common practice to shift payment of the administrative fees from the employer to the participant as the plan matures. After the assets grow, these fees constitute a relatively small percentage of your account balance.

Assume a plan that has 500 participants has accumulated $25 million of assets—an average of $50,000 per participant. The annual administrative fees are $50,000 at $100 per participant. This total fee amount is equal to only 0.2% of the plan assets. This means that if participants cover these costs, their investment return will be reduced by only this small percentage.

Participants don't always realize that they're paying administrative fees. The fee may be clearly shown on the statement, or it may less visibly reduce the investment return participants receive. In the latter instance, participants simply see changes in the value of their shares net of all expenses. The fees that are deducted are totally hidden.

The second type of fee you pay is the investment fee—typically a percentage of the account balance. This percentage varies substantially depending on the type of available funds. Actively managed funds carry the cost of a manager who picks the stocks, and passive "index" funds that do not require human intervention are less expensive. The annual fee for an actively managed stock fund is in the 1.0% range, compared to 0.20% for an index fund. Actively managed stock funds are also more expensive to run than bond funds. Funds that invest solely in international stocks are more expensive to run than those that invest only in stocks of U.S. companies.

You can find the investment management fee for each registered mutual fund in the fund's prospectus. (Look on the fund company's web site, or call them directly for a copy.) Investment vehicles offered by some financial organizations are not required to provide a fund prospectus. As a result, it can be very difficult to get straight answers on fees for some funds.

I've heard representatives of financial organizations tell employees that they do not pay any fees. Don't believe this: no organization that runs a 401(k) plan does so for free. The question is how participants pay the fee—not whether they pay one. Participants don't actually write a check as payment for a fee, but the reduction in their investment return is a powerful form of payment.

The investment management fee that fund companies charge for retail mutual funds is much more than is needed to cover investment-related costs. For a 500-participant plan with $25 million of assets, the typical fund company receives fees of $200,000 to $250,000—or $400 to $500 per participant. Typically, $100 per participant covers administrative fees and the balance covers investment-related costs.

However, this method of covering administrative costs from investment fees creates inequities because not all participants share costs equally. A new participant may only have a $2,000 plan balance at the end of the first year. How does this participant's $100 administrative fee get paid? It's paid by participants who have larger account balances.

I recently spoke on a panel where this type of fee structure was debated. One panelist was a young representative of a major fund company. Another was an age 50+ individual from a consulting firm. The fund representative argued that it's justifiable for participants who have larger balances to subsidize the administrative costs for participants who have smaller balances. Her rationale was that "Someone did this for you at some point." But the older panelist did not agree.

Perspectives on this issue are likely to vary with each person's stage in life. Expecting new participants to pay a $100 administrative fee isn't any more acceptable today than it was when I started the first plan years ago. But there should be a better alternative than saddling participants who have larger balances with this expense.

One alternative is to return to employer payment of the administrative fee for new participants. The primary reason this practice stopped is that there was no perceived value for this invisible benefit. Years ago I suggested that one of my larger corporate clients shift this expense to participants and use their savings for a visible benefit like an increased company match, and they took my advice.

How could employers make their payment of administrative fees for participants who have smaller balances more visible?

It could be included on the participant statement as an additional employer "contribution". Or for the first five years of participation, the employer could cover this expense for employees who are not in the highly compensated group. The added benefit could also help employers pass the non-discrimination tests. And paying the administrative fees for participants who have small balances would be a win-win situation—those who have small balances would continue to receive help and those with larger balances would no longer have to bear an inequitable cost.

It's ironic that employers pay all actuarial and administrative expenses for defined benefit pension plans, even though there is no perceived benefit value. Why is the perceived value of this fee payment such a big issue for 401(k) plans? I know some readers will think I don't realize your company pays these fees out of surplus DB plan assets. But what will your company do when excess pension assets dry up? It's not likely that these fees will be deducted from employee paychecks.

The third type of fee is tied to specific transactions, including loans, hardship withdrawals and benefit payments. The organization that handles the plan most likely deducts an additional fee from participant accounts for each of these transactions. For example, there may be a fee to take out a loan and an annual administrative fee during the period of repayment. Participants commonly pay these fees because they trigger the transaction—it's similar to an ATM fee.

The fourth and last fee is a wrap fee, which is an additional asset-related fee that may be charged for a variety of reasons. Small employers that have less than 100 participants are most often charged this fee. The fee is likely to range between .5% and 1.5%, and it is in addition to the normal fund management fee.

For example, a plan may offer a variety of name brand funds from different fund families. Participants pay the standard fund management fee, which is probably between .7% and 1.5% of their assets annually. The organization that sells and services the 401(k) receives an additional .5% to 1.5% of participant assets. This combination of asset-based fees pushes the cost of investing into the 1.2% to 3.0% range per year.

Wrap fees reduce the participant's investment return even more. Assume one of the fund options is the Fidelity Magellan Fund and the organization that runs the plan charges an extra wrap fee of 1.5%. Each year the participant's investment return will be exactly 1.5% less than the return reported by Fidelity. A 1.5% additional wrap fee reduces 30-year savings by 30%!

It's often difficult to get the full story on fees. I've been pushing for greater fee disclosure because it's tough to make informed investment decisions when the firm that handles the 401(k) plan refuses to disclose their fees.

I was one of many who appeared before the DOL when it conducted hearings on fees a number of years ago. Representatives from several financial organizations that are not willing to disclose fees claimed it is too expensive to do so. They also believe that fee information only confuses participants. (Amazingly, Vanguard and TIAA/CREF are the two lowest cost defined contribution service providers and they both fully disclose their fees.)

This provider attitude does not make sense. Imagine buying a car and authorizing the dealer to deduct the monthly payment from your checking account without knowing the cost. In my opinion, fee information should be included on the participant statement, rather than buried in the fund prospectus. I want participants to know which fees they're paying to whom—and be able to evaluate the services they are receiving versus the costs. Some extra fees may be worthwhile in exchange for valuable services.

If administrative and investment fees are distinguished, it will also be easier for participants to evaluate investment alternatives. When the plan administrative fees have been paid directly by the employer or the participant—rather than buried in the investment management fee—participants can consider less expensive investment alternatives such as index or institutionally priced funds. Even if participants are not paying the administrative fee up front, they usually pay it in the end—so it makes sense to consider more cost-effective options.

Institutionally priced funds are geared to large investors like pension funds or endowment funds of colleges and universities. Employers are increasingly selecting the same investment managers for the 401(k)—but because of the volume of money invested, they pay less. It doesn't cost an investment manager 10 times more to invest $100 million than $10 million. As a result, investment management fees usually drop as more money is invested.

The nation's 401(k) participants are collectively investing $2 trillion. This huge amount of money should give participants access to less expensive investment alternatives than retail mutual funds. The barrier to this is the practice of bundling administrative and investment services and paying for both types of services from asset-based fees. Unbundling the payment for these two different types of services allows participants to explore investment alternatives more intelligently.

A move toward lower-cost investment alternatives began a few years ago, and it will continue. Previously, when there was strong stock market performance throughout the 90s, participants were indifferent to fees. It was hard to get worked up over this issue when net investment returns were 15% or higher. The fact that a participant may have been able to earn another .5% to 1% with lower investment fees wasn't really a big deal. Investment fees become a much bigger deal when investment returns aren't as robust and may even be negative. Few would argue that a 9.5% return is a lot more attractive than 8.0%.

Participants can do little to change the minds of providers who will not provide fee information. On their behalf, I have asked the DOL to modify the Section 404(c) regulations to require full fee disclosure for plans that want to be compliant. I have also suggested a warning label be put on a provider's sales literature and participant information if they don't disclose fees and their product is not Section 404(c) compliant. That suggestion has received a few chuckles, but I do think that it would motivate more providers to disclose fees.

Another controversial issue concerns employer rebates. In some instances when large employers are investing many millions into name brand retail funds, the employer actually receives money from the fund company to help cover internal plan costs or other plan services such as education. This rebate may also be used to cover administrative costs for participants who have selected less expensive investment options. In large company plans participant contributions generate the rebates—so I believe that these fund credits should go back into their accounts. As participants continue to focus on fee issues, employers will be pressured to rethink the rebate situation.

Participant Support

The larger organizations that manage 401(k) plans offer a lot of support. Participants can call an 800 number or log on to the Internet to get detailed information about their plan investments at any time. This should include fee information and historical investment results. Participants should also be able to make changes at any time—move money from one investment to another, change their contribution rates, etc.

The provider should also offer a lot of educational support for retirement planning. At a minimum this support should include:

- A retirement calculator to help participants determine how much they will need when they retire and how they should invest to reach their goals
- Account statements and other tools to help participants measure their progress toward a specific goal
- Information about the various types of mutual funds to help participants understand their investments
- Investment support to help participants formulate the most appropriate asset allocation
- On-site educational seminars.

What can participants do when their plans aren't competitive? Many participants and journalists ask me this question. The answer depends on the reason the plan is not competitive. It's a disadvantage, for example, if a plan does not have any employer contributions, but there probably isn't much that participants can do except save more. In the case of small employers, many simply can't afford to contribute.

When a plan lacks other important features, participants are best advised to gather competitive information about other employer plans. Local information can be obtained from the Chamber of Commerce. National information can be obtained from the profit-sharing/401(k) Council (*www.PSCA.org* or 312-441-8559).

Sometimes the information participants gather can clear up employer misconceptions. A lot of small employers overestimate the cost of a matching contribution. A 25% match limited to the first 4 to 6% of eligible pay costs less than 1% of pay, because not all eligible employees will contribute and some will contribute less than the maximum amount that is matched.

For example, matching the first 4% of pay that is contributed at the rate of $.25 per $1.00 will cost only .75% of pay if 75% of the employees contribute at least 4% of pay. The annual total will be only $750 per $100,000 of eligible payroll.

This is not an insurmountable amount for even a small employer—and it's very probable that the cost would be recovered through reduced employee turnover.

Employers often need to be reminded that the 401(k) not only helps to retain employees, it helps to attract them as well. Information about competitive plans can help employers shape a plan that draws more top employees to their companies.

The most common area of employee dissatisfaction is not contributions, however. Performance and a lack of available information are the two most common complaints, closely followed by the number and type of funds offered.

On the information front, employees are often shocked to discover that employers are required to provide only three things:

- A Summary Plan Description (SPD)
- A Summary Annual Report (SAR), and
- An annual statement of each employee's account.

The SPD explains the general terms of the plan—who is eligible and when, the types of contributions, vesting, etc. The information about plan investments is typically limited to a generic fund description. In some cases an SPD doesn't give fund descriptions and says only that participants are able to split their contributions among various funds selected by the employer.

Distributed annually to each participant, the SAR contains information that is taken from the Form 5500 that is filed with the government. This form is due by the July 31st following the close of the calendar plan year.

The SAR contains general information about the total plan assets for the plan year that ended on the December 31st preceding the filing date. This means the information is very dated by the time you receive it. For example, the 5500 Form filed by July 31, 2002 contains the information from the plan year ended December 31, 2001.

In the SAR you'll find general financial results for the year for the entire plan. It includes the total contributions, interest, dividends, realized and unrealized gains, benefit distributions, etc. for the entire plan. None of this information helps you decide how to invest your money.

The annual benefit statement doesn't have to include detailed information on the actual return and expenses for each participant's investments. The statement may be limited to the beginning balance, contributions, withdrawals, investment gains or losses and ending balance. A growing number of service providers are reporting a lot more information, including each participant's specific rate of return. These voluntary efforts are to be applauded.

Participants often receive a lot of other services and information that employers are not required to provide. These include quarterly statements, the opportunity to call a toll-free 800 number to ask investment and other plan account questions and Internet access to plan information.

It's also important to point out that educational support from employers or service providers is not legally required. I know some readers will say "but what about Section 404(c)?" (Sorry, I promised earlier that this book wouldn't be filled with IRC Code Sections, but this is one of those times when it can't be helped.)

Years ago the Department of Labor issued regulations to provide some fiduciary relief to employers. These regulations are known as Section 404(c). If employers want the fiduciary relief, they have to structure their plan investments in accordance with these regulations. One requirement is that participants must be given sufficient information to make informed investment decisions. But, these regulations are voluntary rather than mandatory. The regulations also do not contain any further guidance about what is adequate information to make informed investment decisions.

Even though participants may get a lot more information than what is legally required, it is probably not enough. What can participants do? They should ask their employers and/or service providers for the information they need. I recommend submitting written requests.

Here's a sample letter:

Dear 401(k) Plan Representative:

Planning for my retirement is a serious matter. I want to do everything I can to be sure that I have an adequate income during my retirement years. I understand this is my responsibility, including how to invest the money I contribute to my 401(k) plan.

Unfortunately, I haven't been able to make informed investment decisions because I can't get adequate information about the fees that I pay. I've called the service center at the Outback Investment Company and their representative told me I don't pay any fees. Perhaps I should consider this wonderful news, but I'm not dumb enough to believe that it's true.

As a result, I'm requesting a written explanation of all the fees that I pay, including those that are deducted from plan assets by the organizations that invest and manage the plan-and reduce the net investment return I receive.

Sincerely,

Participant

A letter to a service provider is one way to get to the bottom of the fee issue, but it's not a guarantee that you will get a detailed response. Another way you can find hidden fees is to compare the annual fund returns reported on your statement with those that are publicly reported for the same funds.

Assume Caroline has money invested in the Janus fund through a 401(k) plan. When she looks at the fund's annual return on her statement, she sees that it's roughly 1% less than the published return for this fund. This is a good indication that she is being charged an additional 1% plus the normal investment management fee Janus charges.

Several years ago I received a call from the president of a company who asked if I would review his company's 401(k) plan. He explained that some of the participants were unhappy with the plan's investments—even though a consultant he hired concluded that they had nothing to complain about. When I read the investment advisor's report, I was surprised that she didn't mention the fact that participants were being charged an extra 1.0% annual wrap fee on their contributions and another 1.5% fee on the employer contributions. As a result, the total fees being charged to participants were in the 2.0% to 2.5% range.

The unhappy participants had suspected they were paying additional fees, but they didn't have any proof because they were buried. The president was motivated to change this situation because some employees had stopped contributing to the plan. This reduced the amount he could contribute and the payment of the additional fees also reduced his own annual returns. Because the participants were not receiving any additional services for the fees that they were paying, they had nothing to lose if the plan was moved to a lower-cost provider. And that is what actually happened.

As you've read in this section, there are not a lot of ways that participants can influence plan sponsors to change their plans. The situation above, however, is an example of participant power. Most employers offer a 401(k) plan to help attract and retain good employees. Senior management wants employees to be happy with the plan so that they'll join the company, stay on and be productive. Realistically, they also want a good plan with low fees for personal reasons. When participants stop contributing, it impacts senior management pocketbooks and it can bring about change.

I caution participants that this action will not *always* bring about change. And missing out on employer and employee contributions can be a high price to pay for change. Participants need to be sure that their dissatisfaction with fees is justified before they take any action.

One example is a participant who called to tell me that he was really unhappy with the service provider for his plan. He had just received his statement, which showed a negative return for the bond fund. I knew that the organization that handles his plan is a quality provider, so I dug deeper.

He told me that outside of the 401(k) he buys bonds that produce a 6%+ return. He said that he never has any losses because he gets his money back when the bonds mature. I then explained that with a 401(k) it's necessary to report the value as if the bonds were being sold as of the statement date. As a result, the return that appears on his statement reflects both income and changes in value for each bond held. This explanation calmed him down and helped him realize that complaining to his employer would not have been justified.

Participants have a better chance of getting their company plan sponsors to listen and take action if they submit detailed written complaints. Generic complaints (either verbal or written) that simply state that a plan's investment options stink are not very useful. It's best to explain why, specifically, there is dissatisfaction. It may be the fact that a particular type of fund is not offered— or it may be due to excessive fees or poor performance.

Here's a sample letter that may get the attention of a plan sponsor:

Dear Plan Representative:

I take 401(k) investing very seriously because I want to do everything I can to be sure I have an adequate income when I retire. As you know, investment return has a major impact on the savings that I and other participants will accumulate.

I am very dissatisfied with the return of our large-cap stock fund, the Outback Super Stock Fund. In the past year the return for this fund was 2.4% less than the S&P 500 index. During the last three years the fund returned an average of 2.6% less than the S&P. This fund has also ranked in the bottom quartile for three years, and it has only a two-star Morningstar rating.

It would clearly be in the best interest of all participants to replace this fund with a similar fund that has a better track record and rating.

Sincerely,

Participant

This letter contains specific reasons for the dissatisfaction supported by Morningstar ratings, an independent source. It also properly identifies the type of fund and compares its performance with the S&P index—an appropriate benchmark for this type of fund. Gathering all this information may appear to be very difficult, but it isn't. *Morningstar.com* (or other similar fund resources) provides all this information.

Participants need to consider the culture of their employers before they start attacking the 401(k), however. They don't want to be labeled as troublemakers if this is how their employers view people who complain.

When participants fail to get the information they need, I encourage them to write to the DOL. Letters should be addressed to the Assistant Secretary of Labor, Pension and Welfare Plans Administration, 200 Constitution Avenue, N.W., Washington, DC 20210. Ann Combs is the Assistant Secretary at the time I am writing this book. Participants should explain what efforts they have made to get the information they need and the responses they received.

In the end, as participants evaluate their 401(k) plans, they are really evaluating the corporate citizenship of their employers. How an employer shapes a 401(k) often reflects how they view and treat their employees. 401(k) attitudes and actions vary widely among companies, and participants need to decide if they're investing their time and retirement savings potential in the right company over the long term.

Some companies simply do not put a lot of emphasis on helping their employees save for retirement. The benefit manager of a company that owned a national chain of restaurants told me about a new board member who was troubled by the fact that less than 50% of the eligible employees contributed to the 401(k)—even though there was a 50% employer match. The benefit manager was asked to develop an educational campaign to increase participation.

The benefit manager presented his proposed campaign to the company's board but they voted it down. Why? Because the board soon realized that a 10% increase in the participation rate would have cost the company $1 million per year.

In contrast, the attitude at CYRO Industries is far more benevolent. Bill Dorcas, CYRO's benefit manager, has a passion for helping employees save for retirement through a comprehensive program of "Choice & Responsibility". CYRO's 401(k) plan objectives are to:

- Aid in affecting good behavior and practices for retirement savings and planning.
- Use investment education and retirement planning to help employees meet their Choice & Responsibility for a successful retirement.
- Give all employees a flexible, convenient way to save for retirement while saving on current taxes.

CYRO goes much further than most companies to help employees understand the impor-

tance of using the 401(k). Here are just a few examples of how CYRO goes the extra mile for employees:

- Mandatory meetings for all employees not enrolled in the plan
- Mandatory investment education and retirement planning meetings for all employees
- 401(k) articles in the company newsletter
- One-on-one employee meetings that include retirement modeling software
- An investment education library
- Annual personal letters to all non-participants
- Personal meetings with all non-participants to discuss the reason why and provide potential 401(k) savings projections
- Requirement that all non-participants sign a waiver acknowledging the potential loss of 401(k) benefits
- Reminders to employees to increase 401(k) contributions when they receive pay increases.

The examples on the next two pages illustrate several ways you can increase your plan participation.

Why does Bill have such a passion about what he does? He says, "One of my personal goals in life is to truly make a difference in the lives of others. By helping our employees save more, invest wisely and strive for financial security in their retirement years, I'm meeting that personal goal." My personal thanks and congratulations to Bill Dorcas and others like him who are truly dedicated to helping employees save for retirement.

SAVING JUST $43 PER PAY PERIOD CAN GET YOU HEADED DOWN THE ROAD TO A MORE COMFORTABLE RETIREMENT!!!

October 23, 1997

EILEEN

Will you be ready to retire when the time finally rolls around? The CYRO Industries 401(k) Employees Savings Plan can make it possible. This summary illustrates your potential "nest egg" at retirement if you were to enroll in the CYRO Plan today. It is based on the following assumptions:

- You are contributing 4% bi-weekly of your current salary of $28,028.
- A 15% Federal marginal tax bracket.
- Company Match contributions based on the following:
    $0.75 for $1.00 on the first 4% of your contribution
- Investment returns are calculated assuming your entire portfolio averages a rate of return of 8%. (Please note that this is not a representation of the options in your particular plan.)
- An annual salary increase of 4%.
- You will retire at age 65.

YEARS OF PARTICIPATION	YOUR "OUT OF POCKET" COST*	ACTUAL CONTRIBUTIONS	COMPANY MATCH	TOTAL ACCOUNT BALANCE
5	$5,161	$6,072	$4,554	$12,864
10	$11,441	$13,460	$13,460	$34,552
20	$28,377	$33,385	$25,275	$125,740
30	$53,446	$62,878	$47,158	$347,171

Your out of pocket cost represents your actual cost of investing money in your pre-tax account. Your actual contributions represent the amount of pre-tax contributions in your account. Projections shown above do not reflect any unusual tax situations such as excise taxes, penalty taxes, or the alternative minimum tax.

If you join the CYRO Plan today, you could have $347,171 at retirement (in 30 years), if all of the above assumptions are met. That translates to $2,193 a month in the form of an annuity to supplement any other retirement income you may have. This monthly payout is determined by assuming you enjoy 25 years of retirement earning a 6% pre-tax rate of return on your money once you retire. Of course, the actual results you may realize will vary depending upon your salary increases, investment results, and other factors. So don't get lost on the road to retirement .... **enroll in the CYRO Industries 401(k) Employees Savings Plan today!**

CYRO INDUSTRIES
401 (k) EMPLOYEES SAVINGS PLAN

ACKNOWLEDGEMENT OF PLAN EDUCATION
AND WAIVER OF BENEFIT

I ALSO CONFIRM THE UNDERSTANDING THAT THIS DECISION
RESULTS IN THE LOSS OF THE COMPANY MATCH MONEY WHICH IS
EQUAL TO AN AMOUNT OF UP TO 3% OF MY CYRO EARNINGS, ALONG
WITH LOSS OF POSSIBLE PERFORMANCE MATCH OF UP TO AN
ADDITIONAL 1% OF MY CYRO EARNINGS. I FURTHER AGREE THAT I
UNDERSTAND THE VALUE OF COMPOUNDING.
I ACKNOWLEDGE THAT CYRO HAS INFORMED AND EDUCATED ME
ABOUT THE BENEFITS OF PARTICIPATING IN THE PLAN. AT THIS
TIME I DECLINE TO PARTICIPATE.

SIGNED ———————————————————————————

NAME PRINTED ———————————————————————

DATED ————————————————————————————

Tips on Recognizing a Good 401(k) Plan

- When you compare 401(k) plans, first look at the amount of employer contributions.
- Compare all employer contributions—not just the 401(k) match.
- Remember that an employer that contributes 10 to 15% of pay to a retirement plan without requiring participant contributions is a better deal than a 401(k). (Even a 401(k) that has a healthy employer matching contribution.)
- Compare apples to apples when you compare plan investments.
- Don't believe that any 401(k) provider does not charge fees.
- Review fees carefully: the expenses you pay directly impact your investment returns and the savings you accumulate.
- Submit written comments about plan dissatisfaction to company plan sponsors and 401(k) providers. Be specific and substantiate your points.

Notes

Joining Your 401(k) Plan

I occasionally get letters and calls from individuals who want to open a 401(k) account. Unlike an IRA that you can do on your own, the 401(k) is available only through an employer.

Employers are not required to have any retirement plan. Employers that do have plans must establish the rules within the guidelines of existing laws and regulations. Congress writes the laws, and administrative agencies such as the Treasury Department and the Department of Labor issue the regulations. Tax laws governing plans like the 401(k) provide the general legal framework. Regulations provide the detail and there's no shortage of that. The regulations are typically much more voluminous than the actual laws.

The fact that your employer offers a 401(k) doesn't mean that you are eligible to contribute. You must meet your employer's eligibility requirements before you can join the plan. Your employer is permitted to exclude those who have been employed for less than one year and/or who are under age 21. In addition, employees who have satisfied the plan's eligibility requirements can be required to wait a maximum of an additional six months until a plan entry date. The entry date is the first date you can actually enter the plan after satisfying the eligibility requirements.

For example, assume you joined your company on January 14, 2002 and your employer requires one year of service before plan eligibility. Further assume the plan has two entry dates: January 1st and July 1st. You will complete one year of service on January 14, 2003. You will have missed the January 1, 2003 entry date so you will have to wait until July 1, 2003 before you can begin contributing. This is almost eighteen months after you started with your employer. As I mentioned previously, the trend has been to move away from these long delays so that newly hired employees can join the plan immediately or within 30 to 90 days of the first pay period.

Full-time and part-time status is another issue that may affect eligibility. The employer is permitted to exclude all employees who have not worked at least 1,000 hours during any year. The following are other categories of employees who may be excluded:

- employees who are covered by a collective bargaining agreement (union),
- non-resident aliens,
- leased employees, and
- a specific category of employees.

Leased employees include those who work for a company on a temporary basis placed through an agency such as Manpower. An employer may also exclude a specific category such as hourly or salaried employees or the employees of a specific business unit, as long as the rest of those covered by the plan satisfy applicable legal standards. For example, your company's 401(k) may be available to only salaried employees if the coverage rules of the Internal Revenue Code can otherwise be satisfied.

Some companies that own many different businesses prefer to let each business unit have their own benefit programs. For example, one of my clients owned a business unit that hired rocket scientists and other business units that hired low-skilled factory workers. The units with low-skilled workers could not afford the same benefit programs that were needed to attract rocket scientists. As a result, each business unit maintains its own plans that qualify under IRS separate line of business rules.

There is a lot of confusion related to the exclusion of union employees. Labor laws pro-hibit employers from offering any retirement or other benefit plan (including a 401(k) that is funded solely by employee contributions) outside the collective bargaining process. The labor laws require union employees who want a 401(k) to include this in their contract demands. Union managers continue to prefer defined benefit pension plans, which is the primary reason why 401(k) coverage is lower among union employees. It also is the reason why 401(k) plans for union employees typically don't include an employer matching contribution.

Getting Started

Probably the most important decision you will make regarding your 401(k) plan is simply to join. Everything else is irrelevant if you don't start contributing to the plan. If money is tight, you will be tempted to wait and to start saving in a couple of years when you might be earning more or have less debt. One of the biggest myths for younger employees is that it will get easier to save in the future. The fact is that it never gets easier. I know because I have been there. Saving is easy for some people and seemingly impossible for others.

You might think that it doesn't really matter if you wait to join the plan for a couple of years. But you lose a lot of potential savings when you wait. Take a look at the difference in Ken, Rasheed and Lisa's account balances after 30 years. Ken, Rasheed and Lisa all earn $25,000 each year and decide to contribute 5% of pay or $1,250 to their 401(k) plan.

Ken waits eight years to begin saving. In years nine through thirty, he contributes $27,500 to the plan and his account balance grows to $71,827. Rasheed starts saving right away, but stops after eight years. He has only contributed $10,000 to the plan but he ends up with $74,897, over $3,000 more in his account than Ken. This surprising difference is due to the magic of compounded earnings over a thirty-year period.

Advantages of Starting to Save Early Through a 401(k) Plan

Year	A — KEN waits 8 years to start saving — Annual Investment	A — Year end value @ 8%	B — RASHEED starts saving early, quits after 8 yrs. — Annual Investment	B — Year end value @ 8%	C — LISA starts saving early and keeps at it! — Annual Investment	C — Year end value @ 8%	WHAT YOU INVEST AND WHAT YOU EARN
1	$0	$0	$1,250	$1,295	$1,250	$1,295	**A - started late 22 yrs. @ $1,250**
2	0	0	1,250	2,694	1,250	2,694	Total saved $71,827
3	0	0	1,250	4,205	1,250	4,205	Amount invested 27,500
4	0	0	1,250	5,836	1,250	5,836	Investment return 44,327
5	0	0	1,250	7,598	1,250	7,598	**B - stopped early 8 yrs. @ $1,250**
6	0	0	1,250	9,501	1,250	9,501	Total saved $74,897
7	0	0	1,250	11,557	1,250	11,557	Amount invested 10,000
8	0	0	1,250	13,777	1,250	13,777	Investment return 64,897
9	1,250	1,295	0	14,879	1,250	16,174	**C - started early & continued 30 yrs. @ $1,250**
10	1,250	2,694	0	16,069	1,250	18,763	Total saved $146,724
15	1,250	11,557	0	23,611	1,250	35,167	Amount invested 37,500
20	1,250	24,579	0	34,692	1,250	59,271	Investment return 109,224
25	1,250	43,713	0	50,973	1,250	94,687	
30	1,250	71,827	0	74,897	1,250	146,724	

The figures indicated reflect employee contributions only. In this example, investment return is calculated at 8%. Your own 401(k) investment return may be higher or lower, depending on the performance of the funds offered and how you invested the money in your account.

Lisa saves for the entire thirty years. She has contributed only $10,000 more than Ken, but her account has grown to $146,724—twice that of Ken's. You can see that it pays to start saving early and to keep saving.

This may be old stuff to those of you who are older, but you can help a younger fellow employee, a child or grandchild learn the importance of developing the savings habit early. One great lesson I've learned is that it's truly how we manage the income we receive rather than how much income we earn. I know this is very difficult for some of you to believe, but I have seen many examples. I have met individuals with incomes in excess of $300,000 who have a huge amount of debt and no savings. I have also met individuals who have built substantial savings and carry little or no debt—despite modest incomes.

The Department of Labor hosts an event annually to celebrate the efforts that have been made by both the public and private sector to encourage savings. I was able to attend the year 2000 celebration. One of the highlights of this event is to honor an individual of modest means who has accumulated significant savings. Earl Crawley, a parking attendant who worked for a bank for many years, was the 2000 honoree.

The fact that Mr. Crawley saved so much money in a low paying job shows that just about anyone can build an adequate nest egg. It's a matter of turning spenders into savers.

I have found that spenders will always spend what they have or more, regardless of how much they earn. A spender who gets a substantial increase in income adjusts his spending habits to the new level within a very short period of time. This is why if you are a spender, you should take a portion of any pay increase and put it into a 401(k) or similar forced savings vehicle before you get used to having it in your hot little hands.

Otherwise you will never break the spender cycle.

Some Easy Ways to Save

I have stated before that 401(k), 403(b) and 457 plans don't work well for most individuals with incomes below $20,000. Many different types of employees fall into this category, including high school and college students, seasonal workers, seniors and other part-time workers who have little interest in saving for retirement. There are also many employees working full-time earning only enough to cover basic necessities.

Even though I know that everyone has to save as early as they can, it's not right to condemn those who have trouble eking out any extra money. But sometimes people don't realize that there are easy ways to save. I'm not suggesting that you give up many of the things that you enjoy in life—but often a few minor spending adjustments can free up money for savings.

It all boils down to making choices. Each of the things on the following list are not necessities—and cutting one or two out or reducing the cost of a few items could begin your savings program.

- $1 each day or week for a lottery ticket
- $25 for a carton of cigarettes
- $3 a day for an alcoholic beverage
- $3 a day for various other beverages of choice (bottled water, soda, coffee, etc.)
- $10 a day for lunch
- a $400 monthly car payment vs. a $250 payment
- a $250,000 home vs. a $150,000 home
- $20 per week for entertainment
- a $500 vacation vs. a $1,000 vacation.

Each of these small expenditures adds up over time. Drinking regular old water with lemon every time you eat out will save $1 to $3. Assume you eat out five times a week or 260 times per year. Your annual savings will range from $260 to $780 depending upon the cost of the beverage you normally select. Next, assume you reduce your non-mealtime beverage consumption by one drink per day. That's one less beer, Starbuck's coffee, bottle of water, etc. This will generate another $260 to $780 of annual savings. Just cutting back on beverages alone could bring you close to $1,500 a year in savings—and in 30 years that savings could add up to $204,450 (assuming a 9% investment return).

Cars are another item that prevent many people from saving. It can cost a lot to own and operate a car, regardless of whether you buy or lease it. If you have a new car, it costs you around $13.00 for a 40-mile roundtrip to the mall—when you consider all operating costs and amortize the purchase price. Sure, you need a reliable car for commuting to work, but there are many good and affordable used cars that are not an embarrassment to drive. Ideally, you should always buy whatever car you can afford with cash. But if this isn't possible, a $250 monthly car payment instead of $400 payment gives you $150 more per month to invest for retirement.

You may be asking if all this nickel and diming is really worth it. I can hear some people saying, "Hey, you only live once, and I want to have all the extras I can afford." I understand this way of thinking, but I also think that giving up a few non-essentials today is far better than struggling without necessities during your retirement years. The fact is that I've never met any 401(k) participants who claim that they've saved too much. I've also never heard participants say that they

Help your children or grandchildren catch the savings habit with a "401kid" match. Add $.25 or $.50 to the amount your child or grandchild saves. The advantages of saving can and should be learned at an early age.

wished they had spent more money. Instead, what many older participants tell me is that they wish they had started saving sooner.

Getting started is the issue. And sometimes the best way to get started is to save a very small amount such as $10 per week or $520 per year. Due to the tax savings the 401(k) offers, your take-home pay is reduced by only about $8 per week when you save $10. I think that just about anyone who is earning more than $20,000 could find a way to save $8 a week. If you keep a record of your non-essential spending for just one week, you would see how easy it is to eliminate one or two things.

Remember that even a small savings makes a big difference over time. Only $10 per week invested for 35 years with a 9% return will eventually be worth $112,320. Any employer matching contribution will increase this amount. Roughly $100,000 won't be enough money to live on during all your retirement years, but it certainly will be a big help.

How Much Should You Save?

After you get started, your goal should be to increase your savings rate each year. Perhaps the easiest way to accomplish this is to boost your savings rate each time you receive an increase in pay. Assume you start by contributing 1% of your pay and you receive a 4% pay increase. Take at least 1% of the raise to increase your contribution rate to 2%. Keep doing this each time you receive a raise until you reach a point where your savings plus any employer contribution is likely to provide an adequate level of retirement income. Don't miss any opportunity to get your retirement planning on track.

When you consider how much you need to save, don't forget about any employer contribution. Employers usually match only a portion of the amount you contribute—so it makes sense to contribute the amount necessary to get the entire match. There are many different ways the match-

ing contribution can be structured, but the most common is for the employer to match the first 4 to 6% of pay that you contribute.

Assume you are earning $30,000 and your employer matches the first 5% of pay you contribute. This means the employer will match the first $1,500 (5% of $30,000) you contribute. You should attempt to contribute the full percentage that is matched by your employer so that you can get as much "free" money as possible. If you can't afford to do so now, start with a lower percentage and increase your contribution rate to the maximum employer level as soon as possible. Remember, you're leaving money on the table when you contribute less than the percentage that is matched by your employer.

One other important point: even though in this example, you will not receive a match for any contributions you make in excess of 5%, you still get a tax break for your entire contribution. It always makes sense to personally contribute as much as you possibly can.

If you are married, you and your spouse should each contribute the maximum amount required to get the full employer match. If you can't afford to do so, then see which plan has the higher match and decide who is likely to stay long enough to get the vested employer contributions. You may also want to consider which plan has the better investment options—and which one permits loans if you expect to tap your 401(k) plan resources in the future.

How the Matching Contribution Boosts Your Savings

Both employees and employers have trouble understanding exactly how the match works. Most importantly, you need to know how to structure your contributions so you don't lose a portion of the match. When you join the plan, clear up any confusion and make sure that you're maximizing your employer contribution.

The matching contribution rate is set by each employer, and a match is not required. The amount may be as little as $.10 for each $1.00 you contribute or as much as $1.00 for each $1.00. The most common matching rates are $.25 and $.50 to the dollar. A few employers match more than $1.00 per $1.00. The highest matching rate I've seen is $4.00 for each $1.00 of employee contributions. I would tell you the name of the employer so you could apply for a job, but they don't want publicity.

Beware of the fact that some employers match only during the pay periods that you also contribute to the plan. Suppose you want to make several large contributions early in the year so that you're sure you've contributed the maximum permissible amount ($11,000 in 2002).

The problem is that your employer may match a fixed percentage of your pay in each pay period—they will not front-end their employer contribution the same way that you do. If your employer uses this contribution method, it means that once you stop contributing, your employer does as well. But at the point you stop, the employer has not yet matched the full percentage of your total salary that you will receive throughout the year. By front-loading your own contribution, you then forfeit some of your employer's contribution.

Assume you earn $80,000 and you decide to contribute 20% of your pay. You will be forced to stop contributing when you reach the $11,000 limit. Matching contributions will also stop at that point if your employer matches only during payroll periods when you're contributing. It makes more sense to reduce your contribution rate so you will be contributing for the entire year and still hit the $11,000 limit. In this

See more detail on contribution limits in Chapter 4.

instance, 13.75% would be the applicable percentage for each pay period. Otherwise you would be forced to stop contributing when you have earned $55,000.

Assume your employer matches the first 6% of pay you contribute and the matching rate is 50%. You should receive an employer contribution equal to 3% of your $80,000 pay or $2,400—if you contribute at least the 6% required to receive the full employer contribution.

However, if your employer match is made only when you are contributing, you would receive only $1,650 of matching contributions in this example (3% of $55,000). You would lose $750 of employer contributions. This arrangement is unfair to employees who don't spread their contributions over an entire year, but it's common practice because it's easier to compute the matching contribution for each pay period that you actually contribute.

You will also need to know how your contributions will be calculated if you receive variable pay due to overtime, commissions, bonuses, etc. Most employers will permit you to have contributions deducted from your entire gross pay, but some will limit contributions to only your base pay. For example, assume your gross base pay is $1,000 per pay period and you want to contribute 5%. Your contribution would be $50 per pay period. Further assume you earn an additional $100 of overtime. Your contribution will be increased to $55 if contributions are deducted from your gross pay including the overtime. If your employer doesn't deduct contributions from gross pay, your contribution will be $50 each pay period regardless of the amount of overtime you earn.

Some employees also like to make larger than normal contributions when they receive a bonus, a large commission or other form of variable pay. For example, you may contribute 4% of your regular pay but you may want to contribute 30% of a special bonus you receive during December.

Naming a Beneficiary

One of the things you will be asked to do when you join the plan is to name a beneficiary who will receive the money that is in your account in the event of your death.

Before you name any beneficiaries you need to understand that by law your spouse automatically receives your 401(k) benefit when you die, regardless of whom you have named as your beneficiary. This is the case unless your spouse signs a benefit waiver that is witnessed by a notary or a plan representative. This provision was added to the law to protect the rights of female spouses, but it works both ways. For example, a married female employee who has children from a prior marriage must obtain an acceptable spousal benefit waiver from her husband before she can name her children as beneficiary.

You will probably be able to name both a primary and a secondary beneficiary. The primary beneficiary will receive your 401(k) money if he/she is living at the time of your death. Your secondary beneficiary will receive your money if your primary beneficiary dies. You should also be able to name more than one primary and/or secondary beneficiary. In this instance, you will need to specify the percentage that each will receive.

You may want to use a more generic secondary beneficiary if additional children are a future possibility. You could specify that all your children are to share equally or you could name a trust as the beneficiary. A trust is advisable if there are minor children, or if you have a large account and you do not want your children to get the money when they reach age 18. Related tax issues are covered in Chapter 10.

You need to know that the beneficiary form you have filed with your employer is the primary instrument that will determine who receives your plan benefit. The provisions of the plan document will determine what happens to your 401(k) money if you haven't named a beneficiary or if the beneficiary you named isn't living. I have met people who have written wills and trusts that they think will control the distribution of their 401(k) assets.

Whenever your marital status changes, you also need to review your beneficiary designation. For example, you may be single when you join the plan. If you marry, your new spouse will automatically become your beneficiary, regardless of who is named on the form you previously filed with your employer. This is fine if you want your spouse to receive the benefit, but it isn't if you want someone else such as your children to receive the benefit. Remember that your new spouse will remain the primary beneficiary unless a spousal waiver is submitted.

One of the questions I have received regarding the spousal waiver is what to do if you are legally married but your spouse is nowhere to be found. If you are in this situation, you should name your children or someone else as your beneficiary—but you need to know that your spouse still has legal rights to claim your 401(k) benefit.

Another question I have been asked is whether a waiver that is part of a pre-nuptial agreement will suffice. There isn't a clear answer. The law states that the waiver must be signed by the spouse. An individual is not a spouse prior to actual marriage. As a result, the spouse could contest the pre-nuptial waiver.

Tips on Joining Your 401(k) Plan

- *Don't wait to join your 401(k) plan.*
- *To find ways to save, for just one week track how much you spend on non-essentials.*
- *Don't give up the chance for the "free money" employer contribution.*
- *Increase your savings rate each time you get a raise.*
- *Time your contributions to get the maximum employer contribution.*
- *Check whether your employer deducts contributions from base or total pay.*
- *Update your beneficiary arrangements when your marital status changes.*

Notes

Notes

How to Build an Adequate Nest Egg

The reason that I am writing this book has a lot to do with my faith, which is a major part of my life. I start each day, other than Sunday, with a 45-minute devotional time. This is the most important part of my day because I frequently receive specific direction during this time I spend alone with God. I was directed during my devotional time on the day I started this chapter to share some of my personal plans for retirement, so that is what I am doing.

My goal in this chapter is to personalize the retirement planning process and show that there are five relatively painless steps that can get you on your way toward retirement security. Too often people are led to believe that all they have to do is to plug their retirement dreams into one of the many retirement calculators. This mechanical calculation will supposedly tell you everything you need to know to hit your savings goals. I know that retirement planning is a very personal issue, and the people who are most successful in reaching their goals don't rely on quick, magical numbers. It's a long process, and the more you think about what will be important to you and your family throughout your retirement years, the better planner you will be.

To help you personalize your retirement planning process, I'm going to tell you a little bit about my own background. I grew up on a dairy farm in Bedford County, part of South, Central Pennsylvania, with a daily view of the Allegheny Mountains. When I was six years old I started milking cows in the morning before leaving for school and in the evening before dinner.

My family worked hard, particularly during the summer months. I was blessed with three older brothers, an older and younger sister. The three stronger older brothers were truly a blessing because they got the tougher jobs. Perhaps even more importantly, my dad ran out of farms before he got to me, so I wasn't raised with the expectation that I would stay in the family business. I was the only male member of the family who didn't study agriculture in high school. As a result, I left the farm to attend college.

I got my first full-time job at age 18 by responding to an ad for a math clerk. This was of interest because math was my major. The position was in the pension department of Provident Mutual Life Insurance Company. I spent over five years there learning the basics of the retirement business and attending college at night.

While I was still in college, I joined Ed and Dave Johnson in the northern Philadelphia suburbs. We spent 25 years together building an employee benefit consulting company from scratch. The Johnson Companies eventually grew to a $25 million firm with approximately 350 employees. We sold the company in 1990, and I was contractually committed to the buyer for three years.

During my time at The Johnson Companies, I had various management and consulting responsibilities, and I became one of the top retirement planning consultants in the country. One evening as I was driving on the Pennsylvania Turnpike, I realized that I had been so focused on wrapping up my assignments that I hadn't given very much thought to the fact that I was soon leaving the firm.

My future was undecided—and as I rode along, I was suddenly made aware that I was being given a clean slate to plan the rest of my life. I was fortunate that the amount of money I received for my stock when we sold the company removed an immediate need to replace my paycheck. But at age 51 I wasn't ready to retire.

The following morning I wrote down the things that I would value most in a future career. It was readily apparent that joining some large organization wouldn't match my goals. That quickly led me to the conclusion that I would be doing something on my own. But the big question was: what? For three years I was prohibited from soliciting any of my former clients or business associates. That plus my general dislike for management activity made me realize that I would have to do something very different.

In 1993 my career took a completely new turn and I established the 401(k) Association. At that time, there was a constant battle to preserve the private retirement system. Many policymakers viewed all private retirement plans as the big black hole that sucked up tax revenue. As I mentioned in Chapter 1, the Reagan team tried to eliminate 401(k) plans in 1985—and the threat to the private retirement system was still very real in 1993. My original objective for the Association was to give participants a vehicle for joining in the fight to save 401(k) plans. Today, because retirement savings plans enjoy a wide level of political and private support, my association now focuses on how 401(k) plans can better serve participants.

Now that you know how I got to where I am today, I can tell you about my personal retirement plans. I am now 59 years old and I've been working since I was 6 years old. Despite my long working career, I've never looked forward to a time when I don't work. I am not consumed by my work, but I've always been thankful to have been given the opportunity to do things that I enjoy.

With an office at home (which was a major adjustment), I save a lot of commuting time. This arrangement gives me room to reward myself with a hike into the mountains (which I can see out my office window), walks to the library, a bike ride, running and most importantly visits with our children, their spouses and our grandchildren. I plan to continue working as long as I am healthy, enjoy what I am doing and I can find something productive to do. I'll reassess my career plans again at age 64. This will take me to the 25th anniversary of 401(k), which may be the ideal time to hang it up—unless there are new challenges that give me a reason to continue.

There are both financial and physical reasons why I'm not anxious to retire. I believe that our Creator did not intend for us to spend 20 years or more in retirement. Of course, I realize that many of you are in situations where you are counting the days until you can leave your job and never look back. Many of you work in jobs that probably entitle you to a 20-year golf game. But most people have a built-in need to be productive and useful. This is not just my opinion—there are endless numbers of studies that show that productivity in the traditional "retirement" years leads to longer and healthier lives.

In my case, I'm not only predisposed to be productive, my family genetics suggest that I may be retired for a long time. At any income level, it takes a lot of savings to live in financial security for 30 years or more without a paycheck. I'm also not confident that Social Security and Medicare will give me the financial help I need 30 years from now.

The best way to avoid outliving your retirement nest egg is to delay using it as long as possible. I plan to do just that. On the 50th anniversary of 401(k), I don't want my grandchildren to find that I've outlived my retirement nest egg and set up camp in the woods!

STEP 1: ESTABLISH...
...a Realistic Retirement Target Date

The most difficult part of planning for retirement is knowing how much you will need. First you need to establish a realistic retirement date target. Most workers want to retire at an age that is considerably younger than what is considered their Social Security normal retirement age. This is the age when you're eligible to receive full

Social Security benefits. The age is 65 for those born prior to 1938 and 67 for those born during 1960 or later. The normal retirement age is between 65 and 67 for the rest of you.

While we're on the subject of Social Security, you need to know that the earliest age that you can receive benefits is 62. If you retire at age 62, you will get 80% of the full benefit if 65 is your normal retirement age and 70% if 67 is your normal retirement age. Although the future of Social Security is uncertain, you need to factor these benefits into your retirement planning.

There is no "right" age to retire—it's a very personal issue. Virtually everyone I talk to who is over age 30 has some general ideas about retiring some day. These may be dreams that include travel or nothing but sitting around. In most instances, people have a target retirement age. At one extreme are those who plan to retire by age 45, but they have saved very little. These people are generally clueless about what it will take to retire. At the other end of the spectrum are 35-year-olds who have very detailed and disciplined plans to retire early.

I doubt that Social Security benefits will disappear during the next 20 to 30 years, but they may be reduced. There's also the possibility that a "means test" will be enacted, whereby only those with incomes below a certain threshold will receive Social Security benefits. Here are some of the more likely Social Security changes that will occur in the next 10 years:

- All earned income will be subject to the full FICA (Social Security) tax
- The normal retirement age will continue to increase
- All Social Security benefits will be taxed if your income exceeds a certain level.

The most important piece of advice I can give you about Social Security is to reduce your expectations.

STEP 2: CALCULATE...
...How Much You Need to Save

Once you have decided on a retirement age, assume that your retirement begins tomorrow. What will your life be like? This is the retirement planning prerequisite question that retirement calculators don't ask. Most importantly, what will you do six months from now after the novelty of retirement wears off and you're tired of golfing, shopping, traveling and other leisure activities? Many people find it difficult to go straight from full-time work to full retirement—particularly when they haven't developed interests outside of work.

As you continue down this imaginary path, consider how you will feel if you no longer have a paycheck of any size. How much income will you need to maintain your current standard of living? Probably close to 100% of your current income.

How much savings will it take to provide this level of income? The answer is a lot. I generally recommend saving ten times the final income you expect to earn when you retire. This formula is a good starting point if you plan to retire at your Social Security normal retirement age. If you retire earlier, you will of course need to save more. If you have a company pension or other sources of income, you may be able to get away with saving a bit less.

As an example, assume you are retiring today and you earn $50,000 per year. This means that you should save a total of $500,000 to hit this ten times goal. This nest egg would be sufficient to provide approximately $30,000 per year of inflation-adjusted income, assuming:
- the rate of inflation is 3%,
- you will need this income for 25 years,
- only a small cushion will be left at the end of 25 years,
- you invest 50% of your nest egg in stocks and 50% in bonds during this period.

Remember that $50,000 represents your gross earnings—you are not actually living on $50,000 because you have to pay taxes. Your taxes will be less when you retire and you will no longer need to save for your retirement. Your income will also be subsidized by your savings and Social Security—the other reasons why you actually need a smaller amount—roughly $30,000—for each retirement year.

STEP 3: ADJUST...
...Your Savings Target for Inflation

Your first reaction is likely to be that you can generate a lot more than $30,000 per year or 6% from a $500,000 nest egg. But the amount that you withdraw for each year of retirement needs to be increased annually to offset the impact of inflation. You will need $60,984 (3 x 20,328 from the inflation chart below) in the 25th year of your retirement to buy what $30,000 will buy in the first year. This is why you need $500,000 to provide $30,000 of inflation-adjusted income for 25 years.

Inflation Chart

This chart uses $10,000 as an example of the income amount you need during the first year after you retire. The amount you need will increase 3% each year after you retire. The sole purpose of this chart is to show how inflation erodes buying power—even at a modest 3% annual inflation rate.

Number of Yrs. After You Retire	Annual Income Needed	Number of Yrs. After You Retire	Annual Income Needed
1	$10,000	13	14,258
2	10,300	14	14,685
3	10,609	15	15,126
4	10,927	16	15,580
5	11,255	17	16,047
6	11,593	18	16,528
7	11,941	19	17,024
8	12,299	20	17,535
9	12,668	21	18,061
10	13,048	22	18,603
11	13,439	23	19,161
12	13,842	24	19,736
		25	20,328

Those who have never done any retirement planning may have trouble believing that you should withdraw only $30,000 per year from a $500,000 nest egg. The following chart shows why you must be realistic about how much you should withdraw.

You will have enough left after 25 years for only another two years. That isn't a very big cushion.

Since you will not be retiring tomorrow, but at some point in the future, the following table helps you project how much you are likely to be earning the year you retire. Assume your retirement goal is age 62—or 20 years from now. You

Managing Your Nest Egg During Your Retirement Years

No. of Yrs.	Beginning of Year Balance	Annual With-drawal*	Invest-ment Return**	End of Year Balance
1	500,000	30,000	33,950	503,950
2	503,950	30,900	34,195	507,245
3	507,245	31,827	34,393	509,811
4	509,811	32,782	34,539	511,568
5	511,568	33,765	34,628	512,431
6	512,431	34,778	34,653	512,306
7	512,306	35,822	34,610	511,094
8	511,094	36,896	34,485	508,683
9	508,683	38,003	34,278	504,958
10	504,958	39,143	33,977	499,792
11	499,792	40,317	33,574	493,049
12	493,049	41,527	33,060	484,582
13	484,582	42,773	32,424	474,233
14	474,233	44,056	31,654	461,831
15	461,831	45,378	30,740	447,183
16	447,183	46,739	29,667	430,111
17	430,111	48,141	28,423	410,393
18	410,393	49,585	26,992	387,800
19	387,800	51,073	25,358	362,085
20	362,085	52,605	23,505	332,985
21	332,985	54,183	21,413	300,215
22	300,215	55,809	19,062	263,468
23	263,468	57,483	16,431	222,416
24	222,416	59,208	13,497	176,705
25	176,705	60,984	10,445	129,166

* Equal to $30,000 adjusted annually for inflation, assuming a 3.0% inflation rate
** 7% return

Inflation Adjustment Table

Number of Years	Assumed Annual Rate of Change				
	3%	3.5%	4%	4.5%	5%
1	1.03	1.035	1.04	1.045	1.05
2	1.06	1.07	1.08	1.09	1.10
3	1.09	1.11	1.12	1.14	1.16
4	1.12	1.15	1.17	1.19	1.22
5	1.16	1.19	1.22	1.25	1.28
6	1.19	1.23	1.27	1.30	1.34
7	1.23	1.27	1.32	1.36	1.41
8	1.27	1.32	1.37	1.42	1.48
9	1.31	1.36	1.42	1.49	1.55
10	1.34	1.41	1.48	1.55	1.63
11	1.38	1.46	1.54	1.62	1.71
12	1.42	1.51	1.60	1.70	1.80
13	1.46	1.56	1.67	1.77	1.89
14	1.51	1.62	1.73	1.85	1.98
15	1.56	1.68	1.80	1.93	2.08
16	1.60	1.74	1.87	2.02	2.18
17	1.65	1.80	1.95	2.11	2.29
18	1.70	1.86	2.02	2.21	2.41
19	1.75	1.93	2.10	2.31	2.53
20	1.80	1.99	2.19	2.41	2.65
21	1.86	2.06	2.28	2.52	2.79
22	1.91	2.13	2.37	2.63	2.93
23	1.97	2.21	2.46	2.75	3.08
24	2.03	2.29	2.56	2.87	3.23
25	2.09	2.37	2.66	3.00	3.39
26	2.15	2.45	2.77	3.14	3.56
27	2.22	2.53	2.88	3.28	3.74
28	2.28	2.62	3.00	3.43	3.92
29	2.35	2.72	3.12	3.58	4.12
30	2.42	2.81	3.24	3.74	4.33

need to project your current income to what you think you'll be earning 20 years from now.

Assume you expect your income to increase at an average rate of 3% per year for the next 20 years. The appropriate factor from this table is 1.8. Multiply 1.8 times your current income ($50,000 in this example), and you'll see that your expected income at retirement is $90,000. This will increase the size of your targeted nest egg to $900,000 (10 times $90,000). This is an easy way to get a rough idea of how big a nest egg you should build—regardless of your current age or income.

STEP 4: DEVELOP...
...a Detailed Savings Plan

How do you accumulate ten times your annual income—and then some—by the time you retire? The first step is to start early. Then there are many retirement calculators and other tools you can and should use to help you develop a workable retirement plan.

A retirement calculator should be available through the financial organization that handles your 401(k) money. Some other resources are:

www.financialengines.com
www.mpower.com
www.quicken.com/retirement
www.money.com
www.asec.org/int-blpk.htm

Each calculator uses different methods and assumptions. As a result, different calculators will give you widely varying results. Check the assumptions each calculator uses to see if they make sense for your situation.

Tools like retirement calculators will help you decide how much you need to save—and then once you begin to save, you have to keep checking that you're on track. There are certain benchmarks that generally help you gauge where you should be at certain points of your nest egg accumulation. The following savings goals are

designed for 25-year-olds who are just starting their savings program.

Most likely you are over age 25, but these benchmarks can still tell you if you're on target with your retirement planning. Many of you will be significantly behind these benchmarks. Remember that these are ideals, and I don't include them here to make anyone feel defeated. Instead, my intention is to motivate you to sit down and develop a workable plan for catching up. This may mean that you have to work longer than you would like—unless you have enough time to substantially increase your savings rate.

Savings Goal By Age 35:
One Times Your Pre-Retirement Income

How To Accumulate $39,000 by Age 35

Age	Your Pay	Your Contribution	Employer's Contribution	Total Return	Year End Value
25	$25,000	$1,000	$500	$68	$1,568
26	26,000	1,300	650	229	3,747
27	27,040	1,622	811	446	6,626
28	28,122	1,687	844	710	9,867
29	29,246	1,755	878	1,006	13,506
30	30,416	1,825	912	1,339	17,582
31	31,633	1,898	949	1,710	22,139
32	32,898	1,974	987	2,126	27,226
33	34,214	2,053	1,026	2,588	32,893
34	35,583	2,135	1,067	3,104	39,199

The above example is based upon the following assumptions:
- 4% annual wage increases
- 4% of pay contributed during the first year; 5% the second year and 6% each year thereafter
- an employer matching contribution equal to $.50 per $1.00, limited to the first 6% of pay that the employee contributes
- an assumed total investment return of 9%

Your goal should be to accumulate one times your annual income by age 35. The previous example shows what you need to do to accomplish this goal.

As you can see, a 50% employer matching contribution is a big help. You would have to adjust your contributions if you are in a plan that has a lower employer contribution or none at all.

Savings Goal By Age 45:

Three Times Your Pre-Retirement Income

Assume in the next 10 years you increase your contribution rate to 10%. You continue to receive a 50% match or a 3% of pay contribution from your employer, your annual pay continues to increase by 4% per year, and your investment return is 9% per year. The following are the results:

Age	Your Pay	Your Investment	Employer's Contribution	Total Return	Year End Value
35	37,006	$3,700	$1,110	$3,744	$47,753
36	38,487	3,849	1,154	4,523	57,279
37	40,026	4,003	1,201	5,389	67,872
38	41,627	4,163	1,249	6,351	79,635
39	43,292	4,329	1,299	7,420	92,683
40	45,024	4,502	1,350	8,604	107,139
41	46,825	4,683	1,405	9,917	123,144
42	48,698	4,870	1,461	11,368	140,843
43	50,646	5,065	1,519	12,973	160,400
44	52,672	5,267	1,580	14,744	181,991

By age 45 you will be ahead of schedule with an accumulation of more than 3.5 times your annual pay! You will be well on your way to accumulating a nest egg equal to 10 times your annual pay at retirement.

Savings Goal by Age 55:

7 Times Your Pre-Retirement Income

Assume that everything stays the same for the next 10 years—except that you increase your contribution rate from 10% to 15% at age 50, your annual salary increases by 4% per year and your investment return continues at 9% until age 50 and then drops to 8% from 50 to 55 because you reduce your stock holdings.

Age	Your Pay	Your Investment	Employer's Contribution	Total Return	Year End Value
45	$54,778	$5,478	$1,643	$16,699	$205,811
46	56,970	5,697	1,709	18,856	232,073
47	59,248	5,925	1,777	21,233	261,008
48	61,618	6,162	1,848	23,851	292,869
49	64,083	6,408	1,922	26,733	327,932
50	66,646	9,997	1,999	26,714	366,642
51	69,312	10,397	2,079	29,828	408,946
52	72,085	10,813	2,162	33,235	455,156
53	74,968	11,245	2,249	36,952	505,602
54	77,967	11,695	2,339	41,571	561,207

At this point you will have accumulated 7.2 times your annual pay. As you near retirement, your goal is within reach.

Savings Goal by Age 60:

Ten Times Your Pre-Retirement Income

Assume that you keep your contribution rate at 15%, receive a 3% employer contribution and your pay continues to increase by 4% per year. Your investment return remains at 8%.

Age	$ Your Pay	$ Your Investment	$ Employer's Contribution	$ Total Return	$ Year End Value
55	81,085	12,163	2,432	45,480	621,282
56	84,329	12,649	2,529	50,311	686,771
57	87,702	13,155	2,631	55,573	758,130
58	91,210	13,682	2,736	61,307	835,855
59	94,858	14,229	2,845	67,551	920,480
60	98,652	14,798	2,960	74,348	1,012,586

Now you have topped your goal with an accumulation of just over 10 times your annual income. At this point you should be in a good position to consider various alternatives—including retirement, working fewer hours at your current job or shifting to some other income-producing activity that is of interest.

Step 5: TRACK...
...Your Savings Progress

The purpose of these examples is to show you how a specific plan gives you a tangible way to measure your progress each year. It's helpful for you to know some assumptions that I've made in the previous savings goal examples:

- There aren't any savings gaps because you should always add to your retirement savings even during periods that you are not eligible to contribute to a 401(k).
- All the money is left in the plan for retirement. None of the money is withdrawn for other purposes.
- The assumed return requires at least 60 to 70% in stock investments up to age 55. After age 55, the stock holdings drop to the 50 to 60% range.

Of course, annual returns on a well-diversified stock portfolio will vary widely from year to year. As a result, your annual investment return will not be consistent. Some years you will earn more than what my examples assume, but in other years you will earn less. Despite these year-by-year variances, you should be able to achieve long-term returns similar to these examples.

Your retirement nest egg comes from your own and your employer's contributions and the investment return that is earned on these contributions. In the example above that shows your savings progress at age 60, this is your final breakdown among these three sources:

Employee contributions	$226,173
Employer contributions	57,812
Investment return	728,601
TOTAL	**$1,012,586**

You've probably heard about the magic of compounded growth. It's very real, but this magic is significant only over long periods of time—20 to 30 years or longer. The above results are accomplished from age 25 to age 60, a period of 35 years. This is why it is so important to start saving at an early age and stick with your program. If you wait 10 years before you start, you'll substantially reduce your investment return. The difference can only be made up by a much larger savings rate or by extending the accumulation period through longer employment. The following chart illustrates the cost of waiting.

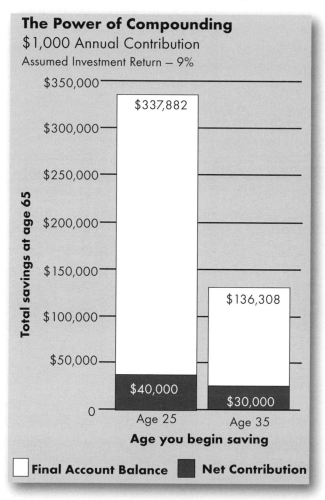

The Power of Compounding
$1,000 Annual Contribution
Assumed Investment Return – 9%

The best reason to do careful retirement planning is that once you know you'll be financially secure, you have the freedom to make life and career choices. You may think that there are only a lucky few who have this luxury. The fact is that most of the people I know who have retired before age 65 weren't professionals or high-paid executives. They are individuals who saved what they needed to enjoy an early retirement. If you achieve this financial security in your late 50s or early 60s, you have the flexibility to continue working, retire totally or shift to something less demanding. If you do some basic planning, you can avoid being trapped into working until you drop at a job you don't like.

Your goal is to retire with an adequate level of retirement income. Even if you really enjoy what you are doing and have no specific plans to totally retire, it is much nicer to have alternatives. It's also good to be ahead in the savings game in case your health forces you to stop working.

Case Studies

Rhonda Hendrix is a Quality Assurance Analyst at Anheuser-Busch in Cartersville, GA. I met her when I was speaking at a 401(k) conference that she attended as a union representative.

Rhonda is only 30, but she has already accumulated $78,000 in her 401(k) account. This amount will grow to more than $1 million by age 60—even if she never contributes another dollar (assuming a 9% investment return). Rhonda saves 16% of her pay and Anheuser-Busch adds 6%. She started contributing to the plan at age 25. This reinforces a point I've made earlier: the importance of working for an employer that has a competitive 401(k) plan.

You're probably wondering (as I did) how Rhonda manages to save 16% of her pay. She and her husband have lived in a garage apartment for about three years. They are currently building a home and Rhonda is expecting their first child. Rhonda says, "I don't believe saving 16% of my pay has impacted my life in any negative way. This savings rate allows me to accumulate a nest egg very quickly without noticing the void in my pocket. We vacation every year at least 2 or 3 times. We own a recreational vehicle, jet skis, a

boat, and two tractors. We do save money where we can. For example, we try to eat out only 2 to 3 times a month and we do not have any expensive habits other than the water toys. For the most part I think we live a very full lifestyle."

Rhonda is not the only saver in the family. Her husband also works for Anheuser Busch in the beer packaging and shipping can lines. He contributes 8% of his earnings to a 401(k) and he receives a 6% match. When there are two savers in the family, you can reach your retirement goals even faster.

I met Danny Brantley, one of Rhonda's co-workers, at the same conference. Danny is a Maintenance Mechanic at the same Anheuser-Busch plant. He didn't start contributing to his 401(k) until age 36, but he is also contributing 16% of his pay. Danny is now 44 and he has accumulated $130,000. This savings, plus a company pension, a separate investment account with Fidelity and the equity in his home, give him a grand savings total that is already close to 8 times his pre-retirement salary. This is a particularly impressive achievement, given that Danny did not start saving as early as Rhonda. (He is also the only saver. Danny's wife is currently a nursing student.) Danny will obviously build his account at a much faster pace than the examples above because he is contributing 16% of pay and is getting another 6% from Anheuser-Busch.

When I asked Danny why he contributes 16%, he said: "I can't afford not to. I save money every way around, because of the tax situation. Our company matches 6% and the other 10% just adds more money to the pot. I don't have to pay earnings tax on the 10%, which is a real savings boost." Most importantly, saving is an essential part of Danny's life: "To me, financial independence is far more important than social status."

Like Rhonda, Danny doesn't feel that a high savings rate affects his lifestyle. "Saving this amount of money from each paycheck makes me feel more confident and secure. I don't go out and spend more because I have this great plan. I spend less, but I also live comfortably and I am looking forward to retirement."

Stories like Rhonda's and Danny's are why I feel good about my involvement with 401(k)s. These are average American workers who are using the 401(k) to help them achieve their retirement dreams.

Notes

Tips for Successfully Managing Your 401(k) *Chapter Six*

Understanding Investment Risk

I'm writing this chapter at a point when the stock market has been battered. The value of a significant number of individual stocks has dropped by more than 50%, a few by more than 90% and a growing number of small, technology companies have totally disappeared. Even some mutual funds have also dropped in value by more than 50%.

Because of the current climate, this chapter is particularly relevant. At this point, I suspect many of you have a much better understanding of the risk involved with stock investing.

In general, there are three types of risk you need to consider when you invest for retirement:

- losing everything
- not having enough savings
- losing more investment value than you can tolerate.

The Risk of Losing Everything

The early days of 401(k) investing were very different from today. The typical plan had only two investment options—a guaranteed investment contract (GIC) and a growth mutual fund or company stock. The stock market was not producing double-digit annual returns. Most participants had little or no experience investing in the stock market, and many also had been raised by parents who feared stock investments.

Participants who invested in GICs earned a guaranteed fixed return in the 7 to 10% range. Participants could typically get an attractive guaranteed return with a GIC compared to a big unknown with stocks. There were a few years when GIC returns were as high as 15%.

The S&P 500 started a 27% decline on November 28, 1980, and it wasn't until the beginning of 1983 that investors recovered this loss. As a result, there wasn't a really strong incentive to invest in stocks, and about 70% of total 401(k) contributions were in GICs. The combination of an attractive, guaranteed return and the fear of losing money in stocks made GICs the logical choice for most participants.

Investment options were typically limited to 25% multiples. You had to split your money between the two types of investments 100/0%, 75/25% or 50/50%. Very few participants put 100% into the growth option. Most opted to invest 100%, 75% or 50% in GICs.

At the time no one told 30-year-olds they were foolish if they didn't put at least 75% into stocks. Because the 401(k) was new, it was important for employees to have a positive experience. GICs were performing well and employees were happy.

The primary concern was to get employees to contribute and to keep contributing. One of my fears was that if participants lost any money during the first couple of years, they would stop contributing. For this reason, some of the first 401(k) plans I designed had only a GIC option. I told these employers to add other options after the plans were a couple of years old. The new investments would be nice plan enhancements after participants had a positive initial experience.

Because participant account balances were small, any additional investment returns that might be gained through stock investments would make very little difference. A $25,000 account balance was a big deal at this point.

Investment attitudes began to shift during the late 1980s for the following reasons:

- Confidence in GICs eroded when a couple of insurance companies failed
- Returns on GICs dropped to the 5 to 6% range
- Mutual fund companies became significant 401(k) providers, offering a wider range of investment options.
- Participants pushed for more options as their account balances grew.

The investment multiples changed from 25% to 10% as the number of options increased—typically from only two to three to five options during the late 1980s. The multiples typically dropped to only 1% as plans moved to a greater number of investment alternatives and record-keeping systems that permitted daily transfers.

The following comparison of the current and early 401(k) investment structure will help you understand the magnitude of the changes.

Comparison of 401(k) Investment Structure

	Early 1980s	2001
Number of options	2	10–15*
Investment multiples	25%	1%
Change frequency	quarterly	any time
How implemented	written	request online
When completed	after next valuation	same day
Transfer value	as of last valuation date	current value

*A growing number of plans are also giving participants access to thousands of investment alternatives through self-directed investment options.

During the bull market of the 90s there was industry-wide concern that participants were investing too much of their money in GIC type investments that would produce lower long-term returns than stocks. A lot of effort went into educating participants about the risks of investing too conservatively.

Participants have generally reduced their fixed-income holdings, but I suspect the fear of losing everything may reemerge as a result of the 2000/2001 carnage. The first point you need to understand in dealing with this fear is that there aren't any risk-free investments. Start with burying the money or stuffing it in your mattress. The money may be stolen, burn or your dog may eat it for lunch. Even FDIC insured bank savings accounts or certificates of deposits (CDs) carry some risk of loss.

You may be able to avoid many investment disasters but one you will never avoid is inflation. The value of your money erodes by more than 60% over 30 years at a 3% inflation rate. This means that the $100,000 that you have today will be worth only $40,000 when you need it at retirement 30 years from now. This loss is just as real as waking up tomorrow morning to find that your account value has dropped by 60%. As a result, you must invest your 401(k) contributions—it's the only possible way to beat inflation.

The first key to dealing with the fear of losing everything is to have a basic knowledge of the risks involved with the different types of investments. These are the major investment categories that are likely to be available to you through your 401(k):

• **Money Market Funds:** These funds invest in short-term debt obligations that are issued by banks and large U.S. companies. If one or more of these businesses fails before the debt obligation is repaid, you could lose money. Interest is owed on the securities owned by the fund. The securities will not increase or decrease in value; therefore, your investment return is limited to the interest earned. The risk is low but so is the return—typically 5 to 6%.

• **Bond Funds:** These funds purchase longer-term debt obligations of the U.S. government or U.S. companies. The long-term return for this type of investment is in the 6 to 7% range. The fund earns

a specific amount of interest income on each bond it owns. The fund manager actively buys and sells bonds realizing a gain or loss each time a bond is sold. The manager may also hold on to the bond until its maturity date—at which time the fund will receive payment for the face amount of the bond.

A company that issues a bond may also be able to pay off the bond early. This is likely to happen when interest rates drop, enabling the company to sell new bonds at a lower interest rate.

The investment return you get will depend upon the:

- interest rate paid on the bonds
- changes in interest rates which result in an increase or decrease in the value of the bonds
- results the manager achieves by trading bonds
- failure of any companies that have issued bonds held by the fund.

The average maturity of the bonds held by the fund will impact both your risk and return. Your return from investing in a short-term bond fund will be 1/2 to 1% lower than an intermediate or long-term fund. But there will be less change in the value while you own a short-term fund.

The manager of a short-term fund buys bonds with a one to three-year maturity, an intermediate fund manager buys bonds with a 5 to 10-year average maturity and a long-term fund manager buys bonds with a 20 to 30-year maturity. The longer the average maturity, the larger the ups and downs in value while you own the fund.

Another factor that will impact your investment results is the quality of the bonds the fund owns. The financial strength of companies that sell bonds is determined by independent rating agencies like Standard & Poor's. They rank companies by their ability to pay the amount that is borrowed. Companies with high credit ratings are able to borrow at lower interest rates, because they are more likely to repay the loan than companies with bad credit ratings.

Many bond funds invest in what are known as "junk" bonds. These are bonds issued by companies with low to medium credit ratings. There is much greater potential that one or more of the companies that have issued these bonds will not be able to repay the loan, particularly during an economic slump.

You need to understand exactly what you are buying when you invest in a bond fund. For example, a fund company is not going to call its fund that invests in junk bonds a junk bond fund. It will more likely be called a high-yield fund or some similar name. Read the prospectus or other material from the investment company carefully.

• **Stock Funds:** You are buying ownership in a company when you buy shares of its stock. You may receive a dividend, but your investment return is determined primarily by what happens to the price of the stock. These are a few of the many factors that make a stock go up or down:

- political events in the U.S. and around the world
- a change in management
- the revenue and profits of the company
- general market trends
- the industry climate
- new products the company has recently introduced
- a company's prominence within its industry
- the opinion of large institutional investors such as mutual fund managers
- the opinion of key analysts
- special events such as the Y2K scare.

Since so many things can impact the price of a stock, you may wonder why in the world you should invest your retirement savings in something that is so uncertain. The answer is because this is how you can get the best long-term investment return. Retirement investing is a 40 to 60-year event that includes both your working and leisure years. You can't afford to accept a safe 6% return over this time period.

If you do invest too conservatively, you are likely to run afoul of one of the other risks: the risk of not enough money to fund your retirement. The best way to reduce your risk of loss, regardless of whether you invest in bonds or stocks or other investments, is to diversify your investments. The most efficient way for most 401(k) participants to do this is via collective investments such as mutual funds.

Assume you invest all your 401(k) money in only one mutual fund—an S&P 500 index mutual fund. When you invest in this fund, you own a small piece of the 500 largest companies in the U.S. The only circumstance that would cause you to lose all your money is if all 500 of these companies folded. This would be a disaster far beyond anything our economy has ever experienced. Most of the largest companies survived the great depression and ultimately recovered.

Aside from the issue of investing too conservatively, there's also the risk of making the wrong investment decision. The advantage of mutual funds is that you shift the responsibility for deciding which stocks to buy to a professional fund manager. With a mutual fund you own a portion of many bonds or stocks.

The important fact is that it is highly unlikely that you will ever lose all your money. But the chances are much greater that you will lose 25% or more of your money when you invest in stocks. Why should you invest where you can lose 25% or more of your money? Because you will also earn more than 25% during some years. You are never likely to ever earn more than 7% in a bank savings account.

Because a mutual fund is a diversified investment, it often has less volatility than an individual stock. This means that the value of a fund you own could increase on a day that a single stock drops by 30%. If your fund manager owns shares of the company that drops by 30%, your account value may drop by only 4% for the day—compared to 30% for a person who owns only this one stock.

Here's an example that shows the importance of diversification. In this example, Manuel and Sophia both have $5,000 in their 401(k) accounts.

EXAMPLE OF DIVERSIFICATION

Manuel and Sophia both have $5,000 in their 401(k) accounts. Manuel chooses to invest his entire balance in a money market with an average annual yield of 5%. Sophia decides to diversify her 401(k) account balance. She invests $1,000 in each of five different investment options. Her first investment choice fails and she loses the entire $1,000. The second option doesn't do well, and although Sophia doesn't lose any money, she doesn't' make any either. Her third, fourth, and fifth investment choices produce average to above-average returns.

25 YEARS

$16,932 Manuel

$22,070 Sophia

Manuel invests $5,000 at 5%

Sophia invests $5,000 and diversifies

Invests $1,000, losing it all	$0
Invests $1,000 at 0%	$1,000
Invests $1,000 at 5%	$3,386
Invests $1,000 at 8%	$6,849
Invests $1,000 at 10%	$10,835

As you can see, even though two of the five investment options Sophia chose performed worse than the money market, Sophia came out with over 30 percent more than Manuel—because she diversified her 401(k) account rather than putting it all into a money market fund.

The Risk of Not Having Enough Money

The most obvious risk is the risk that you will not have enough money when you retire. Your 401(k) retirement nest egg must come from your savings, any employer contribution and investment income. The more you earn on your investments, the less you have to contribute. You will hopefully have additional retirement resources, such as personal investments, home equity, etc. But the hard reality is that increasing your investment return requires taking more risk.

This is why you need to use a good retirement calculator or consult a financial planner to help you get the right balance of risks and returns. The following example shows how drastically your savings increases with an additional 3% return.

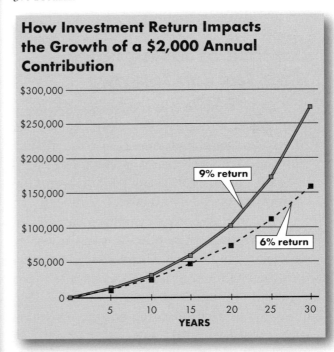

How Investment Return Impacts the Growth of a $2,000 Annual Contribution

As you can see, the additional 3% return brings a total return of $273,000 after 30 years vs. $158,000 at the lower return rate. That means that the higher return would make it possible for you to generate 73% more income from your

401(k) nest egg. To achieve the same result over 30 years at the lower rate of return, you would need to make an annual contribution of $3,460 vs. $2,000 at the higher rate of return.

The major benefit of using a retirement calculator is that it gives you an investment reality check. Will the amount you are saving and the investment mix enable you to accumulate what you will need? A good retirement calculator will answer this question and also help you decide how to close any savings gap. Generally, a gap can be closed by increasing your contributions, adjusting your investments to achieve a higher long-term return or a combination of the two.

The earlier in your career that you become involved with this retirement planning process, the more likely you are to achieve your goals. It's a lot easier to make the necessary changes at age 35 than age 55. Check how you are progressing toward your savings goals every year.

The Risk of Losing More than You Can Tolerate

No one wants to lose any money—but we're all especially fearful of losing more than we can afford. You should find some comfort in the fact that it's very unlikely that you would lose everything in your 401(k) account—but losing to the point of severe pain is a very real possibility.

Of course, everyone's pain threshold is different. At this stage of my life, a loss of 10% on my retirement funds is as much as I can tolerate. Fortunately, I've been able to avoid any losses beyond this point. (I will get into how I've done this in the next chapter.) You need to determine your own risk tolerance, and your 401(k) provider should have the tools to help you. If not, visit one or more of the retirement planning sites mentioned in Chapter 6.

Sometimes people say that you shouldn't be concerned about any drops in your retirement fund value because they are only "paper losses".

This refers to the fact that if you don't cash in your investments on the day their value drops, you haven't actually lost any money. It's true that you shouldn't panic with all the market ups and downs, but you still have to ask yourself if you can handle drops of 20%, 30%, 40%, 50%—or even more.

My retirement plan is disrupted if the value of my account drops from $100,000 to $80,000 because I didn't include a 20% loss in my plan. I could react to such a loss by withdrawing all my money from stock investments, shifting to lower-risk investments and staying there forever. If I do this, I will have to dramatically increase my contributions to make up the loss and the lower investment return I will be getting in the future.

My recommendation is to stick to stock funds that are less volatile for retirement investing. I've come to the conclusion that funds with a heavy industry sector weighting (like those that have recently dropped by 70% or so) are not appropriate for retirement investing. You need to focus on funds that have more consistent, positive returns. Many age 55+ participants have been hammered in the current market because they had either too much in stocks and/or the wrong type of stocks.

The Risk of Company Stock

Although this chapter primarily talks about the risks associated with investments that you choose, you also have to be aware of the risks related to the investments your employer chooses. What I'm referring to is company stock, which can be a very risky investment. At most public companies, it's common for the employer matching contribution to be made in company stock.

Because stock investments are so volatile, and because participants don't always choose a company stock investment, there are politicians like Congresswoman Barbara Boxer who have attempted to change the laws. While I understand that people would want to limit the amount that participants have in company stock, I don't want to create a situation that forces employers to stop their contributions. Remember that employer contributions are voluntary. Prohibiting employers from contributing stock to fund the matching contribution could lead to the reduction or elimination of their contributions. A contribution of company stock is much better than no employer contribution at all.

The real concern for participants is to consider how company stock investments affect their overall asset allocation. If a large percentage of your portfolio is in company stock due to your employer contributions, you need to be sure to balance these equity investments with other fixed-income investments.

This balance is also an important consideration if you are permitted to buy company stock with your own contributions. The fact that many companies prospered and their stock values consistently increased led many employees to invest all their own contributions in company stock. Especially in 2000 when the stock market began to decline, it was not a good idea to have all your eggs in one basket.

Employees often get a big sales pitch on the benefits of owning company stock. This is because the personal wealth of many senior executives is tied to company stock options. Many of them want employees to own as much company stock as possible for these reasons:

- Senior management has greater control of the company when large blocks of stock are owned by employees and other "friendly" investors.

- Employees are more loyal and productive when they own company stock (at least when the stock is doing well).

If you consider your total asset allocation and you make appropriate adjustments, I'm generally

a big fan of employee stock ownership. But I only feel this way if the stock is given to you or if it is sold to you at a discount. We had an Employee Stock Ownership Plan (ESOP) at The Johnson Companies, and all employees were given stock via employer contributions to the plan. Employees received an additional benefit when we sold the company—they got cash for their stock.

Generally, I don't recommend investing your own retirement money in company stock. The risk of a major loss is just too high. It's not just dot.com companies that have tanked during the recent market downturn. Many large, well-known companies have watched their stock prices drop by more than 50%. The entire S&P stock group has experienced some of the most major declines in its history.

You may wonder about the severity of some of the historical market drops. We all know about the great crash of 1929—that drop was 86%. But few are familiar with the 54% drop that started on March 5, 1937, followed by the 45% drop that started on November 11, 1938.

Major Market Drops Since the Beginning of the 401(k)

Date of market peak	% decline
Nov. 28, 1980	27%
Aug. 25, 1987	34%
July 16, 1990	20%
July 17, 1998	19%

How do these drops tie into investments in your company stock? These historical market declines reflect the average change for the 500 companies in the S&P index. As I mentioned earlier, some stocks fare better or worse than the general market decline. This means that the stocks of some S&P companies dropped by a lot more than 34% during the 1987 decline. The big problem with owning a single stock is that your company may be the one that drops by 80% during such a period.

Eventually every stock's value goes down. It seems to be only a question of when and by how much. Some companies have experienced periods of 20 or more years when the value of their stocks have only gone up. But it's virtually impossible to maintain an uninterrupted upward record for 20 years or more.

Unfortunately, many 401(k) investors who have been heavily invested in company stock have experienced this reality at the worst time— when they are in their 50s and nearing retirement. For years they saw the value of their accounts grow as they rode the company stock wagon. Then, seemingly overnight, they watched much of what they gained disappear.

Many experts say that you shouldn't rely on company stock to get you to your retirement goals. The Charles Schwab brokerage firm conducted a study in 2000 showing how single stock ownership performed in comparison to a market index during three and ten year periods from 1926 to 1998. The best average return for a single stock holding was 65% and the worst was minus 60%. This compares to a best of 32% for the index and a worst of 29%. A single stock has twice the potential to move up and down than a diversified portfolio. As a result, you should keep your ownership of company stock to the lowest level permitted by your plan to avoid unnecessary risks.

Company stock can also bring wonderful results. Penelope Wang wrote a very good article about company stock that appeared in the October 2000 issue of *Money*. She described "the accidental millionaire", a woman named Michelle Seymour who built a 401(k) account worth $5 million by age 39 through company stock investments. Michelle started contributing only $400 per year in the mid-1980s. She then increased her contribution rate to 15% of pay and invested primarily in company stock because it was doing better than any of the other plan options.

Michelle obviously totally surpassed the goal I suggested of building a nest egg equal to 10 times your annual pay by the time you retire. I have seen others like her who have really won big by investing heavily in company stock, but achieving these gangbuster results is more luck than good planning.

Another key point that this example illustrates is that when you are in your 20s and 30s you can take more risk. Michelle gradually reduced her company stock holdings from 90% to 35% to reduce her risk.

Tips on Understanding Risk

- Remember that the three different types of risk you face are (1) the risk of losing everything (2) the risk of not having enough, and (3) the risk of losing more than you can tolerate.
- Recognize that there are no risk-free investments.
- Decide what level of risk is tolerable and manage your investments to stay within your comfort zone.
- Diversify your investments to reduce your risks. Invest in a variety of stocks, bonds and other investments.
- Try to increase your return by small increments-even a 1% increase will make a big difference.
- Don't put all your eggs in the company's basket. Remember that investing your contributions in your employer's stock is much riskier than investing in a diversified stock fund.

Selecting Your 401(k) Investments

I was recently asked during a media interview if participants should continue to be allowed to decide how to invest their 401(k) contributions. This question surfaces every time the stock market takes a serious dip. I told this writer that participants won't tolerate giving investment control back to employers.

There are several reasons why it doesn't make sense for employers to decide how employees should invest their 401(k) money:

- Some presume that the employer will do a better job of selecting investments than employees. Over 90% of existing 401(k) plans cover less than 100 employees. The "plan sponsors" at these companies are generally the owners who have their minds on growing a business. And with few exceptions, they don't have any more investment expertise than the average participant. I've seen some of the worst investment results at plans where the employer controlled the investments.

- The typical 401(k) plan includes new entrants into the work place who are just starting to invest and those who are over age 60 with substantial account balances. A common set of investment options for all employees ignores the fact that participants have widely diverse investment needs.

- If employers take control, they would have to assume full responsibility and liability for the results. The fact is that employers don't want this responsibility. As I've said before, why should employers be liable for how employees invest their own retirement savings?

I'm convinced that employees will continue to be responsible for investing their 401(k) contributions. This is not to say, however, that there isn't room for 401(k) participants to do a better job. Employee responsibility for investing has several major flaws:

- We have attempted to convert millions of amateurs into professional investment managers through limited education.
- Participants haven't been given access to professional investment advisors.
- The investment alternatives in most plans are inadequate.

On the education front, employers and service providers have indeed made extensive efforts in recent years. They all have good intentions, but the education has been woefully inadequate. First of all, it's unrealistic to assume that any amount of education will turn the majority of participants into successful investors. One of the problems is that participants don't have the time or inclination to really become students of investing.

The other problem is that those who need the most education are the least likely to take an active approach to learning. It's a common dilemma. At The Johnson Companies, we used to encourage our clients to provide voluntary on-site wellness training for their employees to help reduce health care costs. We soon discovered employees who were already health conscious attended, but those who smoked three packs a day and had Twinkies and coffee for breakfast usually didn't attend.

How did we get into this mess?

In 1992, in response to pressure from employers, service providers and industry trade groups, the Department of Labor issued final regulations that would provide fiduciary relief to employers when investment authority is given to participants. These voluntary regulations under Section 404(c) of ERISA explain how employers should structure the investment options for their plans in order to reduce their liability. Employers that want the protection these regulations offer must provide adequate information to participants so that they can make informed investment decisions.

The Ongoing Education vs. Advice Debate

The 404(c) educational requirement created a new problem for both employers and service providers. An individual or organization that gives specific investment advice is considered a fiduciary under ERISA, and a fiduciary is fully responsible and liable for its actions. As a result, both service providers and employers pushed the DOL for further guidance because they didn't want to become fiduciaries. They were concerned that by providing the information required for 404(c) compliance, they could unknowingly cross the line from education to advice. The result would be to increase rather than decrease their responsibility and liability.

In 1996 the DOL responded to employer and service provider concerns by issuing an interpretive bulletin (I.B. 96-1) that explained how far employers and service providers could go before they crossed the line from education to advice. The bulletin provided the additional guidance employers and service providers wanted, but it also created the perception that it is illegal to give investment advice to 401(k) participants.

This guidance from the DOL provided the framework for employers and service providers to give participants sufficient information to become competent investors. The problem is that many participants really want someone to tell them how to invest—rather than information on how to do it themselves.

Drake Mosier founded a company that is now called mPower to provide investment advice to 401(k) participants. He approached me shortly

after he founded the company and asked me to serve on his board. I'm often approached by individuals who think they have a great, new 401(k)-related idea. It's not always the case, and I'm not always interested. But I thought Drake's idea had merit. His goal was to provide the type of help to 401(k) participants that has historically been provided only to high net worth individuals and institutional investors.

Drake's dream was to make advice available to all participants at a cost of $10 to $30 per year. Drake and I agreed that attempting to solve the 401(k) investment problem by educating participants could not succeed. We were thinking along the same lines, so I joined mPower's Board and served until May, 2001.

During the early stages of helping mPower launch its business, I was instrumental in getting Olena Berg, the former Assistant Secretary of the DOL, to clearly state in an interview that investment advice is indeed legal. She also pointed out that the DOL actually wants participants to receive advice if it is done properly. Olena's interview clarified the situation, but another barrier to investment advice still remains. Many employers are reluctant to offer investment advice to their participants because they think they could be sued by unhappy participants down the road. This attitude is unfortunate because, in my opinion, letting employees invest their money without this support is a lot riskier.

My investment knowledge is probably higher than most 401(k) participants, but I wouldn't pick my own funds without professional help. Frankly, the more I know about investing, the more I realize how ill prepared I am to pick funds totally on my own.

Like the majority of participants, I also don't have the time to evaluate various funds and investment alternatives. My involvement with mPower and other investment advisors has helped me appreciate the value of an investment advisor.

My first exposure to this type of service was when I was a board member of a seminary. We used an investment consultant to help us evaluate, pick and monitor fund managers. Unfortunately, most individuals base their investment decisions solely on past performance and/or input from relatives, friends, co-workers, etc. There are many things to consider other than a fund's investment track record, and you can't always rely on the advice of non-professionals. Participants from the mailroom to the boardroom need advice—and it needs to be delivered by a professional investment advisor.

The addition of investment advice to the 401(k) market has been a slow process, just like

Sample Time Horizon and Risk Tolerance Choices for Option 1

2010
- [ ] Aggressive Portfolio
- [ ] Moderate Portfolio
- [ ] Conservative Portfolio

2015
- [ ] Aggressive Portfolio
- [ ] Moderate Portfolio
- [ ] Conservative Portfolio

2020
- [ ] Aggressive Portfolio
- [ ] Moderate Portfolio
- [ ] Conservative Portfolio

2025
- [ ] Aggressive Portfolio
- [ ] Moderate Portfolio
- [ ] Conservative Portfolio

2030
- [ ] Aggressive Portfolio
- [ ] Moderate Portfolio
- [ ] Conservative Portfolio

2035
- [ ] Aggressive Portfolio
- [ ] Moderate Portfolio
- [ ] Conservative Portfolio

2040
- [ ] Aggressive Portfolio
- [ ] Moderate Portfolio
- [ ] Conservative Portfolio

most new ideas. But it will become a mainstream benefit available to all participants within a few years. I strongly encourage you to take advantage of this service when it becomes available.

The Move to More Investment Freedom

Although investment advice will help you manage your 401(k) more effectively, it can't do much for you when you're in a plan with limited investment options. An investment advisor can add greater value when you have the opportunity to select your investments from not just one fund family, but a large universe of investment alternatives. That's why I've been pushing to give participants more flexibility and options—so they can invest their 401(k) money as freely as they invest an IRA or any other vehicle.

One of the biggest problems in changing the 401(k) investment structure is the fact that most participants already have difficulty choosing among a limited number of funds. Most participants would be in big trouble if they had to choose from thousands of alternatives. If an advisor helps you choose the funds, there's less of a problem.

In the past year my discussions with many people have led me to the conclusion that a major change in the 401(k) investment structure is needed. At one end of the spectrum are those who want unlimited choice, and at the other end are those who have difficulty deciding how to invest in a limited number of options. The increasing number of investment options is due to the demands of those who want more choice—not those who can hardly handle the opposite.

Not all employers, however, have given their 401(k) participants greater investment flexibility. Some are very concerned that participants who incur major losses in an open investment structure will sue their companies. Employers are also concerned that most participants do not fully understand the complexities of more choice. If employ-

ees are overwhelmed, employers think their companies will be exposed to additional liabilities.

In response to these employer concerns, I'm recommending two investment safe harbors that would free both employers and service providers from fiduciary liability. I've recently met with retirement industry and government leaders to discuss this concept. Most have been very interested in my ideas.

Here's what I am thinking:

Option 1: Participants would be given the choice of a) structured portfolios that consider their time horizon and risk tolerance or b) the opportunity to select their own funds from a fund "window". Employers and providers would be freed from liability if:

- Participants may select only one structured investment portfolio.
- Participant-paid expenses for each structured portfolio do not exceed 75 basis points.
- Participants who stay in a structured portfolio for at least 20 years receive a 7% guaranteed minimum average annual return.
- The additional participant-paid fee to access the fund window does not exceed $150.
- 100% of the participant's account can be transferred into the fund window.
- An IRA option allows participants to retain their portfolios when they change jobs, companies are sold, etc.

The structured portfolios would have to comply with yet-to-be-determined industry standards. For example, the process used to build the portfolios would have to be reviewed and approved by an independent entity at least annually. Among other things, this independent entity would monitor fund selections to make sure fund managers do not drift from their investment styles. For example, they would be on the lookout for a small company stock manager who suddenly starts to invest in large company stocks.

Option 2: Participants would be permitted to invest in IRAs under the same rules that apply to SIMPLE-IRAs. The employer would pick a single financial organization to receive all new deposits, but participants could transfer all accumulated money to any other financial organization without penalty.

Although my ideas have generated great interest, there is no guarantee that either option will be adopted. In the meantime, you need to focus on understanding your investment choices.

The most common mistake I have seen 401(k) participants make is to randomly pick their investments without any idea of what they are investing in and why. One young man once told me that his return was above 20% the prior year, and he wanted to know what he should expect during the current year. My immediate answer was that his account value would go up and down. When I questioned him about the specific funds he chose, he didn't have any idea. All he knew was that he had received a good return and he wanted it to continue. A complete lack of knowledge may be okay during the early years of your retirement investing, but this is not acceptable when you have accumulated a larger amount of money.

Becoming more informed does not necessarily require a major time commitment. There are tons of books that cover the basics of investing that you can buy or borrow from the local library. Two notable ones are *Investing for Dummies* by Eric Tyson and *401(k): Take Charge of Your Future* by Eric Schurenberg. You can also get information about your funds from *Morningstar.com* and from *Schwab.com*.

Talk to others about the resources they find particularly helpful. I introduced Danny Brantley in Chapter 6. Danny rarely makes changes to the 401(k) investments he has chosen, but he actively manages his own investments outside the 401(k). He works the afternoon shift, which gives him a couple of hours in the morning to work on his investments. His favorite resources are *The Wall Street Journal*, Wall Street Online, CNBC, *Morningstar.com* and *Business Week*. He says, "I learned a lot about the fundamentals of investing from reading material like Ben Graham's *The Intelligent Investor*, Robert Hagstrom's *Warren Buffet Way* and information from Vanguard's John Bogle."

If you aren't willing to put in any effort to become a more informed investor, access investment advice through your plan or buy some advice outside your plan.

Common Participant Mistakes

Once you become more informed, you have to be sure to focus on the right information. A common participant mistake is to base all investment selections on past performance. Even the mutual fund companies are required to tell you that past performance is no indication of future results. Despite this constant warning, most investors don't break the habit. The major reason that you can't overemphasize past performance is because good results are often fleeting. Many of the funds that appear on "Top 10" lists aren't repeat stars. A fund manager might go through a particularly lucky period, the companies owned by the fund may have a great short run—not all funds have what it takes to stay on top.

Although fund managers work hard to make informed investment decisions, sometimes the results exceed their skill or efforts. The manager may expect a 10 to 20% gain for a certain stock, but actually receive a 50% or larger gain. Picking that stock took skill, but the unexpected additional gain also involved a lot of good fortune.

The other important point is that the performance of any fund is largely determined by the market view of the type of companies that are represented. Those of you who are heavily invested in funds that own a lot of technology stocks learned this lesson. Many of these funds were top performers prior to 2000 and then dropped into the worst performing category in 2000 and early 2001. The Warburg Pincus Japan Small Company Fund, for example, gained 100% during the first six months of 1999 followed by a 114% gain in the second half of 1999. But then when technology companies took a dive in 2000, the fund dropped by 71.8%.

If you were focused only on past performance, you would most likely have chosen to invest in that Warburg Pincus fund at the end of 2000. But if you had more carefully looked at the companies represented in the fund and listened to analyst predictions on the tech sector, you might have considered other funds.

Participants also make the mistake of comparing different types of funds. You must compare a fund's performance to others in its peer group. If you compare a bond fund to a stock fund, a large-cap fund to a small-cap fund, or a value fund to sector fund, you're comparing apples and oranges.

Sometimes it's not easy to identify fund types. You should be able to identify the fund type from the 401(k) provider's materials, but these materials are not always easy reading. An independent source like *morningstar.com* or *schwab.com* can be your best bet.

Once you know the fund type, you can look at the most recent and longer-term (three to five-year) performance and then compare it to others within its category. It's important to get both a short and long-term perspective. This kind of analysis points out if a single year is the major reason for exceptional results. Newer funds often have this history. The manager may pick a couple of stocks that are real winners in the first year or two. The fund appears on the best performer list and begins to attract a lot of money. It's more common to get a 100% return with a $50 million fund than a $1 billion fund, because larger funds

have less investment flexibility and they require much greater research capabilities.

That same Warburg Pincus Japan Small Company Fund rapidly grew due to its stellar 1999 results. The 214% return in 1999 will probably give the fund an attractive three-year average return at the end of 2001. But the manager is not likely to repeat this three-year result in the future. Most importantly, the only investors who did well are those who owned this fund at the beginning of 1999—long before its results attracted attention. The poor investors who purchased this fund after seeing its 1999 results have been hammered. There are many similar examples with other funds.

Another lesson I learned a long time ago is that the fund with the highest average return won't necessarily give me the most money. I learned this when I was helping a client pick an investment manager to run an employer-funded defined contribution pension and profit-sharing plan. All the investment managers he was considering claimed to have only top-performing funds. I decided to look beyond just the historical performance results. Instead, I tried to determine how much money my client would have after investing $10,000 each year with each prospective manager. I discovered that the potential accumulation varied widely, depending upon when I did the comparative scorekeeping.

Here's how I discovered this fact. The following is a year-by-year comparison of two funds:

Net Annual Return

Year	1	2	3	4	5	3 Yr. Avg.	5 Yr. Avg.
Fund A	35.3	22.4	(8.7)	18.5	(7.6)	16.33	11.98
Fund B	21.1	17.3	(0.5)	13.2	2.7	12.63	10.76

The natural conclusion is that Fund A is a better choice because its five-year average return is

11.98% compared to 10.76% for Fund B. If you look at the amount that you would accumulate in both these funds, you would come to a different conclusion.

In the following example $10,000 is invested in each fund at the beginning of each year.

Amount Accumulated					
End of Year	1	2	3	4	5
Fund A	$13,530	$28,801	$35,425	$53,829	$58,978
Fund B	$12,110	$25,935	$35,755	$51,795	$63,463

I was very surprised the first time I worked through this exercise. The results were hard to believe even though I was a math major. The key is when the ups and downs occur and the amount that you have invested at each of these points. I learned several things from this process that have helped me invest my retirement money:

- A fund that has less dramatic ups and downs can outperform a more volatile fund.
- Average performance results are of limited value.
- Don't consider "top 10" listings the end of the story. Look beyond the obvious to find the funds that can sustain top performance.

Fund A would have been listed among the top funds at the end of the third year with a 16.33% average annual return—compared to only 12.63% for Fund B. Fund A would have appeared in the winner's circle after the first three years—and Fund B's 12.63% average three-year return probably would have attracted little or no attention. But when we look at the actual amount accumulated with each fund, we would have a slightly larger amount with Fund B. The difference is even more dramatic after five years. Fund A has achieved an 11.98% average com-

pared to 10.76% for Fund B, but the actual amount accumulated in Fund B is 7.6% more than Fund A.

The robust stock market performance during the 1990s was great, but it created unrealistic expectations. Most 401(k) participants have never experienced a prolonged stock market slump when the market doesn't really do much for five or more years. Some mistakenly expect annual returns in the 15 to 20% range. Returns in this range should never be built into your retirement planning. I personally would not recommend a return assumption of more than 9%. (And you should use a 9% return assumption only if at least 75% of your money is invested stocks. Otherwise you should reduce your expected return to 7 or 8%.)

One of the other things I learned when I did the Fund A and Fund B comparison for the first time is that it can take a long time to get back to where you were after a bad year. Assume you have $100,000 invested in a fund that drops 20% to a value of $80,000. A 20% gain the next year brings your value up to $96,000. But you are still 4% behind. You really have a lot of ground to make up if your retirement plan assumed a 12% annual return. The $100,000 you had invested at the beginning of this two-year period would have had to be worth $125,440 to be on track, but it is worth only $96,000 after the recovery. You need a 46% gain the third year to get on track, which is highly unlikely.

The combination of setting unrealistic return expectations and picking funds that do not do well during down markets may eventually result in a serious savings gap. You can't just be at a break-even point after a couple of bad years. Somewhere along the way you need to make up for the investment gains that didn't occur. This is another reason why it makes sense to pick funds with less dramatic ups and downs.

In the final analysis, the funds you choose must meet your personal objectives. My long-term investment goal is to earn a 9% average return on my retirement savings. I know I have to be heavily invested in stocks to achieve this result. But due to my age, I'm not willing to accept more than a 10% drop in the value of my retirement account. As a result, I have most of my retirement savings in-vested in only two stock funds that have the potential to produce a 9% long-term return and had positive returns in periods of market turbulence.

The average annual returns for these funds are good—but most importantly, the 2000 returns were 7.9% for one fund and 16.3% for the other. So far in 2001 returns are 5.99% and 12.55% respectively. Since most funds have had negative returns from 2000 into 2001, my investments are doing particularly well.

The funds that I have selected with the help of an advisor have less risk exposure than the S&P 500 Index. I'm not yet ready to shift to bonds to reduce my risk even more. I expect to make that shift once I start withdrawing money from my retirement account. I'm also not looking for big winners. I was willing to give up the big gains from the technology sector during recent years in exchange for the reduced risk; however, I have to confess that these big gains were tempting at times. I've made some technology invest-ments outside my retirement account where I am comfort-able taking a higher risk.

Investing most of your retirement sav-ings in two funds in the same category probably is not a good strategy for most investors, but it match-es my goals at age 59. You're not always going to follow conventional wisdom—you need to make in-formed investment decisions that are right for you.

Read the May 14, 2001 issue of Fortune to get some solid information about why the technology sector collapsed. Jason Zweig's article, "Wall Street's Wisest Man" in the June 2001 issue of Money is also particularly insightful.

Tips on Selecting Your 401(k) Investments

- *Know what you are doing and why: don't invest blindly.*
- *Use an investment advisor or other professional help to choose your investments.*
- *Remember that higher risk doesn't guarantee a higher return. Look for lower risk funds that have the potential to give you the long-term return you need.*
- *Don't focus on average returns when you compare funds. A fund with a lower average return can actually give you a larger nest egg.*
- *Avoid the temptation to pursue the high flyers unless you get a kick out of watching the value of your retire-ment account go up and down.*
- *Watch out for funds that have dramatic up and down swings, particularly if you are within a few years of retirement.*
- *Establish realistic expectations and then pick funds that have the potential to meet your goals.*
- *Use your best instincts: learn from how others invest, but build the portfolio that's right for you.*
- *For more information about my proposed 401(k) investment structure, visit 401kassociation.com*

Notes

The Basics on Hardship Withdrawals, Loans and Job Changes

Have you ever wondered why loans and hardship withdrawals exist in a retirement plan? Permitting participants to borrow or withdraw from their retirement accounts seems counterproductive when we so frequently hear that Americans are not saving enough money for retirement.

But many believe that loans and hardship withdrawals actually lead to increased retirement savings. They claim that many younger and lower-paid employees will not contribute to a 401(k) if all their money is locked up until retirement age. Without question, 25-year-olds have many financial needs other than saving for retirement. It's tough for most employees who earn less than $20,000 to find any money to contribute to a 401(k). The opportunity to access these savings when necessary does help to increase participation among lower-paid employees, particularly when there isn't an employer contribution incentive.

Although loans and hardship withdrawals increase the appeal of the 401(k), they are not required plan features. Check your Summary Plan Description for your plan's loan and hardship withdrawal provisions.

Hardship Withdrawals

Virtually all 401(k) plans permit hardship withdrawals; however, the applicable IRS rules must be followed to avoid a plan disqualification. Withdrawals are permitted only when there is an immediate and heavy financial need. There are two different approaches to determining this need: the "facts and circumstances" test and the "deemed hardship" method.

Employers are required to obtain substantial personal financial data to determine the extent of the need for the facts and circumstances test. Among other things, the participant must show that no other resources are available, including loans from commercial sources. The requirements are so extensive and invasive that most employers choose the deemed hardship method.

With the deemed hardship method, withdrawals are limited to this IRS approved list:

- Medical expenses for you, your spouse or dependents not covered by insurance
- Costs related to the purchase of your primary residence
- Payment of post-secondary tuition and related educational expenses for the next 12 months for you, your spouse, a dependent or non-dependent children
- Payments necessary to prevent either eviction from your principal residence or foreclosure on the mortgage on that residence.

In addition, you are subject to the following restrictions:

- The distribution cannot exceed the amount you need (including taxes)
- You must obtain all distributions of non-taxable loans under all plans of the employer.
- Your maximum contribution amount during the year of the withdrawal and the following year is equal to the annual contribution limit
- You may not make any contributions to the plan for at least the next six months following the date you receive the withdrawal (effective in 2002).

Plans that use the deemed hardship approach don't have to ask participants for personal financial data to show that no other resources are available. The government thinks the tax burden plus the other penalties are sufficiently draconian so that no participant of sound mind would withdraw the money unless there really is an immediate and heavy financial need.

This whole issue of restricted access commonly confuses participants: "Why can't I take out *my* money anytime?" The answer is that the government gives you big tax breaks to help you save. They really want you to use this money when you retire. They could have written the law so there isn't any way to get your money out prior to retirement (similar to Social Security). But they opted for limited access instead.

A hardship withdrawal reduces the maximum amount you can contribute to the plan the year after you take the withdrawal. To illustrate this, assume you:

- take a hardship withdrawal on May 14, 2002
- have contributed $4,500 of pre-tax contributions during 2002 prior to the withdrawal
- start to contribute again on January 1, 2003.

The dollar limit for pre-tax contributions is $12,000 for 2003. Your contributions for 2003 will be limited to a maximum of $7,500 ($12,000 minus $4,500).

The amount you can withdraw for a hardship may be limited to just your contributions excluding investment gains, or you also may be able to withdraw vested employer contributions. This is another example where the employer establishes the rules. I usually advise employers to permit only the withdrawal of employee contributions, because your employer is making its contribution to help you retire.

In addition to hardship withdrawals while you are still employed, you can withdraw your entire account any time after age 59 ½ if your plan permits you to do so. A withdrawal after this age can be made for any reason, including rolling the money into an IRA.

The amount you withdraw is taxable as additional income and the 10% early distribution penalty tax applies if you are under age 59½. You may get a tax break if the withdrawal is for medical purposes. I have received questions from participants who think buying a home exempts them from the 10% penalty tax. This is not the case.

Participants who are unhappy with their 401(k) investments also frequently ask me if they can take their money out and roll it into an IRA. This is not considered a hardship withdrawal. You can transfer your money to an IRA only if you are over age 59½ or if you leave your employer and your plan permits you to take the money out.

Unless participants elect out of tax withholding, hardship withdrawals are subject to a 10% tax withholding—rather than the standard 20% withholding.

The mandatory tax withholding has no relationship to the amount of Federal and state tax you will owe when you take money out of the 401(k) for a hardship or for any other reason. The taxes that are withheld are simply a deposit to the IRS. The actual tax due will be determined when you compute your taxes for the year during which you receive the distribution.

Assume your taxable income for 2003 is $45,000 prior to your $10,000 401(k) hardship withdrawal. The $10,000 is added to the $45,000 to make your total income $55,000, which is taxed at the applicable tax rate. You then pay the 10% penalty tax, which is $1,000. Typically 25% to 40% of the amount withdrawn is paid in taxes. If your tax rate is 27%, you need to add the 10% penalty tax and withdraw $15,873 to have $10,000 left after paying Federal and state taxes. You are not likely to have the money sitting around to pay the $5,873 in taxes, so you will probably have to take it out of the plan. This is the first level of tax pain.

The next level of pain is the disruption in your retirement savings. You didn't just lose the $15,873. You lost what this money would be worth by the time you retire. The following example illustrates this loss:

Cost of Withdrawing $15,873 Early

Age on Date of Withdrawal	Lost Value at age 65
55	$37,577
45	88,959
35	210,598
25	498,562

Assuming a 9% investment return

Using Your 401(k) Money to Buy Your First Home

The tax bite and the disruption to your retirement account are two good reasons to avoid a hardship withdrawal unless it is absolutely necessary. But withdrawing money to buy your first home can be a smart financial decision. The first and most obvious point is that buying a home is a better long-term financial deal for most families than renting. Assume you take a hardship withdrawal of $15,000 to buy a $180,000 home with a 30-year mortgage when you are 35. Your goal should be to pay the mortgage off before you hit retirement age. Assume the value of your home appreciates at a rate of 3% per year. It will be worth $435,600 after 30 years. As I explain in Chapter 10, a house can be turned into a valuable liquid asset if you someday find that your retirement nest egg isn't sufficient.

You may be wondering what would have happened to that $15,000 if it had been left in your 401(k) plan. If the $15,000 earned a 9% return until your retirement age of 65, it would have grown to $199,000. This shows the value of home ownership—the same $15,000 invested in a home more than doubles your return. You will, of course, need to put additional money into your home for repairs and maintenance over the years, but you should still be ahead of the game.

It's worth mentioning that these dramatic investment returns are most likely when you are buying your first home. If later in life you withdraw $40,000 from your 401(k) to upgrade from a $200,000 home to a $500,000 home, you will likely lose in two ways. First, this larger withdrawal drills a larger hole in your nest egg that is difficult to replace in fewer years. The second reason is that you likely have fewer years to pay off the $500,000 home, build equity and see your $40,000 investment appreciate in value.

If you are using your 401(k) money to purchase your first home, there's a smart approach to either eliminate or substantially reduce your tax bite. First, you need to time the withdrawal and the home purchase so both occur as close to January 1st as possible. Assume the following facts:

- You are buying your first home for $180,000
- You have to withdraw $15,000 to help cover the initial costs
- The property taxes are $4,000 per year
- The mortgage will be $162,000 at a 6.5% interest rate
- The settlement date is January 15th.

The property taxes you'll pay will be approximately $3,800 and the mortgage interest will be approximately $10,100 in the year you buy the home. This is because you will own it for only 11.5 months. You will start to receive the tax benefits of first time home ownership by deducting the interest and taxes. This combination will give you $13,900 of deductions to largely offset the impact of having to add the $15,000 withdrawal from your 401(k) to your total income.

But this only works if you withdraw the $15,000 during the same year you buy the home. The benefit diminishes the later in the year you buy the home because you have to include the full withdrawal in your income, but you only have interest and tax payments for the period you own the home. The worst possible result is to buy your home in December, because you would only

get the tax break related to home ownership for part of one month. In this case a $15,000 taxable distribution less a $1,000 tax break means $14,000 is taxable.

401(k) Loans

Loans are also legally permitted but not required plan features. They're difficult to administer, which is the primary reason they're not offered by many employers. I've always advised employers to exclude loans until the plan is a few years old. New plan sponsors have their hands full with many other plan administrative matters.

The process of getting a loan has been streamlined and expedited through online services, but the repayment process is still very difficult. The most common way to repay a loan is through payroll deductions. This is obviously much more cost-effective than submitting a personal check each month. One of the challenges of the payroll deduction repayment is calculating the right amount each month. This is difficult when the number of pay periods varies in some months of the year. There may be three pay periods some months instead of two, or five instead of four.

Another problem with payroll deduction repayments is that it becomes impossible to continue repaying the loan after you leave your employer. When this happens, the entire amount of the unpaid loan becomes taxable, unless you are able it pay it off. Few employees are able to pay off the loan since they have used the money for some other purpose.

If you have a $6,000 unpaid loan balance when you leave your employer and you are unable to repay it, you will have to pay tax on this amount. The 10% early distribution tax will be applied in addition to the regular tax if you are under age 59½. This is why it's wise to stay with your employer until the loan is repaid.

Similar to hardship withdrawals, loans must also satisfy all applicable laws and regulations. The following are some of the major items you face:

- The amount you can borrow is limited to 50% of your vested benefit (from both employer and employee contributions), and $50,000 is the maximum. Some plans allow participants to borrow up to $10,000 without any percentage limit.
- The loan must normally be repaid within five years. A longer period may be allowed if the money is used to purchase a home.
- You must pay a reasonable rate of interest, typically the prime rate plus one or two percentage points.
- Your loan must be adequately secured, typically by your vested account balance.
- The loan must be for a reason specified in the plan document.

Your employer can structure the plan to permit borrowing for any reason or for only specific reasons. A common approach is to permit loans only for the reasons that are included on the hardship withdrawal list. You can get the specific details about loans in your Summary Plan Description or from your plan administrator.

The most attractive feature of a loan is that it isn't taxable when you receive the money. This is a way to get your hands on some of your retirement money without having to immediately pay income tax or the 10% early distribution penalty tax. While this may seem to be a great deal, it really isn't because you have to repay both the loan and interest with after-tax deductions from your paycheck. As a result, you really do pay tax on the loan. You just pay it every pay period rather than in a lump sum.

Assume you borrow $10,000 that you will repay with interest at 8% over a five-year period. The monthly deductions from your pay will be $202.76. The total amount you will repay is $12,166, including interest. But you must also pay tax on this money before you start to make the loan payments. You will also pay Social Security and state and local income/wage taxes in addition to the applicable income taxes at this time.

And, by the way, you will pay tax again on this same money after you repay the loan and the money is later withdrawn as a plan benefit.

By the time the $10,000 loan is repaid it has cost you $18,617, assuming a 27% Federal income tax rate, the 7.65% Social Security tax and any applicable state and local income/wage taxes. This is the breakdown:

Loan to be repaid	$10,000
Interest on loan	2,166
Federal income tax (27%)	5,027
Social Security (7.65%)	1,424
Total cost	**$18,617**

On page 115 I explained that it costs you $15,873 to get $10,000 net of taxes out of the plan with a hardship withdrawal. It costs you $18,617 to repay a $10,000 loan. I know the $2,166 of interest goes back into your account reducing the net cost to $16,451, but this still doesn't make a loan a better deal. I realize you have to repay other loans with after-tax money, but I'm not comparing 401(k) loans to other loans. I'm comparing 401(k) loans to hardship withdrawals. With a hardship withdrawal you must stop contributing for six months, but this also is better than missing five years of contributions if you can't afford to repay your loan and continue to contribute. (I have ignored state and local teaxes in these examples to avoid making an already complex analysis even more complex).

The bottom line is that both loans and hardship withdrawals are much less attractive than they first appear. As a result, they should be used only when absolutely necessary, rather than as a convenience. And remember that there's an advantage to the hardship withdrawal if you will lose employer contributions while you repay a loan.

As you can see in the example on page 118, your retirement savings plan will be seriously dis-

Example of How a $10,000 Loan Can Cost You Over $100,000

One of the biggest risks when you borrow from your 401(k) is that you will not be able to repay the loan and continue to contribute to the plan. The following example illustrates this point. Assume:

- A 35-year-old employee, Rob, has been contributing $1,800 and receives $900 of employer matching contributions per year.
- Rob decides to borrow $10,000 from his 401(k).
- The loan repayment is $207.58 per month or $2,490.96 per year for five years using a 9% loan interest rate.
- Rob is earning a 9% annual return on the amount he has invested in the 401(k) plan.
- There is a 50% employer match.

Rob cannot afford to repay the loan and continue to contribute to the plan. So, he stops contributing during the five-year period the loan is being repaid. This creates a lost opportunity that is much bigger than the $9,000 he would have contributed during this five-year period. Rob will also lose $4,500 of employer matching contributions. Even more importantly, had these additional contributions been invested in the plan earning 9% until age 65, they would have grown to $139,340.

rupted if you can't continue your plan contributions while you are repaying your loan.

A 401(k) loan is attractive only if you can't get a commercial loan at a similar interest rate. Of course, borrowing from yourself at 8% is a lot better than paying 22% to a credit card company. You should cut up your credit cards if you need to borrow from your 401(k) to pay off credit card debt.

I had to borrow from my 401(k) when my wife Ellie and I were struggling to handle four tuition payments at the same time. Although it was difficult, I continued to contribute 6% of my pay while I was repaying the loans, because I didn't want to lose the 50% employer matching contribution during those years. I certainly know that borrowing from your 401(k) can be a lifesaver under the right circumstances.

Warning for Employers

Employers must administer hardship withdrawals and loans according to the plan document and the applicable regulations. Not long ago a controller told me his company permits hardship withdrawals for any reason. This approach may make some of your participants happy, but it will lead to big trouble if your plan is audited by the IRS or DOL. The primary penalty for violating the law is to disqualify your plan, which will create major tax problems for your company and all participants. The company will lose the tax deductions it has received and employees will lose the benefits that come with a qualified plan, such as the tax-deferral for investment earnings and the opportunity to roll the money over to an IRA.

Both the IRS and the DOL are likely to review both your hardship withdrawal and loan procedures if they audit your plan. You should retain the application and other paperwork for each hardship withdrawal. I strongly recommend getting some documentation from the participant to support the reason for the withdrawal. For example, get a copy of the contract if the participant is buying a home. The loan application should include a computation that shows that the amount of the loan doesn't exceed the applicable limits. You should also have any paperwork showing the loan approval.

The streamlined processing offered by many service providers for hardship withdrawals and loans may make both these transactions faster and easier for your participants, but you are still required to follow the procedures that are outlined in your plan document. A few years ago one of my clients was audited by the DOL. The agent spent weeks on-site going through all the employer's files. Subsequently, the agent sent a letter to the CFO citing a loan violation. The amount that one participant borrowed supposedly exceeded the 50% limit. The CFO was very upset when he called me, because my firm had computed the loan amount and the letter from the DOL made it sound like this company had committed a horrible crime. We discovered the agent was wrong and we were right—but it was a big hassle to get to that point. Incidentally, my client didn't receive an apology letter after the agent was informed of his error.

You should operate your plan with the awareness that these audits do occur and they are not fun. The agent involved will probably also check to see that your plan's eligibility, vesting, loan and hardship withdrawal provisions are being followed as they are defined in the plan document. Not to mention a check of your compliance tests, Form 5500 filings, timing of plan contributions and investments. It's an exhaustive process that takes you away from important business: do everything that you can to avoid an audit.

When You Change Jobs

Studies show that roughly one-third of all participants invade their retirement savings when they change jobs. Smaller balances are less likely to be rolled over into a new plan, primarily because participants don't understand the long-term impact. Unless you have a serious financial necessity, I'd resist any temptation to spend any amount of your retirement savings.

You might think that spending $5,000 or $10,000 of your 401(k) money won't make a big difference in your retirement savings. As the withdrawal example on page 115 shows, it will make a lot of difference. Blowing $10,000 of your retirement money at age 35 will cause you to have $132,677 less at age 65, assuming a 9% investment return. You'll forfeit $157,047 if you take out $5,000 at age 25.

When you change jobs, your former employer cannot force you to take your money out of the plan, if the value of your vested benefit exceeds $5,000. This includes your contributions plus earnings and any vested employer contribu-

tions plus earnings. After you terminate your employment, your former employer is supposed to give you a written explanation of your options.

Some employers fail to inform employees of the option to leave their money in the plan. The money can be left in your former employer's plan until the normal retirement age specified in the plan document, usually age 65. A forced distribution is permitted at that time, regardless of your account size. Many participants want to get the money out of the plan as soon as they can. Others who are too busy, don't like making decisions, or really like the investment options tend to let the money sit. Both are much better alternatives than just taking the money out and spending it. In any case, you probably will not be able to move the money into your new employer's plan until you are eligible to make contributions.

Regardless of the amount of your benefit, you can transfer the money directly to your next employer's plan or into an IRA. An IRA transfer should be made directly from your 401(k) to the IRA. If the money comes directly to you, your employer will be required to withhold 20% and deposit it with the IRS. In this case, you will still be able to roll over the entire amount, but you will have to make up the 20% penalty by using other funds. You have 60 days to complete a rollover once you receive your benefit payment. The IRS is very firm about this date, so you need to be careful.

This 60-day time limit is applicable only when you receive a distribution directly. There isn't any time limit for rolling your money over from the 401(k) to an IRA or into another plan. For example, you can leave your money in your former employer's plan for several years before you transfer it to an IRA or another employer plan.

I left my 401(k) money in my former employer's plan because I was comfortable with the way it was invested. I decided to transfer it to an IRA when the company was sold a year later because I didn't like the new funds. One of the risks when you leave your money in the plan is that your former employer can change investment funds. Your money is automatically transferred to the new funds without your approval.

When you leave your money in your former employer's plan you could also have trouble collecting the benefit later. The company may go out of business, be sold, or the employees who oversee the plan could be focused on more urgent matters. For this reason, I recommend transferring your money as soon as you can so that you'll have more control. In most instances, the same investments you have in the 401(k) are available for an IRA—and an IRA offers thousands of other alternatives.

Knowing what to do with the 401(k) money you accumulated in your former plan is not the only major issue. There's also the problem of keeping up with your savings while you're waiting for your new plan eligibility to kick in. There will likely be a period when you can't make any 401(k) contributions, and you'll temporarily see more money in your paycheck. My first advice is not to lose the savings habit—don't spend the extra money. If you get used to spending more money, you won't easily get back to your prior savings level once you're in the new plan.

To continue to save at your prior rate, use a tax-favored regular or Roth IRA. If you're not eli-gible for an IRA, or if the amount you want to save exceeds the IRA limit, set up a personal mutual fund account or other investment account. Because some or all of your savings will have to come from your after-tax pay, you may not be able to save as much as you did before. You also won't be receiving any employer contributions during this period. As a result, you should try to save as much or more than the amount you were saving before you changed jobs—particularly if your salary has increased.

Another possibility is to temporarily put your savings into a money market fund until you are able to join the plan. This would allow you to contribute a larger amount of money once you do join the plan. Assume you previously contributed $3,000 per year pre-tax to a 401(k), you have been earning $40,000 and you won't be able to contribute to your new employer's plan for one year. Put the after-tax amount, $2,400, into a money market fund. Increase your contributions to $6,000 the first year you are in the new plan and use the $2,400 you have stashed away in the money market fund to offset the increased 401(k) contribution. This approach will enable you to recover the tax benefits you lost while you weren't eligible to join the new plan. I recommend this solution if you aren't able to make deductible contributions to an IRA.

Tips on Hardship Withdrawals, Loans and Job Changes

- *Consider the real costs of both loans and hardship withdrawals—in dollar and plan contribution terms.*
- *To avoid or greatly reduce the tax sting when you buy your first home, plan ahead so that the hardship withdrawal and the home purchase both occur early in the year.*
- *Don't use your 401(k) money for non-retirement purposes when you change jobs.*
- *Keep up your savings pace while you're waiting to join your new employer's plan.*
- *If you are an employer, maintain loan and hardship withdrawal records in case of an IRS or DOL audit.*
- *Remember, loans are not tax-free money.*

Managing Your Nest Egg During Your Retirement Years

Once you actually retire, your investment job is not over. Now your job is to convert your nest egg into a healthy income stream that will last the rest of your life. This means you not only have to decide how to invest your money—you have to decide how and when it should be spent.

Decide What to Do with Your 401(k) Money

One of your first decisions as a retiree is how to handle your 401(k) money. You will probably have at least two options—to leave your money in your employer's plan or transfer it into an IRA or other personal account. You are legally permitted to leave your money in the plan if you have not reached the normal retirement age (usually age 65) set in your plan and if your vested benefit is more than $5,000.

What you decide to do with your 401(k) money will depend largely on your age when you leave your employer and when you plan to start using the money. If you leave your employer before age 55 and withdraw your 401(k) money before age 59-1/2, you face a 10% early distribution penalty. You can avoid this penalty by leaving the money in the plan until you are 59 1/2, transferring it directly to an IRA or by taking installment payments if your plan permits you to do so.

If your plan permits only lump sum distributions (which is usually the case), your tax bill will be substantially higher than the tax you would pay to withdraw the money over a period of years. If your plan is one of the few that permits installment payments, you can withdraw as little or as much as you want without worrying about the tax penalty—as long as you leave your employer after age 55 and prior to age 70½. Minimum distributions must begin at age 70½.

When you don't have the installment payment option, you can avoid the penalty tax through periodic distributions that qualify under Section 72(t) of the Internal Revenue Code. Periodic distributions spread the tax burden over your lifetime, unlike the single big tax hit of a lump sum distribution. To qualify for this Section 72(t) tax break, you must receive equal distributions for at least five years. A Section 72(t) distribution is the only way to avoid the 10% penalty tax if you retire before age 55 and start withdrawals from your 401(k) before age 59½.

Assume you retire at age 53 and you have to start withdrawing money immediately from your 401(k) account. You must transfer the money in your 401(k) account to an IRA and begin taking Section 72(t) distributions if your plan doesn't permit installment payments. This will enable you to avoid the 10% penalty tax and to spread the tax burden over many years. When you start taking Section 72(t) distributions prior to age 54½, you must continue taking them until age 59½.

To avoid another tax hit, you need to transfer your 401(k) account directly into the IRA. A distribution of your account directly to you results in a mandatory tax withholding equal to 20% of the total distribution. For example, $20,000 will be deducted from your $100,000 account and sent to the IRS even if you intend to transfer the money to an IRA.

Assume you leave your employer at age 56 and decide to keep the money in the plan. Then at age 58 you decide to start taking money out. You will still be forced to move the money to an IRA if you want to avoid a taxable lump sum distribution, unless your employer permits you to take installment payments. But distributions from an IRA prior to age 59½ are subject to the 10% early distribution penalty tax. You will have to roll the money into an IRA and then take a Section 72(t) distribution that must continue for at least five years—until age 63 in this instance.

Another alternative would be to take a partial distribution from your 401(k) and roll over the rest of the money into an IRA. For example, assume you have $200,000 in your account and that you will need to use $35,000 before age 59½. You could take $35,000 (plus enough money to cover the tax) from your 401(k) plan and have the rest of the money transferred directly to the IRA. It is a good idea to have the bulk of your savings in an IRA because it gives you greater withdrawal flexibility after age 59½.

In any event, you must start to take your money out of the 401(k) plan by age 70½, unless you are still working for the employer that maintains the plan. (If you are a 5% business owner, you must start to take distributions by age 70½— even if you are still working.) The government wants to collect tax on your money at some point, which is why you can't leave it in a 401(k) forever. You may always take more money, but you can't take less than the required minimum, which must be computed under the IRS rules. You can calculate the required minimum distribution using tables provided by the IRS—or ask the organization that maintains your retirement account to do it for you.

If you don't need to use any of your 401(k) money for retirement income and your account exceeds $5,000, you can leave the money in the 401(k). Your employer can't force you to take the money out prior to your plan's normal retirement age. Participants who are comfortable with the investments they have in their 401(k) and/or don't like making decisions are more likely to leave their money in the plan. Those who aren't thrilled with their 401(k) investments usually can't wait to get the money into other investments.

There is no right or wrong decision. Either arrangement is fine if your 401(k) investments are satisfactory. One consideration is that money left in a 401(k) has somewhat greater protection from creditors than money in an IRA. This is a worthwhile benefit if you have significant personal liability exposure.

But on the other hand, an IRA offers much greater investment flexibility. Only those who want a lot of investment choices consider this flexibility a benefit. You also have greater flexibility naming a beneficiary with an IRA because they are not subject to the spousal waiver provisions that apply to 401(k) plans.

As you decide whether to leave your 401(k) money with your former employer, you should also consider the fact that the corporate landscape constantly changes. I have a vested pension with a former employer and the company has been sold twice since I left. It's impossible to get any information from the company that is now responsible for paying my benefit—despite numerous phone calls to the plan administrator. In this continuous merger and acquisition climate, I usually advise participants to get their money out of the 401(k) plan as soon as they can. Not only can former employers be elusive, they can also change your plan investments at any time. Your money can be moved from one set of investments to another without your approval.

Develop a Strategy to Deal with the Tax Man

It would be nice if taxes disappeared when you retire, but unfortunately they don't. These are the major tax issues that must be carefully considered during this stage of your planning:

- Which money should you use first? Your tax-sheltered retirement money or other savings?
- How can you avoid the early distribution penalty tax if you need to use your retirement money before age 59-1/2?
- What should you do with the company stock you own in your retirement account?

We've talked about how to avoid the early distribution penalty tax. Another important issue is when to spend your personal savings rather than your tax-sheltered retirement account. Historically, most professional advisors have recommended that you keep as much money as possible in a tax-deferred account. The rationale is that you would continue to benefit from the fact that no interest, dividends or gains are taxable while the money is in the account.

But taxation of Social Security benefits has changed the game. The portion of your Social Security benefits that is taxable depends on the amount of your other taxable income. Your taxable retirement benefits are included in the income that must be counted to determine what portion, if any, of your Social Security benefits will be taxable. As much as 85% of your Social Security benefits can be subject to tax.

Assume you:
- are retiring at age 60
- plan to start receiving Social Security benefits when you reach age 62
- have $100,000 of personal savings
- have $250,000 in your 401(k) account
- will need $35,000 of income after paying taxes during your first two years of retirement.

You could either use your personal savings or withdraw approximately $40,000 from your retirement account during each of these two years. This assumes that the $40,000 withdrawal will net about $35,000 after paying taxes. Withdrawing the money from your retirement account will reduce the size of the taxable distributions you will receive after you become eligible for Social Security. You will still have your personal savings available that have already been taxed.

Taking the money from your retirement account also reduces the amount of your taxable income after you start to collect Social Security benefits. This may be a better tax deal than the tax break you receive by keeping more money in your retirement account.

Taxes also need to be considered when you are deciding what to do with the company stock you may have accumulated in your 401(k) account. You receive a special tax break when you receive company stock as a distribution. Assume you have $100,000 worth of company stock in your retirement account when you retire. If you withdraw the company stock from your retirement account without rolling it over into an IRA, the tax you pay will be based on the value of the stock when it was contributed to the plan.

If the stock had a value of $20,000 when it was contributed to your plan, you will pay tax on $20,000 rather than today's value of $100,000. You must also pay tax on the difference as you sell shares in the future. This will probably be a long-term capital gain tax that is less than the regular income tax rates.

This tax break can be very attractive if you intend to hold the stock for a number of years after you retire. If you pass it on to your heirs, they never have to pay tax on the gain. Assume the $100,000 of company stock grows to $200,000 by the date of your death. The $200,000 value at the time of your death becomes the stepped-up tax base for your heirs—which means they will never pay income tax on the gain from $20,000 to $200,000.

This type of estate planning is feasible only if you do not expect to use the stock during your retirement, and if you are willing to take the risk of having a chunk of money tied to one stock for many years.

As I mentioned earlier, every stock is likely to take a major dive during a 20 to 30-year period. Regardless of how well your company's stock may have done during the years you have owned it, don't expect to avoid a big drop for another 20 plus years. I generally advise people to not let the tax tail wag the dog. Passing company stock onto your heirs is an instance when tax planning can get in the way of good investment planning. As a result, I would recommend selling most of your company stock in order to diversify your portfolio.

Manage Your Investments

Successfully building an adequate retirement nest egg takes most people an entire working career. Investing is even more critical during your retirement years. You can do some really dumb things when you are younger and still recover. A 20% or greater investment loss is a non-event for a 30-year-old, but it can be a disaster when you are 70. Now you really have to pay attention to your investments so that you can convert your retirement account and other resources into an income stream that will last for the rest of your life.

A generation or two ago it was a common practice for retirees to convert all their available funds into income-producing investments. For most, this meant bank certificates of deposit. Those who owned stocks typically stuck to those that were popular for widows and orphans. These were high-dividend paying stocks such as utilities that had a history of steady income with low price fluctuation and modest long-term growth.

Keeping up with inflation wasn't a big deal when the average retiree lived for only 10 to 12 years. A 3% inflation rate reduced the amount of income a retiree could spend by only 23% after 10 years. The actual impact of inflation was even less because at least 40% of an average retiree's income came from Social Security, which was adjusted annually for inflation.

Today, if you retire during your 50s or early 60s, you need to plan for at least 30 years of retirement income. Your buying power will be reduced by 58% after 30 years of inflation at 3%. You undoubtedly have read that you have to retain stock investments during your retirement years to help offset the impact of inflation. This advice makes sense because stocks have produced a higher level of return than other investments over 20 to 30-year time periods. But you also need to know how much stock and which type of stocks to own.

At this point it's necessary to get back to the issue of realistic expectations. I said in Chapter 6 that when you do your retirement planning, you can't expect an annual 12 to 15% return. Unfortunately, too many 401(k) investors came to expect 15% returns during the high performance 1990s. The fact is that the stock market has never rewarded investors with a return in this range for more than a few years. You should expect your return to average 7 to 9% per year during your retirement years—even with stock investments.

There are some return rules of thumb that are helpful for your planning. You can expect stocks to produce a 10% average return and bonds to produce a 6% average return over a 20 to 30-year period. Overall, you can achieve:

- a 7% return if 75% of your money is invested at 6% and 25% is invested at 10%
- an 8% return with 50% invested at 6% and 50% invested at 10%
- a 9% return if you invest 25% at 6% and 75% at 10%.

Remember these are simply rules of thumb to help you establish realistic investment expectations for your retirement years and decide how to split your money among different types of investments. The above guidelines are the level of average returns that could be expected during a 20 to 30-year period. The year-to-year returns will vary, and the amount of the variance is usually higher when you have a large amount invested in stocks.

Professional investment advisors recommend investing less than 75% of your money in stock during your retirement years. This means you should expect an average return in the 7 to 8% range if you follow the most commonly recommended mix of stocks and fixed-income investments for retirees. This mix includes a stock allocation in the 40 to 60% range, depending on your age and risk tolerance. For example, a 60% stock allocation may be appropriate during the early years of your retirement, but in most instances the percentage should be reduced as you get older.

Generally, I recommend stock funds that do not appear on most hot performer lists. I explained in Chapter 8 how a fund with a lower average annual return can actually give you a larger accumulation than one of the funds that appear on the top performer lists. You may decide to invest in the high-octane funds that have more radical ups and downs while you are building your nest egg, but you should not follow this strategy during your retirement years. When you have less time to recover from mistakes, you should stick with funds that have less risk than the S&P index but still produce decent returns. At this point your goal should be to protect your principal.

For the fixed-income portion of your portfolio, you should be able to get a 6% average return by investing in a bond or stable value fund. A Ginnie Mae fund is another possibility for some or all of your fixed-income investments. These are U.S. government-backed mortgages that have about the same risk as bonds but have produced somewhat higher returns.

Manage Your Risks and Maximize Your Returns

Why so much talk of risk during your retirement years? At this point you need to withdraw money from your account to live. The combination of a negative return for a couple of years and regular withdrawals can really reduce the size of your account.

I recently read in *Money* about an early retiree who is withdrawing 10% from his account annually. The value of this individual's almost 100% stock portfolio dropped by 12% during the recent market decline. His nest egg shrank a total of 22% during his first year of retirement! You don't need to be a rocket scientist to realize this guy is in serious trouble.

Assume, for example:

- you start with $250,000
- you withdraw 6% or $15,000 for living expenses the first year and $15,450 the second year
- the value of your retirement investments drop by 10% the first year and another 4% the second year you are retired
- your savings plan was based upon an 8% return during your retirement years.

An 8% return may have looked like a sure thing when you retired, but the market hasn't done well during the first two years of your retirement. The following example shows how much the value of your nest egg drops after two years of retirement, and where you are compared to your original investment plan.

	Your Plan	Your Results
BEGINNING AMOUNT	$250,000	$250,000
Withdrawal		
Year 1	$15,000	$15,000
Year 2	$15,450	$15,450
Investment gain or (loss)		
Year 1	$19,400	$(24,250)
Year 2	$19,734	$ (8,121)
Ending Balance		
Year 1	$254,400	$210,750
Year 2	$258,684	$187,179

I've assumed in this example that your total withdrawals increase by 3% to account for inflation in the second year, and that the withdrawals occur monthly. Although no one can predict when the market will go up and down, you do need a predictable stream of income during your retirement years. But withdrawing money when the value of your investments is declining can be gut wrenching. One way to avoid this problem is to create a special cash reserve fund of about 20% of your nest egg (or enough income to cover your living expenses for two years) in a separate IRA or a low-risk fixed-income investment account. During down periods you can then tap this fund rather than your nest egg.

The risk of a loss during any retirement year is reduced by increasing the allocation to bonds and other fixed-income investments. Assume a 50/50 equity and fixed-income split during these two years with the bond funds producing a 6% return. This would reduce your overall loss to only 2% during a year when your stocks drop by 10%. Your return would also go up by 1% during a year when your stocks drop by 4%. These results would still stray from your original investment targets, but you substantially soften the blow of losses that would occur with a 100% stock allocation.

You may be asking why not avoid any loss and just put the entire amount into fixed-income investments during your retirement years? The answer is, once again—inflation. In the example above, the amount of money you will need to withdraw during the 20th year of your retirement will have increased from $15,000 to $26,300 (including adjustments for 3% of inflation per year). If you are particularly thrifty, you may think that you don't need to adjust for inflation—but that's not the case. You're not living on the same income that you had 20 or 30 years ago, and you will not want to live on today's income 30 years from now. Some argue that despite inflation expenses decrease during retirement years. That's true, but medical expenses usually increase, and you may ultimately need to cover the cost of an assisted living facility. Some stock investments should help you make up the gap that inflation causes.

Avoid Outliving Your Nest Egg

Some people are led to believe that they will never run out of money if the amount they withdraw from their retirement account per year never exceeds the investment return they achieve. First of all, achieving an investment return such as 8% is not a given. There have been extended periods, like the 1970s, when stock returns were almost non-existent. It isn't easy to live through one of these longer-term market funks when you are building your nest egg—but it is much more painful when you are retired and are watching your account shrink. In addition to good planning, a favorable economy during most of your retirement years will certainly help.

Three finance professors at Trinity University in San Antonio conducted a study to determine which types of portfolios would most likely cause retirees to run out of money. The study used historical data from 1926 through 1995 and different mixes of stocks and bonds and rates of withdrawal to determine potential outcomes. As we are often reminded, the past may not be duplicated in the future—but it is foolish to ignore what this type of study shows.

The study considered five types of portfolios:
a. 100% bonds
b. 75% bonds and 25% stocks
c. 50% bonds and 50% stocks
d. 25% bonds and 75% bonds
e. 100% stocks

The professors examined how these portfolios would have fared during 15 to 30-year retirement periods, assuming withdrawals in the range of 3 to 12%. The study showed that the portfolios with a stock/bond mix are most likely to provide an income for the longest period of time.

The following are the results during this study period, using an annual 6% withdrawal rate and assuming a 30-year retirement period:

Portfolio	Probability of Success
100% bond	27%
100% stock	90%
75% stock/25% bond	95%
50% stock/50% bond	98%

With a 100% bond portfolio, the odds of success drop to zero when the withdrawal rate increased from 6% to 7%.

The Trinity study is an excellent resource for your retirement planning. More detailed information about this study appears in Lynn O'Shaughnessy's book, *Retirement Bible,* published by Hungry Minds. This book also contains a ton of great retirement planning information for those who are inclined to do a lot on their own. The entire Trinity study is also available to members of the American Association of Individual Investors, a non-profit financial education group, at its Internet archives (*www.aaii.org*).

The most significant Trinity University study lessons are:
a. Withdrawing more than 6 or 7% from your retirement account per year—regardless of the mix of stocks and bonds you choose—substantially increases the potential that you will outlive your nest egg.
b. You should keep at least 50% of your retirement investments in stocks.
c. The likelihood of running out of money decreases when 25 to 50% is invested in bonds.

Even though you've planned carefully for your retirement, there are some things you can't control. Market ups and downs can change the percentage of stocks and bonds in your portfolio.

If your goal is a 50/50 balance, don't let the percentages wander too far. Rather than making annual shifts to keep this balance, I recommend rebalancing your portfolio when your stock/bond percentage has changed by a small percentage—such as 5%.

How do you rebalance your portfolio? If your stock percentage goes up to 55%, reduce it back to 50% by moving enough money from the stock to the bond fund to get back to a 50/50 split. This move back to a 50/50 split will reduce your loss when your stock investments drop. Likewise, when the bond portion of your portfolio increases to 55% because the stock portion hasn't done well, you should move money from the bond fund to the stock fund to get back to a 50/50 mix. This may be tough to do, but it will improve your results when the stocks move up again.

Create a Predictable Income Stream

IRA Withdrawals

There are several ways you can structure your retirement account to provide a monthly stream of predictable income. One is to take monthly withdrawals of a specific amount from mutual funds that are held in an IRA. You can even have the money deposited directly to your checking account.

For example, assume you have $250,000 in your IRA account and you want to withdraw a total of 6% per year. This $15,000 is divided into monthly payments of $1,250. Then assume that this money is split evenly between a bond fund and a stock fund. You can have the fund company send you $625 from each account.

When you invest in these funds, you receive dividends, interest and realized capital gains. You could elect to have these amounts paid directly to you—but it's easier to have all income reinvested back into new shares. The fund company

then sells enough shares each month to generate the payment you need.

You can increase or decrease your distributions if you have to do so, but you should try hard to stick with your planned withdrawal amount. Remember that your nest egg does not provide a guaranteed lifetime income stream: the checks stop when your account balance hits zero. For example, you can increase the amount you withdraw annually by 3% or whatever inflation rate you have built into your plan; however, I recommend keeping the withdrawal rate at the same level until you really need the additional income.

Keeping your withdrawal amount steady gives you a cushion for later. Your plan for managing your nest egg during your retirement years includes many variables, including a guesstimate of when you will exit your earthly existence. It's highly unlikely that everything will happen exactly as you planned. Living somewhat more frugally during the early years of your retirement reduces the potential that you'll outlive your nest egg.

The Annuity Option

An annuity is another way to get a monthly retirement check. This is a financial product that protects you against living beyond a normal life expectancy. When you purchase an annuity you guarantee yourself income for life—no matter how long you live. It's the reverse of life insurance that you purchase to protect your dependents against the risk that you will die prematurely. An annuity is a good option if you have a limited amount of money that has to last you for many years. For many people, this product provides peace of mind.

The major disadvantage of an annuity is the fact that the insurer keeps your money if you die sooner than expected. You can guarantee payments for a certain number of years beyond your death or for the life of another beneficiary, but the amount payable to you is substantially reduced when you add these guarantees. Financial organizations that sell annuities aren't in the business of giving money away. They take the risk of providing a lifetime income guarantee, but those who beat the actuarial tables and live longer than expected are paid by those who die early.

Another possibility is to split your retirement money between an annuity and other investments. This can be the best of both worlds for some people—they can count on a certain amount of life income from the annuity, plus a monthly withdrawal from the mutual funds or other investments that they make outside the annuity. Once you buy an annuity you can't change the payment structure for some unexpected need. Because of this inflexibility, it's better to put your money in more than one place.

For greater flexibility, I recommend a slightly different product—a variable annuity. With this type of annuity you can invest in many of the same mutual funds you see in the marketplace. But it is more expensive to invest in these mutual funds through a variable annuity. You may wonder why you should pay more for the same mutual funds you can buy on your own—and the answer is that a variable annuity gives you a lifetime income guarantee.

You have to decide whether the lifetime guarantee is worth the extra cost. If you do buy a variable annuity, be sure to choose one that gives you access to mutual funds you prefer. You can in fact buy the annuity directly from most mutual fund companies. Remember to split your annuity investment between stocks and bonds as you do with the rest of your portfolio.

One word of caution: consult a trusted financial planner or other professional adviser to make sure that either type of annuity is right for your situation. Watch out for organizations that use some very clever techniques to sell annuities to anyone who will listen.

Your Home Asset

When you consider financial resources to fund your retirement, you might also wonder about your home. Should you convert your home into an income-producing asset? In some cases, this makes sense—but many people have difficulty selling their family home. You may have to take a less emotional look at this asset, because you may need the equity from your home to achieve a comfortable level of retirement income.

This emotional decision can be particularly difficult for widows. I occasionally do individual financial planning on a voluntary basis, and one widow I advised was a woman named Donna whose husband died when she was 62. Donna worked full-time for an employer where she earned a pension. Her husband's only retirement savings were in a small IRA. The only other significant asset was an older home that required a lot of maintenance. There were a couple of home equity loans that had to be paid, and then the house could be sold for a profit of about $100,000.

I made these specific recommendations to Donna:

- Continue working until age 65 to get the maximum pension benefit and full Social Security benefits
- Move the IRA money from bank CDs into a GNMA fund to get a higher return
- Sell the house as retirement nears
- Look for a nice place to rent after retiring to a lower-cost area.

Donna followed my advice and asked me how to invest the money she received from the sale of the house. I suggested that she put half the money into a short-term corporate bond fund and half into an S&P 500 index fund. She found a nice place to rent close to several family members.

When I tell people about Donna, they often ask why it was better for her to rent when she already owned a home that didn't have a mortgage. The answer is that everyone needs income in retirement, and the sale of Donna's family home made it possible for her to free up some much-needed money.

A home is indeed an asset, but it doesn't produce money—it eats it up. It costs a lot of money to live in your home, even if you don't have a mortgage. Assume you own a $150,000 home. The real estate taxes are probably in the $2,500 range. Your routine annual maintenance costs probably are in the $2,000 range. (Check all your expenditures for a year if my estimates seem high.) Then factor in major periodic repairs such as a new roof. You probably spend at least $5,000 per year for the privilege of owning your $150,000 home—even with the mortgage fully paid. This is okay if you have adequate retirement income, but it's not a wise financial situation if your retirement resources are limited.

You could probably find a nice place to rent for $800 per month in the same area as your $150,000 home. The rental will cost you $9,600 per year compared to the $5,000 it may cost to live in your present home. You're paying almost double for the rental, but you don't have the hassle of home ownership. Most importantly, you can reinvest the money from the sale of your home and make up the difference.

Assume you haven't used your one-time tax exemption and that you have $135,000 left after you sell your home and move. You can reinvest this money in a 50/50 stock and bond portfolio that could generate an 8% investment return of $10,800. You will need $4,600 of this "profit" to make up the difference between the rent you pay and the housing expenses you have eliminated. This leaves you with $6,200 of additional annual retirement income that may enable you to do some things that would not otherwise be possible. You also have access to the $135,000 for emergencies.

It may seem obvious, but the same logic applies if you live in an area where housing costs are much higher than those that I have mentioned above. If you have limited retirement resources, it makes sense to relocate to a lower-cost area so that you can unlock the equity in your expensive home.

All of my recommendations in this chapter have been directed toward individuals. Those of you who are married have probably noticed that I haven't said anything about your spouse. That's because I believe that you both need to do your own retirement planning—unless you operate on a combined income. If you and your spouse have joint accounts and a "what's yours is mine" attitude, a combined plan is fine. But remember that unless you have other resources, both incomes need to be replaced to maintain your lifestyle.

As you decide how to manage your nest egg during your retirement years, I can't overemphasize the importance of consulting a professional. This is probably the best investment you could make for your retirement. Ask co-workers, friends or family members for recommendations on individuals in your area. One good resource on the web is *www.napfa.org*, the site for the National Association of Personal Financial Advisors.

Although I am a big believer in the value of professional investment help, I also recognize the wisdom of everyday people. I recently had the pleasure of attending my Uncle Roy and Aunt Fran's 90th birthday celebration. They are both in good health, which added to the joy of this occasion. Their son-in-law, Tom Hendricks, told me that my aunt and uncle taught him a very valuable lesson. This lesson was simply to live moderately. He explained that they were frugal but not stingy. They have enjoyed doing the things they want to do, but they also have used their financial resources wisely. As I wind up this chapter, I leave you with Uncle Roy and Aunt Fran's wisdom: enjoy your life well into your retirement years, but be prudent and manage your resources wisely.

Case Studies

My brother-in-law, Rick Hahn, recently retired at age 53 after spending his entire career at

Caterpillar. Rick was an operations manager and the plant where he worked in York, PA closed. Rick decided to retire early rather than relocate. This was possible because he began his retirement savings at age 28. By the time he retired, he was contributing 6% to his 401(k) plan.

Despite his relatively young retirement age, Rick had to make the same decisions his older counterparts face. He now receives a reduced pension, which he started to collect when he retired. He also received separation pay, which he took as a lump sum. This lump sum supplements his pension until he starts to collect Social Security at age 62.

Rick left his 401(k) money in the Caterpillar plan for about a year while he searched for a financial planner. He then rolled over his entire 401(k) account, and he doesn't plan to touch it until age 59½. He must, of course, take the required minimum distributions starting at age 70½.

Rick interviewed four financial planners before selecting one that he and his wife Sue trust. The planner they selected was recommended by several friends and a couple of business owners that Rick knew. With the help of the planner, he has invested 55% of his retirement nest egg in stocks and 45% in bonds.

Richard Tofte didn't start saving for retirement as early as Rick. His savings began at age 51 when he was hired by Pepsi Cola as a building start-up supervisor. He decided to start contributing 10% of pay to his 401(k), the maximum amount permitted. He also purchased Pepsi stock through a company purchase plan and started to build a pension benefit. Unfortunately, Richard lost his job at age 59 due to corporate downsizing. Unlike Rick, he hadn't built up sufficient resources to retire.

Richard is now 65. He has started to collect the pension he earned at Pepsi and his Social Security benefit. He and his wife sold their home in New York and relocated to North Carolina where they rent an apartment. Richard went to two CPAs and a financial advisor who didn't work out before a friend hooked him up with a great CPA.

Richard hasn't made any withdrawals from his retirement savings at this point. He has invested the proceeds from the home sale to build a larger nest egg because he is about $15,000 per year short of what he needs to retire. He plans to continue working 32 to 40 hours per week as a security guard until he has enough saved to boost his annual level of retirement income to around $40,000.

Tips on Managing Your Nest Egg in Your Retirement Years

- *Move your money out of your 401(k) into an IRA where you have more flexibility.*
- *Consider tapping some of your tax-deferred retirement funds rather than depleting all your other savings .*
- *Consider mutual fund automatic withdrawal plans or variable annuity monthly payments.*
- *Expect to earn between 6 and 9% on your investments during your retirement years.*
- *Establish a fixed-income/stock investment mix that is likely to generate the retirement income you need.*
- *Don't be lured by high-octane stock investments during your retirement years.*
- *Avoid being too conservative: you'll most likely outlive your money if you invest 100% in bonds.*
- *Keep at least 50% of your retirement investments in stocks.*
- *Rebalance your portfolio when your stock/bond percentage shifts more than 5%.*
- *Plan to withdraw only 6 to 7% of your retirement account each year so that you don't run out of money.*

Notes

The Small Employer's Challenge

Especially during periods of low employment, small employers have a tough road to hoe. One of their biggest problems is maintaining a high-quality work force. Small employers must compete with the big guys for good employees. When prospective employees decide which company they want to work for, they compare features such as pay scale, working conditions, career potential and benefits.

The quality of a company's benefits is a key issue. Start-ups that do not offer benefits can sometimes attract top talent, but not for long. As soon as a growing business begins to scale up, once "entrepreneurial" employees tend to become more "bureaucratic" and expect competitive benefit programs. One of the benefits that is most important to them is a retirement plan.

But for a small employer, establishing a retirement plan can seem like a daunting challenge. Most small employers have their hands full with the "A to Z" requirements of building and managing a successful business. I know this is true because I've been heavily involved with a number of start-ups. The typical small business owner wears many hats in the start-up stages—often including human resources manager and chief financial officer. There's usually no one else who can assume the responsibility for developing a retirement plan.

If you are faced with this situation, the first thing that you have to do is be realistic. Running a retirement plan, particularly a 401(k), can require a lot of your precious little time. You shouldn't trust sales people who tell you otherwise. I have heard many sales professionals tell small business owners that all they need to do is send the plan money to their organizations once a month. They make it seem like their organizations handle everything else—but it's not true. Most dangerous of all are some Internet-based providers who offer to design and get your plan up and running in five minutes.

All consumers need to be aware—but small employers that are considering retirement plans need to be even more informed. You are the one who will be responsible for complying with the law, not the person who sells you the plan, or the organization that manages it. If you take some time to learn about your retirement plan options—and pay special attention to basic legal requirements—you should be able to avoid costly mistakes. The primary purpose of this chapter is to help you determine if a retirement plan is right for your business (2 to 25 employees), and then decide which plan would most benefit you and your employees.

Please note that for ease of reading purposes I've given you general information about each plan rather than a comprehensive, precise profile. Once you decide which type of plan is right for your company, you will need to get more detailed information about administrative, compliance and investment issues from an organization that will help you set up and manage the plan.

The Standard 401(k) Plan

Unfortunately, there are many very complex compliance requirements governing tax-qualified retirement plans. Especially for the standard 401(k) plan, the laws and regulations are voluminous. You might be surprised to learn that the 401(k) is not the easiest plan to operate and that it's not your only option. Although the 401(k) plan is very popular in corporate America, it's not right for many small companies.

Compliance issues are the dark clouds that hang over any retirement plan—and the plan you choose will depend on your tolerance for various requirements. The first compliance issue relates to employer contributions. This is a big issue for small business owners—particularly for start-ups. When you have more expenses than revenues, you might like to avoid employer contributions to a retirement plan. But this is not always possible.

In the case of a 401(k), technically you do not have to make employer contributions. This may seem like a major plus until you see that there are many other compliance requirements that compel small business owners to consider less complex options.

Sometimes small business owners are forced to make employee contributions to a 401(k) plan. This happens when a plan becomes "top heavy" because more than 60% of the money accumulated in the plan belongs to the owners and certain family members. When small employers do not have employer contributions, this situation is common.

For example, if you are an owner and you contribute 3% or more of your pay to a plan that is top heavy, your company must contribute 3% of pay for each eligible employee. This 3% minimum employer contribution must be made for all eligible employees—including those who do not contribute to the plan on their own. Matching employer contributions may be counted toward this 3% required contribution for plan years beginning after December 31, 2001.

Many of the organizations that sell 401(k)s to small employers ignore this employer contribution issue. In my opinion, the first thing you should consider is the likelihood that more than 60% of the money in the 401(k) plan will belong to the owners—and cause a "top heavy" situation.

There's another important consideration related to both employee and employer contributions: at the end of each plan year they must also pass special non-discrimination tests. The amount contributed by highly compensated employees (HCEs) must be compared to the average percentage of pay that is contributed by the non-highly compensated employees (non-HCEs). Typically, employees who earn more than $85,000 and 5% owners are HCEs, regardless of the amount they earn. The spouse and lineal family members of 5% owners are also HCEs, regardless of the amount they earn.

Many individuals, including professional business advisors, commonly confuse these tests with the top heavy requirements. Plans that have a lot more employees than owners are not likely to be top heavy, but all 401(k) plans have the possibility of failing non-discrimination tests.

Non-discrimination tests follow a precise formula. The average percentage of pay contributed by the HCEs may not exceed the lessor of (1) the average percentage of pay contributed by the non-HCEs plus two percentage points or (2) twice the non-HCE percentage. Assume the eligible non-HCEs contribute an average of 4% of pay. The HCEs may contribute an average of 6% (the non-HCE percentage plus 2). The HCEs may contribute an average of only 3% of pay, if the non-HCE contribution average is only 1.5% (1.5% times 2). In this example the HCEs would only be able to contribute an average of 3% because it is the lesser amount.

Another aspect of the non-discrimination test relates to the employee contribution maximum. There is a common misperception that all eligible employees are permitted to contribute the $11,000 maximum. The non-discrimination tests often force HCEs to contribute less than the $11,000 maximum. Assume you are a small business owner and the eligible non-HCEs in your plan contribute an average of 4% of pay.

Once you do the calculations, you find that you're permitted to contribute only 6% of pay (the non-HCE % plus 2). HCEs are commonly limited to 6% or less. You can contribute only $4,800 if your gross W-2 income for the year is $80,000. This may be much less than the amount you wanted to contribute—and of course less than the $11,000 maximum.

Although you want to create a retirement plan to keep your company competitive and reward your employees' hard work, the plan still needs to work for you, too. You won't be happy if most of your employees can contribute the $11,000 maximum and you cannot. Before you start a 401(k), it's a good idea to ask your non-HCEs how much they plan to contribute. This will help you get a rough idea of how much you will in turn be permitted to contribute. Typically, the average non-HCE contribution range is 2 to 8% of pay.

That's the situation with employee contributions. Then there's the matter of employer contributions. Plans that do not have an employer matching contribution tend to have significantly lower participation and contribution rates. Typically, no more than 50% of eligible employees contribute when there is no match. Plans with an employer match equal to $.25 per $1.00 of the employee contribution usually achieve 70%+ participation rates.

The crux of the problem is that all eligible employees must be included when the non-discrimination tests are performed. Those who decide not to contribute pull down the employee contribution average—and reduce the amount that HCEs can contribute. It may be difficult for you to eke out employer contributions—but you have to weigh that expense against the potential HCE contributions lost due to low non-HCE contributions.

Another important point is that all eligible employees must be included in the non-discrimination testing—regardless of how many hours they work. This is the case unless your plan document has a provision that excludes employees who work less than a specified number of hours. The law requires that you include employees who work at least 1,000 hours during any year. This is only an average of 20 hours per week.

With all these considerations you're probably debating whether you should have an employer contribution. The real question is how much it actually costs. Maybe not as much as you think. A $.25 per $1.00 match will cost 1% or less of eligible payroll. Assume all your eligible employees earn a total of $200,000 per year. The entire employer matching contribution will cost you only $1,400 if 70% of employees participate and contribute at least 4% of pay. The employer contribution can vest over a period of up to six years. Unvested amounts that are forfeited can further reduce your cost, because the money may be used to reduce future contributions.

Aside from all the compliance hassles, don't forget that with a 401(k) you also need to find an organization to handle your plan. Finding a quality provider for a new plan is a challenge for a small employer because all the major providers are interested in existing plans that already have significant participant account balances.

Alternatives to the Standard 401(k) Plan

For small business owners, there are easier alternatives than a 401(k). Two great options are the Simplified Employer Plan (SEP) and the Savings Incentive Plan for Employees (SIMPLE-IRA). Both of these plans are much easier and less expensive to set up and run than a 401(k).

A SEP is funded solely by employer contributions. It's a good plan alternative if you are the only employee or if there are a number of owners and only one or two employees. A SEP will not be your best alternative if you have more employees and/or you expect to expand your work force in the future.

If your income is less than the maximum amount that is subject to Social Security tax, the SEP has the advantage of no payroll taxes. All employer contributions to any retirement plan are exempt from Social Security and other payroll taxes. Assume you earn $60,000 per year. A $5,000 employer contribution to a SEP (for yourself) will save you roughly $1,000 in payroll

taxes. If you contributed the same amount to a 401(k) or a SIMPLE-IRA plan, you would have to pay payroll taxes on your own contributions. Consider if the payroll tax savings would help you fund any contributions for the SEP for other employees. If so, this would make the SEP a good choice for your company.

If you don't think that a SEP will work for your company, you have three other retirement plan choices: the 401(k), the SIMPLE-IRA and the Safe Harbor 401(k). Each of these plans are funded solely or primarily by employee contributions. And each plan has its own set of pros and cons. The SIMPLE-IRA and the Safe Harbor 401(k) are largely compliance-free, but they do require employer contributions. The 401(k) doesn't require employer contributions (if your plan isn't top heavy), but there are major compliance hassles. The cost of setting up and running a 401(k) or Safe Harbor 401(k) is much higher than a SIMPLE-IRA.

So how do you choose? In the following decision-making tree, answers to five questions will help you narrow your search.

1. Do you want to contribute more than $7,000 per year?
2. Are you willing to contribute 1% of each eligible employee's pay?
3. Are you willing to contribute 3% of each eligible employee's pay?
4. Are plan fees and administrative simplicity important?
5. Are you and the other owners likely to contribute more than 60% of the total plan assets?

The following is a key to the answers:
• When (5) is yes, consider the SIMPLE-IRA or Safe Harbor, regardless of any of your other answers.
• When (1) is yes, you will need a 401(k) or Safe Harbor 401(k).
• When (1) is no, you should consider the SIMPLE-IRA.

- When (2) is yes and (3) is no, consider the 401(k) or SIMPLE-IRA.
- When (2) is no, consider a 401(k).
- When (3) and (1) are yes, consider the Safe Harbor 401(k).
- When (3) is yes and (1) is no, consider the SIMPLE-IRA.
- When (4) and (2) are yes, and (1) is no, the SIMPLE-IRA is probably best for you.
- When (4) and (3) are yes, consider the SIMPLE-IRA and the 401(k) Safe Harbor.
- When (5) and (3) are no, consider a SIMPLE-IRA or 401(k).

The SIMPLE-IRA Plan

This is a very good plan for small employers, particularly during the first couple of years of a new business. A SIMPLE-IRA can be established by completing a one-page form from any financial organization that offers this type of plan. You don't have to pay any fees to set it up, and you also don't have any administrative or compliance fees. Avoiding these costs and headaches are a big plus.

The maximum amount you can contribute to a SIMPLE-IRA is $7,000. Since the maximum contribution to a 401(k) is $11,000, this may not seem like a good deal. But, unlike the 401(k), you can contribute this amount regardless of how much your employees contribute. There is no non-discrimination testing with the SIMPLE-IRA. Another advantage is that you personally receive the mandatory employer contribution that must be at least 1% of pay. (That's an additional $800 if you earn $80,000.)

The 1% employer contribution is required during the first two plan years. Assume the total pay of eligible employees is $100,000. You will have to contribute $1,000 for these employees if they also contribute at least 1% of their pay to the plan. You may not like having to make this contribution, but it is less than what it would cost you to set up and administer a 401(k).

Some employers feel that the SIMPLE-IRA plan is a good starting point. After the second plan year, you have the option to increase your employer contribution to 2% of pay or to change to a 401(k) to maintain a lower contribution level. Employer contributions are fully vested at all times.

The Safe Harbor 401(k) Plan

The Safe Harbor 401(k) plan has special features that can eliminate the top heavy and non-discrimination problems associated with a standard 401(k). A minimum employer contribution equal to either 3% of each eligible employee's pay or a matching contribution of up to 4% of pay is required. If you do either for all eligible employees, you satisfy the top heavy requirement and exempt the plan from non-discrimination tests.

	401(k)	401(k) Safe Harbor	SIMPLE
Max. Employee Contrib.	$11,000	$11,000	$7,000
Min. Employer Contrib.	None	3%	1%*
Vesting	Over Time	Immed.	Immed.
Loans	Yes	Yes	No
Non-Discrim. Testing	Yes	No	No
Subject to Top Heavy Rules	Yes	No	No
Plan Design Flexibility	Yes**	Yes	Some
Install. Fees	$1,000	$1,000	None
Annual Admin. Fees	$1-3,000 Min.	$1-3,000 Min.	None

* Must be increased to 2% of pay after two years.

** Design flexibility may be adversely impacted by top heavy and non-discrimination test requirements.

With a Safe Harbor 401(k), you and any other owners can contribute the $11,000 maximum, regardless of how much the other employees contribute. Although this is more than you could contribute to a SIMPLE plan, remember that the Safe Harbor 401(k) requires a 3% or 4% rather than a 1% employer contribution. You, too, receive this contribution in addition to the $11,000 you are permitted to contribute. Employer contributions are fully vested at all times. The cost of setting up and running the plan is similar to a 401(k).

The Cost of a Retirement Plan

Many employees have a general perception that there isn't any cost to the employer with a 401(k) because the employer receives a tax deduction for its contribution. It's true that the employer can deduct a retirement plan contribution from its taxable income, if it has any. But many businesses are not profitable in the early years, which means that the tax deduction is of no help.

In the case of a new business, the entire cost of the 401(k) plan is paid by the employer. With a more mature and profitable employer, the tax deduction covers only a small portion of the plan cost. The entire cost must also be paid by a not-for-profit employer.

Regardless, retirement plans are not too expensive for small employers. There is an affordable alternative for just about every employer. I'm speaking from experience as a small business owner rather than some policymaker who hasn't been in the real world. Each of the small businesses I've had an ownership stake in has had a retirement program. In some instances you can't afford not to have a plan because you have to hire and keep top-notch employees in a highly competitive environment.

Case Studies

Even with all this comparative information, it's probably still difficult to choose among your four retirement plan options. These actual examples of how other small businesses owners have found attractive and affordable plans may help.

The Simplified Employer Plan (SEP) Meets the Needs of a Three-Employee Business

Steve and Laura run the Kettle Lodge and Susquehanna Cabins that cater to those who enjoy outdoor activities such as hunting, fishing and hiking. They have only one employee who works less than 10 hours per week.

Both Steve and Laura have annual earnings that are less than the Social Security maximum taxable wage base. As a result, any contributions they would make to either a 401(k) or SIMPLE (rather than a SEP) would be subject to FICA and other employer payroll taxes.

Steve and Laura decided to establish a SEP through a mutual fund company. All they had to do is complete one easy form. Contributions to the plan are deposited into IRA accounts set up for this purpose. They can choose from any of the mutual funds the company offers for retirement plans. There wasn't any fee to establish the plan, there aren't any annual fees and there are no compliance hassles. It's just a matter of sending the money to be invested.

The amount that can be contributed to the SEP is very flexible—up to a maximum of 15% of pay. The business can contribute up to 15% of Steve and Laura's gross pay, but there isn't any required contribution. They can make contributions during the year, or they can wait until the end of the year to determine how much to contribute.

The following are the reasons why a SEP is the ideal plan for Steve and Laura:

• They are the only eligible employees

- The contributions required for their part-time employee will be low if she becomes eligible and they make a contribution for themselves
- Their earnings are below the FICA maximum taxable wage base
- They avoid Social Security taxes through their business contribution—and they also pay only income tax on their eventual distributions.
- There aren't any fees to set up or run the plan.

Doctors Reach Personal Contribution Goals With the SIMPLE Plan

Manoj and Sarla are medical professionals who have three full-time employees. Each owner has earnings of $100,000 that exceed the FICA maximum wage base. The gross annual pay for the three employees is $82,000.

The two doctors want to contribute around $10,000 each to a retirement plan. The three employees are willing to contribute a total of $4,400 to the plan. This means Manoj and Sarla will be contributing more than 80% of the total employee contributions during the first year. This would create a "top heavy" situation with a 401(k), so they realized that their best alternatives were a SIMPLE-IRA or Safe Harbor 401(k).

Either plan would permit them to meet their contribution goals, offer an attractive plan that would help to retain their employees and save administrative time. Manoj and Sarla decided to go with a SIMPLE-IRA rather than the Safe Harbor 401(k) to avoid the cost of setting up and running a 401(k).

To start the plan all they had to do was complete a couple of forms supplied by the organization they selected and have each employee complete an IRA application.

Manoj and Sarla also decided on a dollar-for-dollar employer matching contribution limited to the first 3% of pay. They could have matched only the first 1% of pay that their employees contribute, but the higher percentage allowed them to get to their own desired contribution level and provide a great plan for their employees.

The following chart shows how Manoj and Sarla's plan works:

	Employee Annual Income	Employee Contribution	Employer Contribution	Total Contribution
Manoj	$100,000	$7,000	$3,000	$10,000
Sarla	100,000	7,000	3,000	10,000
Lela	28,000	1,960	840	2,800
Alicia	27,500	1,375	825	2,200
Monica	26,500	1,060	795	1,855

Manoj and Sarla's employees can select any of the funds that are appropriate for an IRA. They simply need to send the money in to be invested at the end of each month. Employees receive detailed statements directly from the investment company.

Manoj and Sarla selected a SIMPLE-IRA because:

- A top heavy situation would have occurred with a 401(k), because they would be contributing more than 60% of the total plan assets.
- They could hit their personal contribution goals—regardless of how much the other employees contributed.
- They could avoid fees to establish and operate the plan.
- The SIMPLE plan required less time to operate than a 401(k).

A Growing Small Business Adopts the Standard 401(k)

Margaret left her employer six months ago to start her own business producing training programs for the medical community. Her clients are drug companies that want effective educational materials that will inform the medical community how to best use specific drugs. Margaret and an outside investor own the business.

Due to the highly technical nature of her training programs, Margaret had to recruit seasoned personnel. During the interviewing process, she promised candidates that she would set up a 401(k).

Because her business couldn't handle the additional expense, Margaret wasn't willing to make an employer contribution. She would be the only participating owner. Three non-owner employees would be eligible and this number was expected to grow. One of the employees earned $65,000, and he wanted to contribute the maximum amount. Another one of the other employees wanted to contribute 8%. The third employee was not interested in participating.

Margaret's contributions were expected to be well below 60% of the total employee contributions, so a possible top heavy status was not a concern. The amount the other employees wanted to contribute would permit Margaret to contribute the $11,000 maximum amount. As a result, she decided to go ahead with a 401(k).

This summary of the plan's first year contributions illustrates how employee contributions impact owner contributions:

	Employee Annual Income	% of Pay Contribution	Employee Contributed
Margaret	$110,000	$11,000	10.0%
Alan	65,000	11,000	16.9
Pen-Li	28,000	0	0
Cheryl	26,000	2,080	8.0

The three non-owner employees contributed an average of 8.3% of pay (24.9% divided by 3). This unusually high average enabled Margaret to contribute the $11,000 maximum and to pass the 401(k) non-discrimination test. If Alan contributed a more typical 6% instead of 16.9%, the average for the three non-owners would have dropped to 4.67%. Margaret could then have contributed only 6.67% (4.67% plus 2) or $7,337. It helps to have an Alan in your plan.

Margaret selected a 401(k) because:
- She did not want to make any employer contribution.
- She wanted to contribute $11,000.
- Her personal contributions were expected to be below 60% of the total, eliminating a possible top heavy situation.
- She was able to lure top-level employees with the promise of a 401(k).

Margaret liked the mutual funds she invested in with her prior employer's 401(k) plan. As a result, she set up the plan using a third-party administrator that enabled her to use the same investments. (Sometimes a mutual fund company doesn't handle 401(k)s for small employers, so a third-party administrator is necessary to get low-cost funds.) The fee was $1,000 to set up the plan, and the annual administrative fee is $1,000. Employees may invest in four funds that have been selected for the plan.

An Engineering Firm Attracts Employees With a Safe Harbor 401(k)

Rocco and Wes own and run a consulting engineering firm. There are 10 other employees. The owners are in their 50s and they earn $85,000 each. They were interested in contributing the $11,000 maximum amount to a 401(k). Rocco and Wes were also willing to contribute 3% of each eligible employee's pay to help attract and retain good employees in a highly competitive area.

The decision to go with a Safe Harbor 401(k) was based on the amount that the two owners would be able to contribute. Their employees were expected to contribute an average of around 5% of pay. As a result, Rocco and Wes would be able to contribute only approximately 7% of pay—or $5,950—to a regular 401(k). The Safe Harbor 401(k) allows them to contribute the

$11,000 maximum, regardless of how much the other employees contribute. They and all other eligible employees will also receive the 3% automatic employer contribution.

The following summary of the first year contributions shows how the combined employee/employer contributions actually work. Note that the employee who doesn't contribute still gets the 3% contribution.

	Employee Annual Income	Employee Contribution	Employer Contribution	Total Contribution
Rocco	$85,000	$11,000	$2,550	$13,550
Wes	85,000	11,000	2,550	13,550
Shreesh	60,000	6,000	1,800	7,800
Willard	55,000	3,300	1,650	4,950
Denise	54,000	3,780	1,620	5,400
Laxman	47,300	0	1,419	1,419
Russell	43,450	2,607	1,303	3,910
Irene	36,930	4,432	1,108	5,540
Darren	32,110	963	963	1,926
Sandi	28,725	0	862	862
Indu	25,850	1,034	776	1,810

Rocco and Wes selected their local bank to set up and administer the plan because they preferred to work with a local organization and they wanted to strengthen their relationship with the bank. The set-up fee was $1,000, and the annual administrative fee is $1,200 plus $30 per participant.

Rocco and Wes selected a 401(k) Safe Harbor plan because:

- This is the only plan that allows them each to make the maximum $11,000 contribution.
- They were willing to contribute 3% of each eligible employee's pay to help the business attract and retain the top-notch engineers they needed.
- They didn't want their contributions limited to the amount the other employees contributed.

Visit my web site, *401(k)association.com* if you are a small business owner and you need additional help determining which is the best plan for your company.

Tips on the Small Employer's Challenge

- Make sure you understand the basic legal requirements before you establish any retirement plan.
- Consider the financial and time cost of establishing and running the different types of plans.
- Stay away from people who tell you can set up a 401(k) plan in five minutes using their Internet site.
- Before you start a 401(k), ask your non-highly compensated employees how much they plan to contribute—so that you'll get an idea of how much in turn you'll be able to contribute.
- Don't immediately dismiss the idea of an employer contribution—it can be more affordable than you might think.
- A Simplified Employer Plan (SEP) or Savings Incentive Plan for Employees (SIMPLE-IRA) may be a better alternative than a 401(k)—particularly for a start-up business.
- Buy a plan from a well-known organization or professional advisor who will evaluate your situation to help you determine which type of plan is best.
- Visit 401kassociation.com if you would like additional help from me.

Notes

PART TWO

200 Frequently Asked Questions and Answers

Plan Eligibility

1. Why do I have to wait to join the 401(k) plan?

Each employer is permitted to establish the rules for plan eligibility within acceptable legal limits. It's permissible to exclude employees who are not yet 21 and those who have not completed one year of service. However, employers aren't required to exclude these employees.

In the early days of the 401(k), newly hired employees were commonly excluded during their first year of employment. The trend now is to include newly hired employees immediately or within 30 to 90 days. Employees under age 21 are still commonly excluded because they usually have less interest in saving for retirement and most don't stay at a company for very long.

2. Why do I have to wait until an "official" entry date to join the 401(k) plan?

You can't start making contributions to the plan until the first entry date after you become eligible. Again, it's up to the employer to determine how many entry dates there are and when they will occur. There may be only one entry date per year or each pay period may be an entry date. Some other possibilities are the first of each month or the first day of each quarter.

Entry dates are chosen for administrative reasons. Your employer may only want to sign employees up for the plan four times a year on January 1st, April 1st, July 1st and October 1st quarterly entry dates. Newly eligible employees are often invited to attend a meeting that explains various plan details and investment options—and not every company can handle more than four of these meetings per year.

Although I understand the administrative hassles, I recommend permitting immediate entry after an employee becomes eligible. Employees don't like to wait several months for an entry date. You can explain the plan basics to new employees. You can have a representative from the company that manages the plan give a more detailed explanation of the investments to new employees quarterly or annually.

The maximum period you may be excluded, counting both the one-year eligibility period and the wait for an entry date, is 18 months.

3. My plan requires a year of service before I'm eligible to join the plan. What is a year of service?

There are two methods for determining years of service as defined in ERISA. The first is the hours of service method. Typically, an employee must work at least 1,000 hours during the first 12 months of employment to receive credit for a year of service.

You have to satisfy this 1,000-hour requirement only once. You will always be eligible thereafter, regardless of how many hours you work—but the number of hours you work may impact your eligibility to receive a contribution during a specific year and your vesting.

The other method for determining a year of service is known as the elapsed time method. Service is measured from your date of employment to your date of termination. Once you have been employed for 12 months, you receive credit for a year of service—regardless of how many hours you work.

4. What happens if I don't work at least 1,000 hours during my first 12 months of employment?

Your employer must continue to track the number of hours you work from either your employment anniversary date or the start of each plan year.

Assume you were hired on February 5, 2002. You will satisfy the 1,000-hour requirement if you work at least 1,000 hours by February 5, 2003. If you don't work at least 1,000 hours during this period, your employer must continue to track your hours either from February 5th of one year to the next or during each plan year. You will receive credit for a year of service if you work at least 1,000 hours during any eligibility computation period.

Most plans operate with the calendar year as the plan year. It's a lot easier to track hours using this time period rather than your employment anniversary. As a result, after the first 12 months of employment, most employers switch to the plan year to track eligibility service.

5. I work about 25 hours per week, but my hours vary. Do I have to work at least 1,000 hours each year to be eligible for the 401(k) plan?

The "hours of service" method is generally used to determine initial plan eligibility—usually when there are many employees who work less than 1,000 hours per year.

In all instances that I know of employees who initially satisfy the 1,000-hour requirement are eligible to contribute in future years—regardless of how many hours they work. This is the only approach that makes sense with a 401(k), because you don't always know at the beginning of the year if you'll work 1,000 hours. Waiting until the end of the year to tally hours also isn't viable because at that point you would not have been able to make any contributions to the plan.

6. I want to start a 401(k) for only my full-time employees. We have a lot of part-timers, but most are not interested in retirement benefits. What are the requirements for part-time employees?

Most employers would prefer to include only full-time employees, but this isn't permitted. Once employees work at least 1,000 hours during an eligibility computation period, they are eligible to join the plan. Employees have to work an average of only 20 hours per week to hit 1,000 hours during a 12-month period.

7. I want to start a 401(k) plan for our 10 employees. I'd like to include all current employees, but require that new employees wait 90 days for eligibility. Is this permissible?

Yes, when you start a 401(k) you can have different eligibility requirements for current and future employees. Of course, the requirements for both groups must fit within the legal time limits.

8. I own three different businesses. I would like to set up a 401(k) for employees of one of the businesses without including the employees from the other two businesses. My broker told me I can't do this. Is he correct?

Maybe. The correct answer depends on the specific facts. Because the three businesses are commonly owned, all employees must be considered—but they all don't necessarily have to be covered by the plan. The specific rules are pretty complex, but the following are some general guidelines.

You may cover only the employees from one of your businesses if it employs more than 70% of the total number of employees. You should also be able to include only the employees of this business if it doesn't have a disproportionately high percentage of highly compensated employees.

I recommend having the specific facts

reviewed by either an attorney or a retirement plan consultant who is familiar with this area of the law. Ask the person you select for a written explanation for your records.

9. I left my employer and then came back six months later. My employer told me I have to wait a year before I can start contributing to the plan again. Is this correct?

Your employer may not require you to satisfy the eligibility requirements a second time—despite the fact that you left and came back to the company.

10. I'm a union employee. Other employees at my company can contribute to a 401(k) and get a matching contribution. Why can't I contribute to the plan, even if I don't get matching contributions?

Any retirement benefits, including the ability to contribute to a 401(k) without matching contributions, must be provided to union employees through the collective bargaining process. As a union employee, you have the right to bargain for additional wages, benefits, better working conditions, etc. Through collective bargaining. To protect this right, the government enacted labor laws prohibiting employers from giving union employees any benefits that aren't included in its contract with union employees. As a result, if you want a 401(k), it must be part of the wage/benefits package that is included when you renegotiate your contract.

11. I can't afford to contribute to my plan now. What happens if I don't join my plan as soon as I am eligible? Do I lose my right to contribute to the plan at a later date?

Unless it is totally impossible, I encourage you to contribute to the plan—even if you start with only 1% of your pay. You can then increase your contribution a bit each time you get a raise. But if contributions are out of the question at this time, you can join the plan as of any pay period or entry date. It depends on the administrative rules your employer establishes.

12. A top-notch candidate I'd like to hire wants to start contributing to the 401(k) immediately. Our plan requires newly hired employees to wait for one year before they join the plan. Can I waive the eligibility requirement to help my company get this new employee?

No, the eligibility rules you set in your plan must be followed in all instances. You can't waive the normal provisions for any reason. One of the requirements for a tax-qualified retirement plan is that it must be operated in a uniform, non-discriminatory manner for all employees.

13. I have a new employee who wants to immediately roll over money from his old 401(k) plan into ours. Our plan requires six months of service for eligibility. Can I permit this?

Employees who are not yet eligible to contribute are legally permitted to roll over money from a prior plan—but only if this provision is included in your plan document. If not, you need to amend the document to permit immediate rollovers.

An alternative is to have the new employee leave the money in his prior plan or transfer it to an IRA rollover account until he is eligible to join your plan.

14. I'm only 20 but I realize how important it is to start saving for retirement. The 401(k) at my company doesn't allow anyone under age 21 to join. This doesn't seem fair. Are they allowed to do this, and if they are, why?

Employers are permitted to exclude employ-

ees who are under age 21, those who have been employed for less than one year, and employees who have never worked more than 1,000 hours during an eligibility computation period. These exclusions are permitted because most employees who fall into these categories are less interested in saving for retirement.

The turnover rate is also commonly much higher for these employees. It's an administrative hassle to sign employees into the plan and then pay them out when they leave just a couple of months later. Most employers want to avoid this large expense for very little benefit.

You are to be congratulated for realizing how important it is to start saving at an early age. Learning to save early and keeping at it will give you big rewards later. I recommend contributing to a ROTH-IRA until you are eligible to contribute to the 401(k). You won't get a tax deduction, but your investment income will grow on a tax-sheltered basis. In addition, your investment gains are never taxed—even at withdrawal. This is probably a better tax break than you would get from a regular IRA.

15. We hire a lot of employees who are over age 65. Do we have to include them in the 401(k)?

All employees who meet the years of service requirements are eligible to join the plan—regardless of age. There isn't any maximum age limit with a 401(k).

16. My company is changing the status of several employees to independent contractors. Up until this point they have been contributing to our 401(k). What do we have to do so they will be able to continue their contributions to the plan?

Actually there is nothing you can do because only employees are permitted to contribute to your plan. Independent contractors are self-employed. These new contractors do have other alternatives, however. The simplest is a SEP-IRA, which can be set up by signing a one-page form. This form and everything else that is needed can be obtained from a financial organization that handles this type of plan.

17. My company is transferring me to a division that doesn't have a 401(k). I'm not very happy about this because it will disrupt my retirement planning. Is this permitted? How can they exclude this division?

Employers may exclude specific groups of employees in addition to those who haven't met the age and service requirements—as long as certain coverage rules are satisfied. Generally, these rules can be met if the excluded group is less than 30% of all employees. For example, assume there are 400 employees in the excluded division and the company has a total of 4,000 employees. The coverage requirements are satisfied because the excluded group involves only 10% of all employees.

Your Plan Contributions

18. How much money may I contribute to my 401(k)?

There are two primary limits that apply to all employees. The first is the maximum annual dollar limit that is $11,000 in 2002. This limit will increase to $15,000 by 2006. Only employee pre-tax contributions count toward this limit. Any after-tax contributions you make or contributions your employer makes are not counted toward this limit.

Your contributions may not exceed 100% of pay. There also are special non-discrimination rules for 401(k)s that link the amount that highly compensated employees (HCEs) may contribute to the amount that the non-highly compensated employees (NHCEs) may contribute. (See

Question 33.) It may be necessary to lower your contributions if you're an HCE.

19. What happens to the money I'm contributing to the 401(k) plan? How do I know it isn't being used to buy company cars for executives?

Your employer is legally required to put the money into a separate trust that is used only for the 401(k). A trust is a separate legal entity similar to a corporation. The assets of the trust must be used exclusively for the benefit of plan participants and their beneficiaries.

The money cannot be used for the benefit of the company or any of the people who oversee the plan. Of course, there are some dishonest people and there have been a few instances of 401(k) abuse which have led to prosecution. The Department of Labor is responsible for enforcing this area of the law and they have done so pretty aggressively. The employer is also required to carry a fidelity bond, which insures a minimum of 10% of the plan's assets from loss in the event of abuse.

20. I am 23 and my budget is really tight. But I want to start contributing to my company's 401(k) because I realize how important it is to start early. I'm not sure how much I can afford. What is the smallest amount I can contribute to a 401(k)?

First, you are to be congratulated for getting started at such a young age. Starting the saving habit early is an important step.

There isn't any legal minimum 401(k) contribution. It's up to each employer to set this minimum. For most plans 1% of pay is the bottom level. A lower amount would be possible, but it doesn't make sense due to significant administrative costs associated with your plan participation. These basic costs are essentially the same regardless of account size—similar to a bank checking account.

21. I am a 43-year-old single mom without any retirement savings, and I earn only $27,000. I can't afford to contribute more than the 1% minimum our plan allows. Is this worth it?

This level of savings certainly won't be enough for you to retire in luxury, but even a small retirement nest egg is better than nothing. If you're able to achieve a 9% investment return, your 1% contribution of $270 each year will grow to $13,770 in 20 years. Your goal should be to increase your contribution percentage by at least 1% each year, until you hit a point where you can't go any higher.

If you can't go any further once you hit 5%, you should still be able to build a nest egg of perhaps $75,000 or more by your early to mid-60s. You'll feel a lot more secure knowing that Social Security is not your sole source of retirement income. Watching your nest egg grow over the years will also give you a sense of accomplishment.

22. I'm working in the U.S. for two years. I expect to return to my home in another country at the end of this period. What's the point of contributing to a 401(k) for this short time period?

Your contributions will give you a tax break for the short time you are in the plan. If your employer matches your contributions, you'll also benefit from this "free" money. Of course, you must check the vesting schedule for your employer match to see if you will get any of this money when you leave after two years. You may also be able to roll the money over to a tax-favored retirement vehicle in your country.

23. I am 57 years old and I earn $64,000. I would like to contribute the maximum of $11,000, but my employer limits my contributions to 15% of pay. Why doesn't my employer permit me to contribute the maximum amount?

Each employer sets a maximum contribution limit when the plan is established. This limit should be set so that employees have the opportunity to contribute the maximum amount that is permitted. Prior to 2002, both employee and employer contributions to all defined contribution plans had to be considered when this limit was set. Some employers contribute as much as 10 to 15% of pay to their defined contribution plans. As a result, employee contributions had to be limited to 10 to 15% so the combination didn't exceed the 25% combined limit. This may be why your employer has limited you to a maximum of 15%. But the law has changed and your employer should modify the plan so that you may contribute the $11,000 maximum.

There isn't any reason for an employer to restrict non-highly compensated employees to less than the 100% limit less any employer contributions and whatever is needed to pay applicable taxes and cover other payroll deductions. Any additional contributions that are made by increasing this percentage will help the plan pass the non-discrimination tests at no added cost.

24. I changed jobs last year and I was able to contribute to two 401(k)s. When I got my W-2s I saw that I contributed $900 more than the maximum permissable amount. What should I do?

You can leave the extra money in the plans, but this doesn't make sense because you will pay tax on the excess amount twice. Your deduction for the year will be limited to the maximum amount when you file your tax return. You will also have to pay tax on this money again when it comes out of the plan unless you withdraw it now.

First decide from which plan you will withdraw the money. You can take it all from either plan or split the withdrawal between the two plans. You should base this decision on the plan that will give you the best financial results. For example, one of the plans may have a better matching contribution than the other. Any applicable matching contributions will be taken away when your excess contributions are returned. This means your first preference is to withdraw the contributions that weren't matched or those that were matched at the lower rate.

Another factor to consider is the vesting schedule of both plans. If the employer matching contributions to your prior plan are fully vested, you have to consider if you are likely to be with your current employer long enough to get the match. If everything is equal, I would probably take the money out of your prior employer's plan. This is because every dollar counts in helping your new employer pass the non-discrimination tests (unless you are a 5% owner).

Once you decide which plan to withdraw the excess from, you must notify the employer by March 1st of the year following the close of the year in which the excess occurred. The refund must be made prior to April 15th of this year, including applicable investment income. Your notice to the employer should include a request that the refund be made prior to April 15th. If the refund isn't made before April 15th, the additional tax burden is yours rather than the employer's—so you want to keep after them to complete the refund on time.

25. I earned $68,450 last year. I contributed the maximum amount to my 401(k) plan. My contributions and my employer's contributions exceeded 25% of my pay. What should I do?

It is up to your employer to keep all plan participants within the percentage of pay limit—regardless of their income level. Failure to do so could trigger a plan disqualification, which would create serious tax problems for all participants and your employer.

The plan document contains provisions that are to be followed to correct this problem. Your employer may already be working on it, but you should check with your plan administrator in case they haven't discovered this problem. *Note:* For plan years commencing after December 31, 2001 the 25% limit has been increased to 100%.

26. I recently stopped contributing to my plan because my car needed some big repairs. When can I start contributing again?

This situation is governed by the rules and administrative procedures for your plan. Some employers permit re-entry at any time. Others require waiting until the next plan entry date or the beginning of the next plan year. The major factor is how you employer feels about letting employees get in and out of the plan.

When you stop contributing, don't make the common mistake of assuming that your money can be taken out of the plan. This isn't the case. Your money has to stay in the plan whether or not you are contributing.

27. When and how often may I change the amount I contribute?

This is another instance when the employer establishes the applicable rules and administrative procedures. The employer can permit a lot of flexibility or be very restrictive. The most flexible approach is to permit increases or decreases in any pay period. The most restrictive approach is to permit changes only at the beginning of the plan year. In this instance, whatever contribution level you choose will apply for the entire year.

Your employer may also limit the number of times you can change your contribution level during the year. This is probably more trouble than it is worth, however, because it's a hassle to track all the participant changes during the year.

Note to employers: I recommend that you give participants as much flexibility as possible. Allow them to stop contributing and to change their contribution level at any time. The fact is that employees don't change that often. You can tell those who abuse this privilege that they could cause you to make the plan more restrictive.

28. I want to contribute the maximum amount as early in the year as possible. What is the best way to do this? Is there any disadvantage to "front-loading" my contributions? I earn around $72,000 per year.

The way to get your contribution into the plan as fast as possible is to contribute the maximum percentage of pay you can afford. For example, assume you can afford to contribute 20%. You will hit the $11,000 maximum by the time you have earned $55,000, but there may be a downside if your plan has an employer match.

Some employers match only during pay periods when you make contributions to the plan. Others contribute the applicable percentage of pay, regardless of when you make your contributions during the year. To illustrate this difference, assume your employer matches 50% of the first 6% of pay you contribute. None of your contributions in excess of 6% are matched. This means your employer should contribute 3% of $72,000 or $2,160, if you contribute at least 6% of your pay for the entire year. But, you will get only 3% of $55,000 ($1,650) if your employer only matches during pay periods when you contribute. In this situation you would lose $510 of the employer contribution.

To avoid similar losses, check with your employer to see which matching contribution method they use. You should contribute 15.3% of your pay if the employer matches only when you're contributing. This percentage will spread out your contributions and enable you to hit the $11,000 maximum when you have earned $72,000 for the year. You'll need to reduce this percentage if your earnings increase during the year.

29. I am responsible for running the 401(k) at my company. I'm having difficulty understanding how to calculate the match.

Ironically, I've found that the matching contribution is frequently messed up, regardless of which method is used—matching only during pay periods when employees contribute or matching based upon an employee's contributions for the entire year.

Assume the employer match is equal to 50% of the first 5% of pay that you contribute. When the match is computed separately for each pay period, the employer contribution should be equal to 50% of the amount you contribute—if you contribute less than 5% of pay. It should be equal to 2.5% of your pay if you contribute 5% or more.

The matching contribution is computed on your year-to-date pay when the match is determined on an annual rather than per pay period basis. For example, you may not contribute anything the first six months of the year and then contribute 20% of pay during the last six months. Another possibility is for you to fund the entire contribution for the year from a year-end bonus. The entire amount you contribute in these instances should be matched—as long as the year-to-date match doesn't exceed 2.5% of year-to-date pay. This is the case even though the match for the current pay period will exceed 2.5% of current pay.

Assume you don't make any contributions during the year but contribute $10,000 from a $15,000 bonus. Next assume your total earnings for the year are $87,000. The $10,000 amount deducted from the bonus exceeds 5% of your $87,000 annual earnings. As a result, you are entitled to a match for the year equal to 2.5% of $87,000 which is $2,175. In contrast, the match would be only $375 if your employer matches only a maximum of 2.5% from the pay that is applicable to your contribution ($15,000 in this instance). As you can see, the difference is substantial, which is why you need to know which way your employer determines its match.

Note to employers: Whichever method you use, it must be applied uniformly for all participants and it should be consistent with the provisions of your plan document.

30. I would like to contribute 50% of my bonus to the 401(k) but the payroll person at my company told me I can contribute only 15%, our plan's maximum percentage of pay. Is this correct? I'm not a high-paid employee, and I haven't made any other contributions during the year.

This probably is incorrect. The applicable percentage of pay and the maximum dollar limit should be applied on an annual rather than a per pay period basis. You should be permitted to contribute 50% of your bonus up to the maximum dollar limit for the year. This is true as long as your compensation hasn't exceeded the $200,000 annual limit. By the way, you should ask your employer to increase the 15% to a much higher percentage such as 80 or 90%.

31. What is the annual compensation limit and how does it work?

The annual compensation limit is $200,000 for 2002 adjusted periodically for inflation. Neither employee nor employer contributions may be made with respect to compensation in excess of this limit. This means you must plan your contributions so you have contributed the desired amount for the year by the time you hit the compensation limit.

You must contribute at least 5.5% of your pay from January 1st on to hit the $11,000 limit by the time you earn $200,000.

32. I'm getting a big bonus in December. I want to increase the amount I contribute to my 401(k) plan that month. What do I have to do?

You must complete a new contribution authorization form instructing your employer to deduct the desired amount. You may also be able to submit this change electronically. Ask the person who oversees your plan for your company's procedure. Be certain that the increased percentage is applied to only the bonus and not your regular pay. This may require two separate requests.

33. My employer told me I can only contribute 6% of my pay because I am a high-paid employee. I am 53 and I need to save as much as possible for my retirement. Why am I limited to only 6%, and what can I do about it?

The amount you are permitted to contribute is restricted because this is the way the law is structured. Through what is known as non-discrimination testing, the government has tied the amount that highly compensated employees (HCEs) may contribute to the amount that non-highly compensated employees (NHCEs) contribute. In most instances, the amount HCEs may contribute is limited to the average percentage of pay NHCEs contribute—plus an additional two percentage points.

For example, HCEs may contribute 6% if NHCEs contribute 4% (which apparently is the case in your situation). The amount you can contribute will increase if eligible NHCEs, including those who don't currently contribute, put more into the plan. This is one reason why employers should encourage more employees to join the plan and contribute as much as possible.

How can your employer make it possible for you to save more money?

- add an employer matching contribution if there isn't one
- change the plan to a Safe Harbor 401(k), which is exempt from non-discrimination testing

- conduct an educational campaign to help employees understand the impact of their savings over time and why they should save even more.

34. I recently changed jobs and my new employer doesn't have any retirement plan. Can I continue to make contributions to my old 401(k)?

You can't make additional contributions to your old 401(k) account because you are no longer an employee of your former company. Since your employer does not have any retirement plan, you're eligible to make deductible contributions to an IRA. You can probably open an IRA account with the same financial organization where your old 401(k) is invested if you want to continue investing in their funds.

35. My employer won't let me make contributions from my overtime pay. Is this legal?

This is legal if your employer's plan document excludes contributions of overtime and other forms of non-base pay. Most employers allow contributions of total W-2 cash compensation because this makes compliance and plan administration easier. The plan must pass a special non-discrimination test when contributions are limited to only base pay.

Some employers count only base pay because they don't want to increase the cost of the match or any other employer contribution. It's possible to use base pay for employer contributions and total compensation for employee contributions, but this makes plan administration somewhat more complex.

36. I'm eligible to contribute to my new employer's 401(k), but I won't get any matching contributions until I have been here a year. Is this legal?

Yes, your employer may have different eligibility rules for employee and employer contribu-

tions. Although you would obviously prefer to get employer contributions during the first year, this is better than having to wait a year before you can contribute.

37. I've always wondered when my employer has to deposit my money in the plan and when the money has to be invested. I notice on my statements that there is a delay of several days before my money is invested.

The answer to this question is a bit fuzzy because the Department of Labor regulations are also fuzzy. Employers can get into big trouble if they don't deposit the money by the 15th working day after the end of the month that the money is deducted from your pay. This date would be roughly the 17th of the month following the month the money is deducted.

But this isn't the whole story. The DOL regulations require employers to transfer your contributions into the plan as soon as it's possible to determine how much should be deposited. For most employers, this is the day the payroll register is delivered to the payroll manager, because the total amount of employee contributions typically appears with the other totals at the end of the ledger. The employer has to deposit a sufficient amount to the payroll account to cover net pay. The 401(k) contributions could be deposited into the payroll account and be transferred to the plan account the same day at most companies. But this is not what normally happens.

The employer typically sends all the payroll data to the recordkeeper. The recordkeeper throws the data on its system, does a data scrub and determines investment splits. The employer is informed of data problems that must be checked. Once these problems are resolved, the money is sent to be invested. Some employers go through this cycle every payroll period. Others deposit contributions once a month. Depositing contributions each payroll period is safer, but monthly deposits are common.

The fact that the regulations are fuzzy leaves the door open for a DOL auditor to hassle employers that make monthly deposits—even if the money was deposited into the plan account in advance of the 15th business day deadline. As a result, I always tell employers to get their money in within several days after the end of the month.

38. I plan to retire later this year. I have six weeks of accrued vacation time that will be paid after I retire. Am I permitted to have contributions deducted from this pay, even though I will no longer be working?

You're permitted to make contributions from any cash compensation you receive unless the plan document specifies otherwise. This should include the various types of compensation that may continue beyond your employment date, including accrued vacation and sick pay. You should delay taking your money out of the plan until after all contributions have been made to avoid the hassle of two distributions.

39. I want to contribute $100 per pay period, but they tell me I must pick a specific percentage of pay. I prefer contributing a specific dollar amount. Why won't they let me do this?

It's easier administratively to deduct a percentage of pay than a fixed dollar amount. Deducting a specific dollar amount can create problems, particularly when the amount of gross pay varies due to hours worked. There may not be enough net pay to cover the fixed contribution during a specific pay period. This problem is usually avoided by deducting a percentage of pay.

Most employees who receive variable pay such as overtime, bonuses, commissions, etc. prefer to have the applicable percentage deducted from whatever amount they're paid.

40. I sent the paperwork to my employer to increase my contributions three months ago. I just discovered when I received my statement for the quarter that this change was never made. What can I do?

Mistakes like this happen, which is why it's important to check your pay stub when you change your contributions. This is as much your responsibility as it is your employer's. It isn't possible to make a change after the fact because the applicable payroll taxes, etc., have been reported for this period. Your best bet is to contribute a larger amount than you intended until you make up this difference.

41. My company has a Section 125 cafeteria plan in addition to a 401(k). My 401(k) contributions are deducted from my pay after my contributions to the Section 125 plan. Is this correct? I would prefer to make contributions from my gross pay.

It depends how compensation is defined in the plan document. Your employer may not be aware that contributions can be deducted from gross pay. It's easy to amend the plan, but if this does not happen, you may be able to achieve a similar result by contributing a larger percentage of your post-Section 125 contribution pay. For example, assume your gross pay is $500 each pay period and you contribute $50 to the Section 125 plan. Further assume you want to contribute $30 per pay (6% of $500) to the 401(k) but your employer deducts only $27 (6% of $450 pay after the Section 125 contribution). Increasing your contribution percentage to 7% of $450 will result in a $31.50 contribution per pay which is closer to your desired amount.

42. I currently contribute 6%, which is the maximum amount that is matched by my employer. Should I be contributing more?

Your goal should be to have enough money to live comfortably when you retire. The amount you will need depends on many factors, including when you plan to retire, your income needs at the time, etc. You should use one of the many retirement calculators to determine how much you will need and the amount you need to save to hit your target. A rough goal I recommend is a nest egg equal to 10 times the amount you are earning at the time you retire.

Employer Contributions

43. I've always wondered why my employer provides a 401(k) plan. Do they get a tax break or something?

It actually costs your employer a significant amount of money to have a plan. First, there is the cost of any employer contributions. Your employer is permitted to deduct these contributions, but this covers only part of the cost at best. The tax deduction reduces an employer's cost only if the company has taxable profits. Not all businesses are profitable, particularly those that are new.

The fact that any employer tax break covers only a portion of their contribution cost is similar to your own pre-tax contributions. The tax break helps you make your contribution, but there still is a cost because you have to contribute the difference out of your pay. For example, you may save $.25 in taxes for every $1.00 you contribute. The remaining $.75 reduces your take-home pay.

A 401(k) plan also creates additional administrative costs for your employer—even when the basic plan fees are deducted from plan assets. Someone at the company must spend time overseeing the plan, and this is a cost.

Rest assured that employers have no hidden agenda. They offer 401(k)s because this is the plan of choice that attracts and keeps good employees. Today's top-notch employees don't want to be limited to an IRA.

44. What is a matching contribution?

This is a contribution that is made by your employer, and you get it only if you also contribute to the plan. An employer contribution isn't required—so this is a plus if you have one. A $.25 or $.50 match for each $1.00 you contribute is most common. The matching contribution is usually capped so that only the first 3% to 8% of pay that you contribute is matched.

For example, with a 6% cap and a $.25 match, your employer will contribute 1.50% of pay (6% times .25) if you also contribute 6%. Any amount you contribute in excess of 6% isn't matched.

45. I'm thinking about starting a 401(k) for my company. We have 20 employees and their pay ranges from $18,000 to $45,000. How much will it cost if I include an employer match?

You should expect around 70% of your eligible employees to contribute if you offer a $.25 match for each $1.00 the employees contribute. I recommend matching only the first 6% of pay that employees contribute.

For example, you will contribute $450 for an employee who earns $30,000—if the employee contributes at least 6%. Assume your total payroll is $600,000 and all employees are eligible. Assume the annual pay of the 70% who contribute is equal to $500,000. The matching contribution would cost 1.5% of this amount or $7,500—if each employee contributes at least 6%. Some will contribute less. For an even faster calculation, just assume that the match will cost you about 1% of eligible payroll—$6,000 in this case.

46. Should I stop contributing when I contribute enough to get the full employer match?

Your goal is to have enough money when you retire. This may require contributing more than the amount that is matched by your employer. You continue to get the full tax breaks for the amount you contribute above the match level. You are probably getting $.25 or more in tax breaks for every $1.00 you contribute. If you aren't an HCE you can contribute as much as you want to the plan, up to the $11,000 maximum (plus the catch up contribution if you are over age 50).

47. Once I contribute enough to get the full match from my employer, wouldn't I be better off saving additional money in a Roth-IRA?

The most important thing to do is to keep saving. I don't mean this as an insult, but most of us aren't very good savers when we have to do it on our own. The biggest benefit of the 401(k) is the semi-forced savings through payroll deductions. Alternatives to a 401(k) are worth considering only if you're able to achieve and maintain a similar level of savings on your own.

From a financial standpoint you'll get the same results with either a 401(k) or a Roth-IRA if you are in the same tax bracket when you withdraw the money as you are when you are contributing it. You will get a better result with the 401(k) if your tax bracket will be lower when you take the money out. A Roth-IRA offers somewhat greater flexibility and its distributions do not count when you have to determine whether your Social Security benefits are taxable.

Of course, everything that I've just said could change when tax laws inevitably change. I personally believe that tax increases are more likely over the long term. Since nobody knows how tax laws will change, my wife and I are covering all our bases—we have a 401(k) and we also invest in Roth-IRAs.

48. My plan has a variable matching contribution? What is this?

A variable contribution gives your employer the flexibility to determine the match based on financial results such as company profits. The best way for employers to do this is to have some minimum employer matching contribution that you know you will get (such as $.25 per $1.00), with the potential for an additional contribution if the company has a good year.

One of the reasons for a match is to encourage employees to contribute. A variable match works best when employees know at the beginning of each year that they will get some match so they can decide how much to contribute themselves. I have helped design plans where there is a minimum $.25 match with the potential of a $1.00 per $1.00 when the company has a great year. This generally works well for both employees and employers.

49. What's the difference between a variable matching contribution and a profit-sharing contribution?

Typically, all eligible employees get a portion of a profit-sharing contribution without having to contribute to the plan. These are contributions determined at the end of the year based upon the company's financial results. The company is basically sharing a portion of its success with eligible employees.

A profit-sharing contribution is usually divided among eligible employees in proportion to total earnings. For example, if you earn $50,000, the total payroll is $500,000 for all eligible employees and the company made a $25,000 profit-sharing contribution, $2,500 (10%) of this amount would be deposited to your plan account.

In contrast, only employees who contribute to the plan receive a portion of the variable matching contribution. I used to tell employers who were deciding between these two types of contributions a story about two workers. They both earn the same income. Phil is married with three children. He's a great worker, but he can't afford to contribute to the plan. Dave is single and a marginal employee—but he contributes 8%

of his pay to the plan. Both employees would receive the same profit-sharing contribution, but only Dave would get a share of the variable matching contribution. Phil is the better employee, but because he does not contribute to the plan, the variable matching contribution wouldn't reward his efforts. This could cause a morale problem for Phil if he sees his less committed co-worker get more financial benefits from the company.

50. My company is not doing very well. I just got an announcement that they are stopping the 401(k) matching contribution. Is this legal?

Your employer can change the matching contribution at any time. This is true unless there is a contractual obligation such as a collective bargaining agreement that requires a specific matching contribution. The plan document could permit your employer to change the match without notice—otherwise they are obligated to tell you when they make a change (which is advisable).

51. Since I have a start-up business, I'm a little worried about establishing a 401(k) with a matching contribution. If my business goes through rough times, can I reduce or stop the match?

You can do either, but you need to make sure your plan document gives you this flexibility so you don't have to amend it each time you make a change. The best way to do this is to structure the document so that you are permitted to make a discretionary match. This enables you to set the match at any level you want and to change it as necessary.

The other issue is how to manage your employees' expectations. Tell employees how much you will be contributing, but also explain that you will notify them in advance if you have to change the amount or stop the match.

52. Our company has a 401(k) with matching and profit-sharing contributions. What is the maximum amount we may contribute during a plan year?

You must consider both the limit that applies to employees and the amount that your company can contribute. The maximm amount that an employee can receive is 100% of pay, including all employee and employer contributions and forfeitures that are reallocated. There is also a combined maximum dollar limit per employee, which is $40,000.

You must also consider the maximum amount the company is permitted to deduct, which is 25% of covered payroll. This is the pay that employees receive for the period they are eligible during the applicable plan year. Include total pay, regardless of the plans definition of compensation. For example, the 25% is applied to total pay rather than base pay, even if contributions are tied to only base pay.

53. What's an automatic employer contribution, and why would a company have one?

There are various types of employer contributions that eligible employees can receive, regardless of whether they contribute. The profit-sharing contribution is one type. Another is an automatic contribution—such as 3%. This type of contribution is paid to all eligible employees—usually as a percentage of pay. It can also be determined in some other manner such as a specific amount for every hour worked.

It's possible to have several different types of employer contributions within the same plan. For example, a plan with a profit-sharing or an automatic contribution may also include a matching contribution.

An automatic employer contribution is frequently used when a company has discontinued a defined benefit pension plan. All employees received benefits under the pension plan without contributing.

Note: An automatic employer contribution is also one of the design options with a safe harbor 401(k) plan.

54. My company has always contributed 15% of my pay to a profit-sharing plan. Now they are changing to a 401(k) plan. Why are they doing this and how will this change impact employees?

Several of my clients went through this type of change. The change was usually made because the companies could no longer afford to contribute 15% of pay to a profit-sharing plan. This is a common problem as businesses grow. It's very difficult to fund growth and continue to make contributions at this level as the payroll continues to increase. You're very fortunate to have received this benefit for the years that you did. Few employees get this level of retirement help from their employers for even one year.

When this type of plan change is made, employers typically design the 401(k) to include pre-tax employee contributions, a matching employer contribution and a reduced profit-sharing contribution. For example, the employer match may be $.50 per $1.00 limited to the first 6% of pay you contribute, plus a profit-sharing contribution in the 5 to 10% of pay range. This combination is still a very attractive retirement package. You should continue to have the opportunity to invest 15% of your pay for retirement—but not all of the money will come from your employer.

55. My company is eliminating our defined benefit pension plan and replacing it with an additional contribution to the 401(k). We already have a match, so I don't understand how this additional contribution will work.

I have found there's a lot of misunderstanding about what typically happens when a company eliminates a defined benefit pension plan.

The common misperception is that this benefit is taken away. The pension benefit is usually replaced by an additional employer contribution to the 401(k) or another type of defined contribution plan.

The amount of the additional 401(k) contribution is usually equal to the average percentage of pay the employer was contributing to the pension plan—usually ranging between 3 and 5% of pay. All eligible employees receive this contribution without having to make contributions to the plan. This is why this contribution is in addition to the match.

Assume you earn $40,000 and your employer has a 50% match for the first 5% you contribute to the 401(k). Next assume the new contribution will be equal to 4% of your pay. To make up for your defined benefit plan, you will get $1,600 (4% of $40,000) without having to make any contributions. Then you will get a 401(k) match equal to 2.5% of pay—if you contribute at least 5% (which will be $1,000). The total employer contribution will be equal to 6.5% of pay.

When you add in your own contributions, you're saving 11.5% of pay—which is a nice total. You can, of course, contribute more.

There's one other important issue when a defined benefit plan is being terminated. The annual current value of the benefit a 55-year-old earns with a defined benefit plan is much larger than the benefit a 30-year-old earns—even if they have the same incomes. This is because the cost is tied to how soon the benefit will be payable. As a result, it's best to structure the pension replacement contribution so that older employees get a higher percentage.

The following is an example:

Age	Contribution Percentage
Less than 40	3%
40 but less than 50	4%
50 and over	5%

This age-related contribution structure will provide benefits that are more closely related to the defined benefit plan structure. But since these plans are very different, there will not be an exact benefit match with the 401(k).

When the contribution varies by age, testing may be required to assure that the benefits HCEs receive in comparison to non-HCEs are within acceptable limits.

56. My company has a 401(k) with a matching employer contribution and a discretionary profit-sharing contribution. Only employees who work at least 1,000 hours during the year and who are still employed on the last day of the year get these contributions. This doesn't seem fair. Is it legal?

Your employer is permitted to set these eligibility requirements for employer contributions—assuming coverage tests are met. I realize this may seem strange since you are eligible to contribute to the plan. Giving the profit-sharing contributions only to those who work a minimum number of hours or who stay the entire year enables employers to give a share to those who they feel are more deserving.

57. It's now the middle of April and my employer still hasn't made its contributions for last year. Obviously, I'm losing money because these contributions aren't invested in my account. This just doesn't seem right. What can I do about it?

The law permits each employer to make its contributions for a given year at any time prior to filing of its tax return for that year. This deadline is March 15th of the following year for corporations that operate on a calendar year. But this date can be pushed all the way to September 15th via filing extensions. Your employer may legally delay making its 2002 plan year contributions until September 15, 2003. Employers must

make their contributions by the date their tax return is filed to get a tax deduction for the applicable year.

58. The salespeople at our company make a lot of money. As a result, I don't want to increase my costs by giving them the matching contribution our other employees receive. Is this possible?

There will be compliance issues to consider. It's easy to exclude these employees from the match if they are all highly compensated employees. Discrimination against this HCE group is permitted—at least in qualified retirement plans. If some or all don't fit the definition for HCEs, it may also be possible to exclude them from the match, but some special testing will be needed.

In any event, you'll probably need an individually designed plan document because the prototype documents usually aren't able to handle this type of special design. You should contact an ERISA attorney or a retirement plan consultant who does this type of work.

59. Our company has many different business units with varying levels of profit. Is it possible to have varying matches for these business units?

You can have different benefit structures for different business units, but you will need help from a professional advisor to determine the best method. One approach I have used is to reduce the employer contribution to the qualified plan to the lowest level for all highly compensated employees. Special benefits are then provided for these HCEs though a non-qualified plan. This approach eliminates the need for somewhat expensive special non-discrimination testing. (By the way, high fees paid for special non-discrimination testing don't provide additional benefits to any of your employees. That's one reason why I always look for solutions that don't require this testing.)

When all HCEs within your business enterprise get the same basic retirement benefits, it's much easier to transfer them from one business unit to another. You'll need help from an ERISA attorney or a retirement planning consultant.

60. What is a non-qualified plan and how do they work?

A non-qualified plan is one that can be structured to provide retirement benefits that are very similar to those in a qualified plan. One of the reasons for having a non-qualified plan is to enable HCEs to tax-defer amounts that can't be put into the 401(k). Plan benefits can be funded by employer or employee contributions or both. Similar to a 401(k), participants do not pay taxes on contributions until the money is either received or when it becomes available.

Unlike a non-qualified plan, the timing and the form of distribution must be decided in advance, and distributions may not be rolled over. In addition, the "assets" of a non-qualified plan are owned by the employer—so there's a risk of losing the benefits if the company fails. Participants also lack other protection that is provided under ERISA—such as vesting.

The financial benefits to the company are very different for a non-qualified plan. Employer contributions and employee deferrals aren't tax deductible until the benefits are paid. Any income earned is taxable to the company as it is earned unless specific investment vehicles are used to defer the tax. Despite the less attractive corporate tax treatment, these plans are used by most large employers.

61. We would like to establish a 401(k) for our small company. I'm concerned that the lower-paid employees won't contribute, making it difficult for us to pass non-discrimination tests. I'd like to include a match that doesn't cost very much. What is the best way to do this?

There are several common approaches for limiting the cost of the match. The first is to limit the amount of the match. The smallest amount I have seen is $.10 for each $1.00 an employee contributes. The most common match is $.25 or $.50 per $1.00.

Another common way of limiting your cost is to match only a portion of the amount that employees contribute. For example, you may match only the first 4% of pay that employees contribute. This means that employees who earn $30,000 would receive matching contributions for only the first $1,200 they contribute.

A less common alternative is to include a dollar maximum. For example, the maximum match per employee could be $500 per year. Or highly compensated employees could be excluded from the match. As you can see, you have a lot of flexibility and you can design a plan with a match that costs only approximately 1/2 of 1% of eligible pay. This is only $500 for each $100,000 of eligible pay. Your cost is this if you include a $.25 match limited to the first 3% of pay an employee contributes, assuming 70% of eligible employees participate.

Investing Your 401(k) Money

62. I'm really an investment novice. What in the world do I need to know about the funds my plan offers?

This is a tough question because there is so much you need to know. The following are some of the basics you should focus on:

- the type of fund: fixed-income/bond, stock, other
- what type of bonds and stocks each fund buys
- whether the fund is actively managed or if it is a passive index fund

- the total investment fee for each fund
- the historical performance for each fund
- for each managed fund, how long the manager has been running the fund
- how the fund's performance, expenses, etc. compare to similar funds
- the size of the fund.

One common mistake is to look only at the average returns when you compare fund performance. You should look at year-by-year results to see how the funds perform during both up and down periods. Basically, you want to see how the average return was achieved. Did the manager have one or two great years that have inflated the results? I recommend using an independent source like Morningstar when you compare funds because you can't count on your service provider or the fund company to put the fund in the right category.

63. What happens to the money I invest in the 401(k) plan?

Your employer must establish a separate legal entity that holds all plan assets for the benefit of participants and their beneficiaries. This separate entity may be either a trust or a group annuity contract that is arranged through an insurance company. A trust has either a corporate trustee (typically the investment organization that runs the plan), or individuals who serve as trustees. Individual trustees are usually officers of the employer.

All contributions must be deposited into the trust or the group annuity contract within the time period required by law. The money is invested after it is deposited according to the investment structure for your plan.

64. My employer just started a new 401(k) plan, but participants aren't able to choose their investments. I was able to pick from 16 different funds in my old plan. Is what my employer doing legal

and fair?

It's a surprise to many participants that employers aren't required to let you choose your own investments. The employer is permitted to determine with the plan trustees how the money will be invested. This arrangement is very unusual for 401(k)s, but it is legal.

Why would your employer structure such an inflexible plan?
- It's easier and less expensive to administer
- The need to educate employees about different types of investments is eliminated
- The employer may think that the bulk of your co-workers aren't capable of making informed choices.

One important point is that the employer assumes full fiduciary responsibility when it maintains investment control. Most employers don't want this responsibility—but they take on another responsibility to educate employees when they relinquish control.

Most plans give employees the opportunity to split their contributions among a number of different funds. This method allows each participant to structure an appropriate investment allocation among stocks and bonds. Since each participant has a different time horizon and risk tolerance, it makes sense to avoid "one size fits all" investment structures.

65. The minimum amount that I can invest in any one investment option is 10%. I would like to invest 5% in a couple of our funds to get a broader diversification among the different fund types. Is a 10% investment multiple normal? What can I do to get my employer to lower it?

In the early days of the 401(k) when there were only two options, investment multiples were typically set at 25%. The multiple was generally lowered to 10% as the number of options grew. Today 1% multiples are the most common due to the continued expansion of fund options and the ability to make easy electronic transfers via touch tone phones and the internet.

I recommend showing your employer the total investment allocation you would like and why. There are probably other participants who would like greater flexibility. Ask your employer to do a survey if your opinion isn't sufficient to make a change.

66. My 401(k) is managed by a bank. I'm having a lot of trouble finding out how my funds are doing. What can I do?

This can be very frustrating. You're responsible for managing your money and building an adequate nest egg—yet you can't get the information you need to do a good job. Knowing how your money is being invested, the applicable expenses and how the funds are doing is essential. Unfortunately, there aren't any industry-wide information requirements.

There are Department of Labor regulations under Section 404(c) of ERISA that require employers to give participants adequate information to make informed investment decisions. But these regulations are voluntary, so not all employers and financial organizations comply.

Since your employer selected the bank, try to leverage the relationship. Explain to your employer what additional information you need and why. If you still don't have any luck, look for fund performance results in the financial section of the newspaper. If the funds are registered, you can also obtain information about them through *morningstar.com* or *schwab.com*.

67. My employer was recently sold. The new company has told us our money will be transferred into their plan. I don't like the investments for the new plan. Why can't I leave my money in the old plan or transfer it to an IRA?

The situation you have described is common when a company is sold. The buyer typically wants all employees in the same plan with the same investments. This is usually accomplished by forcing the participants of the acquired company to move their money into the new company's plan and investments.

The terms of the purchase agreement between the two companies is a key factor governing what happens to the old 401(k). The purchase agreement will frequently provide for an automatic transfer of the 401(k) money from the old plan to the new plan. A single transfer to the new plan is much easier for your old employer than having to process a lot of individual benefit payments or IRA transfers. Your old and/or new employer may also want to avoid making these funds available for fear that employees will have the opportunity to blow their retirement savings.

68. I've never invested in a 401(k) before. I know I need to save for retirement, but I don't want to lose my money. How safe is my 401(k) account?

First, congratulations for joining your plan, despite your investment concerns.

The first fact that you need to understand is that any type of investing involves risk. You can reduce risk, but you can't eliminate it. The best way to reduce your risk is by diversifying your investments. This is accomplished by spreading your money among different types of investments. Ask your employer and the company that runs your 401(k) to help you choose an investment mix that's right for you.

69. Does the government guarantee my 401(k) money as they do pension plans?

Defined benefit pension plans are guaranteed by the Pension Benefit Guaranty Corporation (PBGC) because the assets in these plans may not be sufficient to provide the benefits that have been promised to employees. This isn't possible with a 401(k) unless someone runs off with some of the money illegally. The assets of the plan are always equal to the benefits that are to be paid.

For example, when you receive a statement showing how much you have in your account, the money is really there. When you retire or leave the company for some other reason, the investments you have are sold and you get your money. It's that simple.

But there is some potential for abuse. The person at your company who has control over these funds could in theory do something dishonest. Your company is required to maintain a fidelity bond equal to at least 10% of the plan assets. This bond insures the plan in the event of dishonesty.

70. I'm 46 and I know I should invest in stocks because they've produced the best long-term return. But I'm uncomfortable with the way that stock values go up and down. I want to have enough money when I retire, but I also don't want to lose money uneccessarily today. I read that my employer has to have insurance for the plan. Does this provide an investment guarantee?

The only insurance your employer must carry is a fidelity bond that protects your plan from dishonesty. This coverage doesn't provide any protection for investment losses. Investing does involve risks, but the risk of not having enough money when you retire should be as much of a concern to you.

How you invest impacts your chances of having enough money throughout your retirement. For example, a mere 1% additional return will increase the amount you accumulate by 20% over 30 years. A nest egg of $100,000 would instead be $120,000 with this small additional return.

Of course, taking greater risks to get higher returns also increases your potential of loss. The key is to stay within your risk comfort zone and accept the customary ups and downs. The worst possible situation would be to take more risk than you are comfortable taking—and then retreat into the most conservative investments after a major drop in the value of your investments. Your employer and the organization that runs your plan should be able to help you choose your investments.

71. My company offers its stock as an investment option. How much of my money should I invest in company stock?

Chances are you already are invested in company stock through your employer's matching contribution. You may also be able to buy company stock via a stock purchase plan and you may even have stock options.

Your company may be a great place to work and its stock may have done really well, but you should limit the amount of your 401(k) contributions that you invest in company stock. In fact, I don't recommend putting any of your 401(k) contributions in company stock. You should choose from other investment options that have less risk.

My recommendations are not based on the fact that you will increase your overall investment returns—they're based on the fact that you will reduce your overall risk. Your company stock may in fact produce a higher return for some number of years than any other plan investment. But every stock hits the wall at some point. These points are usually very painful—losses in excess of 50% are the norm.

Outside of the 401(k), I'm a big fan of company stock. Take as much stock as your company gives you. You should also buy stock via the stock purchase plan if you can afford to do so. Use your stock options to buy more shares if the stock does well.

Use your "insider" knowledge to determine how much you should invest in your company's stock. Does your company make quality products? Do you and other employees buy their products? Would you recommend their products to family members and friends knowing how the products are made? Does the senior management team seem to know what they are doing? Are there any new products in the works that have the potential for success? When you invest in company stock outside of the 401(k)—and you take the time to objectively view your company's potential for long-term success—you're more likely to boost your nest egg savings.

72. When I invest in company stock, why don't I receive actual shares?

Plans have different ways of handling company stock. Some grant actual shares of the stock. Each time you invest, additional shares are purchased and they will show as shares of stock on your statement. The other method is to create a stock fund similar to a mutual fund. This fund holds some cash as well as company stock. The investment return will not be exactly the same as owning shares of stock, because a portion of the fund is held in cash. The company stock fund appears on your account statement as units of the fund rather than shares of company stock.

Service providers often prefer a stock fund because daily movements of money in and out of shares of company stock are more difficult to handle. The settlement rules are different for stock than for mutual funds. Assume you want to sell shares of stock and re-invest the money into one of your other investment options. The proceeds from the stock may not be received for a couple of days. Waiting for the cash before buying the fund creates operational problems. This problem can be avoided with a stock fund because on the same day that you submit instructions a portion of the cash held by the stock fund can be used to buy shares of the new fund.

73. What benefits does my employer get by contributing stock rather than cash to our 401(k)?

Most publicly owned companies contribute their stock to the 401(k) plan because they want employees to have an ownership interest in the company. Studies show that employees who own stock are likely to be more productive and to have more pride in their work. Senior executives prefer to have as much stock as possible held by employees and other "friendly" shareholders. Stock contributions also enable your company to use its cash for other business purposes.

74. I've done well buying stocks on my own outside my 401(k). My plan has decided to give us the option to buy stocks with our 401(k) money. What do you think of this idea?

First, congratulations for doing well picking stocks on you own. This isn't easy to do, which is why I don't generally recommend picking your own stocks when you are investing your retirement money. Picking your own stocks takes a lot of time and knowledge. I know what effort it takes, which is why my retirement money is all invested in mutual funds. I use my non-retirement money to play around with stocks. I tend to buy larger, market dominant companies that have been battered. My biggest problem is which ones to buy and when to sell.

To play it safe, I would suggest limiting your 401(k) stock picking to 25 or 50% of your 401(k) investments. See how well you do for a few years compared to the funds where you are currently invested.

75. My 401(k) plan limits me to 12 funds that are chosen by my employer and also company stock. Employees who leave the company can roll their money into an IRA where they can pick from thousands of funds. Why are ex-employees treated better than active employees, and what can I do about it?

Your point is one that I increasingly hear

from participants. Many participants say it's my money, I'm responsible for having enough money when retire, and I should have the same investment flexibility with the 401(k) that I have with any other investment. It doesn't seem to make sense that a significant percentage of their assets is tied to relatively few 401(k) investment options —and just a few thousand dollars outside the plan can buy access to thousands of funds.

The fact is that your employer could give you this investment flexibility by adding a mutual fund window to your 401(k) plan. This is becoming a very popular alternative.

76. We're considering offering a mutual fund window in our 401(k) plan that will enable participants to choose from thousands of funds. I have read conflicting information about how this will impact our liability. What's the real story?

You're correct that opinions vary on this subject. Those who say that a mutual fund window increases liability believe that some participants will blow their money unnecessarily and then sue the employer for not preventing the calamities. The other concern is that in order to get the limited fiduciary protection under 404(c) regulations, employers are required to provide sufficient information for employees to make informed investment decisions. How is this possible when there are thousands of funds that are constantly changing?

I'm not that concerned about the first issue because the risk of a mutual fund window can be reduced by requiring a participant to sign a waiver. The waiver should require participants to:
- acknowledge that they consider themselves to be knowledgeable investors
- waive their right to sue if the investment results are bad
- acknowledge that they are assuming the full responsibility to secure whatever infor-

mation is needed to make investment decisions.

I also think giving participants additional investment flexibility reduces liability because there is less risk that participants can say that they aren't satisfied with a limited number of funds that the employer has selected

77. We're thinking about offering investment advice to our participants. Although we've done a lot of things to educate our employees, many are still having trouble. What's the best way to provide advice without increasing our liability?

This is another area where there is disagreement about potential liabilities. I believe that investment advice will reduce your liability if it is done right. Providing this additional level of help for your participants is better than letting them decide how to invest on their own. We've learned that education is not enough—all the educational materials in the world have not turned amateurs into professional investors. This is an impossible goal—but adding investment advice to your plan should bring better results.

The best way to offer advice is to hire an investment advisor who doesn't have a financial stake in how your participants invest their money. The advisor should be paid a flat amount per participant. You should use the same care when you select the investment advisor that you use when you select other service providers for your plan.

I also strongly recommend obtaining indemnification from the advisor to protect you if there is a problem. The primary advantage of such an agreement is that you and the advisor would work together to resolve a participant lawsuit. If you don't get indemnification from the advisor, you'd most likely be in a very difficult situation. The advisor would probably deny responsibility or even claim that they were not giving investment advice.

78. What is the difference between investment advice and generic allocation models?

Allocation models are used to help employees structure their investments. They're used either as a guide or a template for actual investments when participants don't want to create their own fund mix. Participants may be given tools such as risk tolerance tests to help them make their investment decisions, but ultimately they must make their own decisions. The generic allocation models commonly recommend specific types of investments rather than a specific fund.

With an investment advisor, participants are actually told how to invest. The investment advisor will tell the participant to buy or sell specific funds. The advice is specific rather than general. Even though participants are told what to do, they still must decide whether or not to follow the advice. This may be accomplished by simply clicking "yes" when you're asked whether you want to implement the changes suggested by the advisor. Some advisory firms will actually run your account for you.

79. Some of my co-workers have turned the management of their 401(k) over to an investment advisor who actually runs their investments. The advisor makes all the investment decisions, including moving the money from fund to fund. I am considering this possibility. What do you think?

This can be a good alternative if you don't have the time or the skill to manage your own account. The two major keys are the cost and the methods the advisor uses. I recommend using an advisor who charges a flat fee rather than a percentage of your balance. I would avoid an advisor who uses any market timing techniques. Focus

on the methods the advisor uses for establishing your allocation among various types of investments and for picking the specific funds.

80. What's the difference between investment advice and financial planning?

Financial planning is a much broader activity—covering budgeting, debt management, estate planning, the funding of education and home purchases, insurance needs, etc. You also normally do extensive financial planning and then put it on the shelf to be dusted off and reassessed when a major life event occurs.

The primary goal with investment advice is to tell you how to invest. This is a much more active, ongoing process. For example, you want to know what your investment advisor has to say if the market drops by 10% or if you read something unfavorable about one of your funds in the newspaper. Your advisor should also be feeding you relevant information that you may have missed.

81. I've read that I should rebalance my investments. Why is this important?

For those who aren't familiar with this term, rebalancing means keeping your investment mix within a desired range. When you made your original investment choices, you selected a specific percentage that would be invested in each type of fund. This should have given you a specific split between stocks and bonds and between different types of stocks.

Assume your original plan resulted in 60% stocks and 40% bonds. Because your different funds don't move up and down at the same time, you will not always maintain this balance. For example, you may find that 75% of your money is in stocks and only 25% is in bonds after 10 years. You will be tempted to leave this as is because the stocks have done better than bonds; however, you have substantially increased your risk by moving from 60% to 75% in stocks. You also are ten years older—and as you age your allocation to stocks should be somewhat less rather than more. When stocks take a big drop, your loss will be much larger than if you had rebalanced your stock allocation to 60% or less.

82. I've read that it isn't good to try to time the market by constantly moving money from one fund to another. Is this the same as rebalancing?

Those who are involved in market timing think they know what direction the market is moving. For example, you listen to several news reports and become convinced that stocks are going to drop—so you decide to sell all your stock holdings. This decision is not based on fact—no one truly knows when the market will go up or down. Market timing is risky because it's impossible to be on top of all the factors that impact the market.

Rebalancing involves shifting money from one type of investment to another in order to maintain a specific ratio such as 60% in stocks and 40% in bonds. These shifts are made to maintain consistent risk exposure rather than guess which direction the market is heading.

Other than the occasional rebalancing, experts advise participants to be long-term investors: choose the investment mix that will most likely get you to your retirement goals and generally stay put.

83. How often should I rebalance my account and what's the best way to do it?

The reason that you rebalance is to keep your risk exposure within an acceptable range. Automatically rebalancing on specific dates is one approach. This may be done quarterly, annually or at some other interval. The approach I prefer is to rebalance whenever your investment allocation strays outside a pre-determined range such as 5%. For example, if 60% is your desired stock allocation, you would shift the appropriate

amount when the percentage goes above 65% or below 55%.

84. How often should I check to see if I'm on track to hit my retirement income goal?

It depends on how close you are to retirement. I recommend at least every year when you are within 10 years of retirement. Otherwise every three years should be okay.

When you set your goals, you assume an annual rate of investment return. Most retirement calculators assume you will get this return each year. It doesn't happen this way. For example, if you assumed a 9% annual return, you will have to invest heavily in stocks to have a chance of hitting this return. Since stocks go up and down, some years your return will be much better than 9% and other years you will fall behind.

As a result, when you're younger, I recommend looking at your three-year average return to track your progress. This will give you a more realistic snapshot of how you're doing than an annual check. You also have enough time when you are younger to make the necessary investment adjustments.

85. My plan offers lousy funds. None of them ever appear in any of the top performer lists. Why doesn't my employer give us a better fund line-up?

Your employer may be doing a better job than you think, because most funds that appear on the top performer lists are not necessarily appropriate for 401(k)s. If you watch these lists over several years, you'll probably find that most of the top-performers are only one-time stars. You don't see the same names on the lists from year to year.

Funds that have the highest return in a given year usually invest in one type of stock that did particularly well. For example, the fund may own the stock of a lot of technology, healthcare, or financial service companies. The market goes through cycles—one type of stock does well, then fades out. Another type of stock hits the limelight, then fades out—the cycles go on and on. Fund managers are not smart enough to consistently predict the cycles.

I've also done mathematical studies that show that a fund with a lower average annual return can actually give you a larger eventual balance. I realize this may be hard to believe, but the key is the magnitude of the ups and downs and when they occur. Owning a fund that has smaller year-to-year ups and downs is likely to give you a better long-term result.

86. What is style drift and how is it relevant to 401(k) investors who choose their own investments?

Institutional investors usually pick a specific fund or hire a specific investment manager due to the types of investments the fund or manager makes. For example, an institutional investor may want to invest some money in mid-cap value stocks. Those involved in selecting the manager will look at funds or managers who have this investment expertise. The manager is hired with the understanding, usually in writing, that this is the only type of stocks he is authorized to buy.

The retail funds used in 401(k)s are not required to stick to a specific style. As a result, the manager may drift into other investments or be forced there if the fund gets too big for its intended category. As a 401(k) investor, you have no control over the fact that your original fund choices no longer look the same. Style drift changes your allocation among different types of stocks and shifts your risks.

87. What does risk-adjusted return mean and how can I find this information?

This term refers to the amount of risk the fund manager took to achieve the applicable

return. This is determined by comparing the stocks the fund holds to an appropriate benchmark. Assume you pick a managed, large-cap fund. The benchmark for evaluating this fund's risks and returns would be the Standard & Poor's 500 index.

First, you see if the fund produced a return that was better than the S&P 500 average for the year. Then you look at how much risk the manager took to get the return. Was the risk higher or lower than the S&P 500? The worst possible result is for the fund you pick to produce a return below the S&P 500 while taking a higher risk. The only reason to take additional risk is to achieve a higher return. The manager would have failed in this instance.

You may be able to get a comparative risk profile from the fund company. Otherwise, go to *morningstar.com.*

88. My plan offers both managed and index funds. Which is better?

Wiith an index fund, you will receive an investment return that is the same as the applicable index —less the management fee. For example, if you invest in the S&P 500 Index, your return will be the same as if you invested in a portfolio of these 500 companies, less the management fee. The management fee should be in the .10% to .30% range.

By comparison, the fee for a managed, large-cap fund is likely to be around 1%. This additional fee results in a lower return. This means the manager must pick stocks that outperform the index by at least this amount to beat the benchmark return. As a result, the manager is likely to take additional risk.

It's very difficult for large-cap managers to beat the S&P index, which is why the amount invested in large-cap index funds continues to grow. At age 59, I personally like large-cap value funds. With this type of fund, I'm still heavily invested in stocks, but there's less risk than I would get with an S&P 500 fund. As a result, I am willing to take a lower potential return in exchange for the lower risk.

89. I'm having trouble choosing my own investments. Don't you think it would be easier if we returned to the days when the employer ran everything?

Picking your own investments can be tough, but I don't think letting the employer run everything is the right answer. This would put the full responsibility and liability on the employer and most of them don't want this any more than you do. This also presumes the employer is better equipped to handle this responsibility than participants. With few exceptions, employers don't have any better investment skills than the average participant. In fact, some of the worst investment results I've ever seen have involved plans where the employer ran the investments.

It made sense for employers to manage plan investments with defined benefit plans because the benefits weren't tied to investment results. In this situation the employer also took all the investment risk. With a 401(k), you assume all the risks and your benefits are largely determined by the results. It's critical that your investments reflect your situation at each stage of your life. Your investment mix at age 62 shouldn't be the same as it is when you first started contributing to a 401(k) at age 25. Most employers have employees of all ages, risk tolerance levels, etc. Combining them all in a single investment pot controlled by the employer ignores these individual needs.

Fees

90. I read that I should check to see what fees I am paying when I invest in my 401(k). When I called my service provider, I was told I don't pay anything. This is hard to believe. How do I find out

whether this is correct?

How much you are paying in fees should influence how you invest. It isn't the only factor to consider, but it is an important one. It's highly unlikely that you aren't paying any fees. Some providers will lead you to believe this because they don't want to scare investors away from their funds. Unfortunately, there isn't any universal standard for disclosing fees. Mutual funds include this information in the prospectus because they are required to do so by the NASD. Other financial organizations may not be subject to this disclosure.

The person who told you aren't paying any fees was either intentionally deceiving you or splitting hairs. Some providers are comfortable telling you that you don't pay any fees because you don't actually have to write out a check to pay the service provider. The correct answer, however, is that you do pay fees—but more often than not, they are hidden. Remember that the organizations that run 401(k)s are businesses with big overheads. They obviously don't provide free services.

Where are these fees hidden? The fees are in fact buried through deductions from your investment return. These deductions can be investment management fees for the organization that runs the funds. Investment management fees are equal to a percentage of the amount you have invested and they vary by type of fund. They may range from .20% or less for an index fund to 1.7% or more for an emerging market international stock fund.

There may be an additional fee that is charged by the organization that administers the plan. This additional fee may be as small as .25% or as much as 1.5%. When you add these two types of fees, your investment return in just one fund could be reduced by from as little as .10% to as much as 3.2%! This is an extremely large spread and you should know where your expenses fall in this range.

The higher the fees, the less likely it is that a service provider will disclose its fees.

To learn more about fees that you pay, read the DOL brochure that can be accessed via *www.dol.gov*. Click on agencies, then click on PWBA and then fees.

91. I've been tracking the investment return for my funds and they appear to be consistently about 1% below the returns that are listed in the newspapers. Why is there a discrepancy?

Your plan probably is managed by a service provider that charges an additional wrap fee that reduces your investment returns. You're probably paying a 1% fee in addition to the standard investment fee charged by your funds. This additional fee is charged by your service provider to cover administrative, marketing and other costs.

92. I've read that additional fees can dramatically reduce the amount of money I accumulate. My plan uses variable annuities that have an additional fee that is equal to 1% per year of the amount I have invested. What can I do to get my employer to change to something less expensive?

I agree that a variable annuity isn't a good 401(k) investment during the period when you are building your retirement nest egg. A variable annuity may make sense after you retire if you want a guaranteed life income that you can't outlive.

I always recommend explaining to your employer in writing why you aren't satisfied with your plan. It also helps to get supporting evidence from third-party sources that can help your cause. Most employers are open to constructive input because they know the plan helps to attract and keep good employees. Simply telling them the plan stinks usually doesn't work.

Remember, too, that the top people at your company probably have the most money invested in the plan and they're taking the biggest hit from these additional expenses. If lower-paid employees stop contributing, these top people may not be able to contribute as much as they could in the past. It's in everyone's best interest—except the service provider—to reduce fees.

93. I've read that it is bad to invest in funds that have 12(b)1 fees. What are they and are they really that bad?

You're correct that the media tends to make a big deal about 12(b)1 fees. These are expenses that a fund may charge to cover marketing expenses. For example, the 12(b)1 fee may be paid to a broker for sending business to the fund company.

These fees are neither good nor bad. The real issue is the total amount of fees participants pay. For example, the total expense for a fund that doesn't have a 12(b)1 fee may be 1.4%, compared to 1.2% for a similar fund that has a 12(b)1 fee.

94. A speaker at a conference I recently attended said that an increasing number of 401(k) plans are offering institutional rather than retail mutual funds. What is the difference?

One likely difference is pricing. Retail funds must charge the same fee to large investors as they charge small investors. An individual investing $2,000 into a retail no-load fund will pay the same fee as a 401(k) that is investing millions of dollars into the same fund. Institutional investors are large investors such as pension funds and colleges and universities that invest large endowments. The fees these large investors pay typically decrease as the amount they invest increases. An increasing number of 401(k)s are looking for funds that have this pricing advantage.

95. I'm the benefits manager at my company. Overseeing the 401(k) is one of my responsibilities. A panel at a conference

I recently attended focused on the issue of having administrative and other non-investment fees paid by plan participants. Panelists discussed the fact that participants with larger balances pay a larger share of these fees. What's wrong with this practice?

It is legally permissible to have the plan pay administrative expenses for services such as participant recordkeeping. This practice is common after the plan assets become large enough to absorb these expenses. The investment companies are able to pick up the cost of non-investment services when assets become sufficiently large because they are being paid more than what it costs to run the investments.

For example, a 401(k) that is investing $25 million into retail funds is paying the same fee as an individual who is investing $5,000. The average participant balance for the 401(k) may be $50,000. This will generate a $500 fee per participant—compared to $50 fee for each individual who invests $5,000.

A problem with this method of fee payment is the fact that participants with larger account balances pay a disproportionate share of the non-investment fees. The cost for plan administrative services are essentially the same for a participant who has a $100,000 balance as they are for a participant who has a $1,000 balance. This cost is in the $100 to $150 per year range, depending on the specific services involved. A participant with a $100,000 account balance is paying a 100 times larger portion of the plan's administrative fees than the participant with the $1,000 balance—but he isn't receiving any additional services.

This practice is not tax-efficient for senior executives or owners because they are paying these costs from tax-sheltered funds. Granted, someone must subsidize the cost for participants with small balances. A better alternative is to have the employer pay the administrative costs for these participants. This change should enable

participants with larger balances to reduce the cost of investing by .25% and increase the investment return by the same amount.

Your Plan Benefits

96. I'm thinking about changing jobs. How do I know whether I will get the money my employer has contributed?

You are asking about an area that is known as vesting. This is a term that refers to your right to receive the money that your employer has contributed for you.

You will always get back your own contributions—adjusted for investment gains or losses. Your right to receive the employer contributions may depend upon when and why you leave your employer. Some plans provide full vesting of employer contributions in all instances. Most plans vest the employer contributions upon the occurrence of a special event or based upon your years of service.

With conditional vesting, full vesting of employer contributions usually occurs at death, disability or age 65. If you leave for some other reason, your right to this benefit will be determined by how long you have worked for your employer. With the cliff vesting method you go from 0 to 100% vesting when you complete a specific number of years of service.

Check the Summary Plan Description you received when you joined the plan to see specifics on your plan's vesting arrangements.

97. I started working for my employer on July 13, 1998. Our plan requires three years of service to be fully vested. My statement shows my vested percentage as 0% even though I have worked for more than three years. What's wrong?

There are two permissible methods for determining years of service. One is the elapsed time method that simply counts the time you've been employed by your company. With this method, you would have been fully vested on July 13, 2001.

The other method counts the number of hours you work each plan year. You must work at least 1,000 hours during a plan year to receive credit for a year of service. This may be the method your employer uses—and you probably didn't work 1,000 hours during the 1998 plan year. You may have worked more than 1,000 hours in 1999 and 2000—counting as two years of service. You may have already earned the additional year by working 1,000 hours during 2001, but this may not be reflected yet on your statement. Your employer probably only reports hours worked at the end of the year.

Check your Summary Plan Description to see how years of service are defined for your plan. Speak to your employer if my explanation doesn't clear up the confusion. It's possible that the recordkeeper has the wrong employment date for you or there may be some other error.

98. I'm a contract employee who works on government projects for a private employer. My employer recently lost the contract and I will be terminated. Since this is considered a partial termination, am I entitled to get the employer's 401(k) contributions?

You are correct that full vesting is required whenever a partial termination occurs; however, there aren't specific rules that define a partial termination. This provision in the law was designed to protect employees when a division or plant is closed immediately or over several years. In the latter situation, only employees still with the company when it closes would be fully vested—unless the partial termination rules apply. This provision gives the IRS the authority to rule that a partial termination occurred several years before the company ceased to exist. The result would be to fully vest employees who left during this period when the company was declining.

The IRS generally becomes interested in a situation like yours when more than 20% of plan participants are involved. In your situation the number of participants affected by the lost contract must be compared to the total number of plan participants. For example, there may be 120 employees in your group—but 3,500 participants in the plan.

In any case, ask your employer whether this event will be treated as a partial termination. Your employer also has the option of amending the plan to allow full vesting for all employees in this situation—but this isn't likely to happen.

99. I left my employer but I've been told I won't get any of the 401(k) money the company contributed. Why did they give me statements showing this money in my account if I don't actually get it?

Your employer was required to deposit its contributions into your plan account, even though you weren't yet entitled to receive the money. The fact that your statements included this money doesn't mean it actually belonged to you when you left the company. Your plan contained a vesting schedule that required you to stay with the employer for a specific number of years before the money belonged to you. This fact should have been explained to you when you joined the plan, and it should have been included in the Summary Plan Description you received.

100. I've read somewhere that I should have received a Summary Plan Description. I don't remember ever getting one. What is it?

The Summary Plan Description explains the primary provisions of your plan. The employer was supposed to give you one when you joined the plan. It explains when you are eligible, what types of contributions may be made to the plan, how and when any employer contributions vest, how the money will be invested, when money may be taken out of the plan, etc. Request a copy from your employer.

101. What 401(k) information is my employer required to provide? I get a quarterly statement and not much else.

You will probably be amazed at this answer. The only three things your employer is required to give you are the Summary Plan Description, a Summary Annual Report and an annual statement upon request. That's all. The Summary Annual Report contains general financial information about the plan—but these plan totals are of no real value to you. For example, knowing the total interest the plan earned doesn't help you pick your investments.

Of course, most participants get a lot more than this cursory information—such as materials to help them understand their investment options, general investing terms, etc.

102. I haven't received a statement for over six months. I was told a couple of weeks ago that I would get it soon. I'm wondering if something is wrong. What should I do?

How serious the problem is depends upon the facts involved. This is a pretty long delay if you normally receive quarterly statements. There may be a number of reasons for the delay. The following are some possible explanations:

- The company that is doing the recordkeeping may be having trouble.
- Your employer may have changed to a new recordkeeper.
- Your company may still have to make some employer contributions that haven't been deposited to the plan.
- Your employer may be having financial difficulties, which may include not having paid its fees for the recordkeeping.

You may have to take further action at some point. One possibility is to tell your employer you will request help from the Department of Labor if you don't receive your statement or an acceptable explanation for the delay. Contact your local DOL office—check locations by logging on to *www.dol.gov.*

103. I recently left my employer. When I asked about getting my 401(k) money out, I was told I have to leave it in the plan for three years. Is this right?

There isn't any requirement that your money must be distributed to you immediately after you leave your employer. Most 401(k)s do distribute the 401(k) money in a reasonably short time— but the fact is that your former employer's plan document could permit them to hold your money until retirement age.

Remember, one of the reasons employers have a 401(k) is to help attract and retain good employees. Some employers put a delayed distribution into their plans to discourage employees from leaving just to get their hands on their 401(k) money. Yielding to this temptation is much less likely if you have to wait three years after you leave to get the money.

104. I was recently re-employed by a company where I had a 401(k) account. I took my money out and lost all the employer contributions. I've been informed I can get the employer contributions back if I re-deposit the money I took out. But if I do this, I won't get the investment return. Why not?

Your employer is required to permit you to recover the employer contributions you forfeited when you took out your 401(k) money, but that is all they are required to do. Obviously, you should put your money back into the plan to get the employer contributions restored—even though you don't get any retroactive investment return.

105. I have often wondered what happens to forfeitures—the employer matching contributions that are never vested and given up when employees leave. Our plan requires five years before everything is 100% vested.

The plan document must specify what happens to employer contributions that are forfeited. Forfeitures of employer matching contributions are most commonly used to reduce future employer matching contributions. For example, if $500 of matching contributions are forfeited, the employer would reduce its next contribution by this amount. Other employer contributions, such as profit-sharing, are frequently re-allocated to the remaining participants. This obviously benefits those that stay with the company.

106. We plan to start a 401(k) at our company with a $.25 match. We've been considering various vesting alternatives. One of the reasons for having a plan is to help us attract and retain employees. What are your thoughts about vesting?

Attracting and retaining are two separate issues. Fully vesting the employer contribution makes the plan appear more attractive when you are attempting to attract new employees. The match also increases participation, particularly if newly hired employees know they will get this money regardless of how long they stay.

The vesting schedule that you choose depends a lot on the type of employees you hire. Many of those who are fresh out of college or younger can't imagine spending three years with their first employer. The fact that it may take three years for 100% vesting is likely to keep such employees from participating. The plan is likely to be a useful tool to help attract and retain employees only if they join the plan. As a result, full vesting is your best option.

The amount of the employer contribution often influences an employer's vesting decision. With a $.25 match the amount that you will recover through forfeitures is likely to be rather small. The forfeitures will, of course, be considerably larger with a $1 per $1 match. The retention value is also influenced by the amount of money that employees would leave on the table.

A speaker at a conference I recently attended conducted a study that showed that employees tend to stay longer and be more productive if they're in the 401(k). He was an HR executive for a large hospital group. As a result, his employer has determined they can save a lot of money in recruiting fees, training, etc. if they can increase plan participation by just 10%.

107. The company I work for appears to be in serious financial trouble. I'm concerned about what will happen to my money if they shut down.

This is a common concern that employees have when they aren't confident their employer will be able to stay in business. Your employer is legally required to put your contributions into the plan no later than 15 days after the end of the month during which the money is deducted from your pay. Unfortunately, some employers that are in serious financial trouble abuse this area of the law and hold on to the money for longer periods.

As a result, I recommend keeping as close a watch as you can on when the contributions are deposited into your plan account. Your ability to do so will be governed by the administrative structure of your plan. For example, it will be easy to tell when money is added if you have daily web or voice response access to the current value of your account.

Your money is safe from the company's creditors once it is deposited into the plan. Contributions that haven't been put into the plan are at risk if the company goes out of business. In this case the money is considered to be a plan asset, but it will take you a while to get it. You should consider stopping your contributions if:

- the administrative structure for the plan doesn't enable you to track when money is being added to your account, and
- you think there is a strong likelihood your company will go out of business.

108. My employer went out of business six months ago and I'm still waiting to get my money out of the plan. The former plan administrators are no longer around. The service provider tells me they can't pay my money to me. But since it's my money, what can I do?

What you are experiencing is rather common when a company goes out of business. This usually is a difficult time for everyone, including the former owners. There probably are many creditors and others who want to find them. The good news is that if your money has actually been deposited into the plan it should all be safe. Legally, the service provider can distribute benefits only with instructions from a plan representative. But this authorization can't be provided if the plan representatives have all disappeared.

The court should have appointed someone to liquidate the business, including shutting down the 401(k). You will get your money, but it may take a while longer. Ask the Department of Labor for help through their local office listed on *www.dol.gov*. The offices of your local senators or congressmen are other potential sources of help.

109. I'm helping my wife start a business. Can I use my 401(k) as collateral for a business loan to help her get started?

You can include your balance as an asset when you submit your financial statement to the bank, but you are legally prohibited from assigning this as collateral. This anti-assignment provision of the law protects your 401(k) and other

retirement benefits from the claims of creditors.

The lender may still be willing to give some consideration to this asset when they make their decision regarding the loan. They can't get at your retirement money if you default, but they may expect you to access it rather than default on the loan.

110. I've been working in this country for two years. I'll be returning home shortly. What can I do with the money that's in my 401(k)?

You have the same options as any other employee—except you may not have the opportunity to transfer the money to your next employer's plan. Check the tax laws of your home country. If you cannot transfer the money, your options are to let the money sit in the 401(k) if your vested benefit exceeds $5,000, roll it over into an IRA, or withdraw the money after you leave your employer. Regardless of what you decide to do, you will eventually have to pay U.S. income tax when you receive the money. You can defer the tax by leaving it in your employer's plan or by rolling it over into an IRA.

It probably makes sense to take the money out of the plan and reinvest it in your home country, but you should wait until the calendar year after you return home. The amount of tax you will have to pay should then be greatly reduced if you don't have any other U.S. income.

Loans and Hardship Withdrawals

111. I had to stop contributing to my plan due to some unexpected expenses. When I asked to get my 401(k) contributions back, I was told this isn't permitted. It's my money—why can't I get it when I need it?

It is your money, but a 401(k) isn't like having a personal savings account at your local bank. You are given big tax breaks when you invest in a 401(k), which is why access to the money is restricted. The government has given these tax breaks to help employees save for retirement. It's a heck of a lot tougher to build your retirement nest egg without these tax breaks.

112. The investments in our plan stink. Can I take my money out and roll it into an IRA where I can pick whatever investments I want? I've been doing much better investing in my IRA.

Your pre-tax contributions may be withdrawn while you are working for your current employer only if you meet one of the following criteria:

- You are over age 59½ and your plan permits withdrawals for any reason after you reach this age.
- You are willing to borrow and repay the money (if your plan permits loans).
- You qualify for an IRS approved hardship withdrawal—but this type of withdrawal can't be rolled over into an IRA.

If you don't meet one of these criteria, you may want to encourage your employer to change funds or to add additional ones. But you shouldn't necessarily give up on the funds in your 401(k)—there's no guarantee that the investments you've made outside the 401(k) will always produce good results either.

113. I'm in a plan that allows both pre-tax and after-tax contributions. What are the rules for taking out the after-tax money while I'm still working at my company?

After-tax contributions may be withdrawn at any time for any reason if your plan permits you to do so. You don't have to pay any tax on these contributions when you take them out because you have already paid tax on this money. You are required to withdraw a portion of the investment income which will be taxable, and you'll incur the 10% early withdrawal penalty tax if you are under age 59½.

114. Our plan permits participants to withdraw their own contributions for an IRS approved financial hardship, but we aren't permitted to withdraw the employer contributions. Is this a legal requirement?

The decision to prevent you from withdrawing any employer contributions was made solely by your employer. Many employers limit withdrawals to only employee contributions because they've put their money into the plan for your retirement. They don't want you to use this money for some other reason.

115. I've read that I may not be able to get my money out of my account without my spouse's consent. Is this correct?

Whenever an annuity is one of the forms of benefit payment, the spouse is given specific rights that can restrict your access to the 401(k) money. Most plans permit only lump sum distributions in order to avoid the very complex rules that must be followed whenever the plan provides for annuity payments. Your spouse's witnessed, written consent is required when the plan has this feature and your benefit is at least $5,000.

116. I read my SPD and it says I can take my money out only if I have a heavy and immediate financial need—and that the withdrawal must be necessary to satisfy the need. This sounds like I must really be in trouble to get my money out. Is it really that tough?

It depends upon how your employer has set up your plan. You may have to prove the financial need exists and funds are not otherwise available. In this instance, you're required to submit detailed financial information and evidence that the need exists. Your request to withdraw money must also be approved by your employer.

Most employers don't want to get this closely involved in an employee's personal financial affairs, so they opt to use another method known as the "deemed hardship safe harbor". You don't have to prove that funds aren't otherwise available, but the withdrawal must be for one of the following IRS approved reasons:

- medical expenses for you, your spouse or dependents who are not covered by insurance
- costs directly related to the purchase of your primary residence—typically the downpayment and closing costs
- payments required to prevent either eviction or foreclosure from your primary residence
- payment of tuition and related expenses for the next 12 months for you, your spouse, or dependents, or for children who are no longer dependents.

In addition, the withdrawal is deemed necessary under these circumstances:

- the distribution doesn't exceed the amount you need
- you have obtained all distributions (other than hardship withdrawals) or nontaxable loans that are available under all plans of your employer
- you do not make any contributions for a period of six months to any plan your employer maintains
- the maximum amount you contribute during the following calendar year is limited to the applicable dollar maximum for that year reduced by the amount you contributed during the year you took out the money.

117. I'm considering taking money out of my account to buy a home. How much am I permitted to take out?

A home purchase qualifies for a hardship withdrawal. The IRS permits you to withdraw only the amount that is needed to cover the downpayment, closing costs and the additional tax you will have to pay when you withdraw the money.

Both the IRS and your plan have rules about withdrawal amounts. When employers permit hardship withdrawals, they commonly limit the withdrawal to your contributions only, without adjustments for investment gains. Some plans also permit vested employer contributions to be withdrawn.

118. I once read that withdrawing money from my account to buy a home makes sense only if I do it in a certain way. I don't remember the details. What's the deal?

This idea works only for first time home buyers. The first and most important step is to time your home purchase so that the withdrawal and the closing both occur in the same year. The second step is to complete the home purchase as early in the year as possible. The tax break you'll get by owning the home will wipe out all or most of the extra tax that would otherwise be payable due to the distribution.

Assume you:

- withdraw $12,000 to be used toward the downpayment on January 4th
- complete the purchase of your $150,000 home on January 15th
- pay $2,400 in property taxes during the year
- pay $12,450 of interest on your $135,000 mortgage.

In this example, the $12,000 withdrawal will be added to your taxable income, but this will be offset by a $14,850 deduction for the interest and property taxes.

119. My husband and I are both contributing to a 401(k). We plan to borrow 401(k) money to buy our first home. Does it matter from which plan we borrow?

There are two primary issues that come to mind. The first is the potential that either of you will change jobs during the loan repayment period. If this happens, you'll be forced to repay the unpaid balance in a lump sum in order to avoid paying taxes. If you plan to stay at your job, then borrow from your plan.

The other issue involves your ability to handle the loan repayment, the mortgage payments and continued plan contributions. If it will be necessary to reduce your plan contributions below the maximum match amount, consider which plan has the larger match. Make sure contributions continue to that plan up to the full amount that is matched. Then the other spouse should contribute whatever additional amount you can afford.

120. I've read that loans for home purchases may be repaid over a longer period than five years. My plan requires repayment in full within five years. Why isn't my plan more flexible?

Loan repayments are so difficult that most employers don't want the trouble of dealing with them for longer than five years. Many employers don't permit loans at all—so be thankful that you have this opportunity.

121. I'm planning to use a 401(k) loan to cover expenses for home improvements. Can I deduct the interest payments?

It's my understanding that you're permitted to deduct the interest if the home is the only security that is pledged for the loan. The loan must also be recorded as a lien against the property. Most loans are secured by your account balance, which makes it easy to recover the unpaid balance if you default. Otherwise your employer would have to foreclose on your home, which is a messy and expensive situation most employers want to avoid.

122. I'm considering taking money out of my 401(k) to cover my tuition. How much am I permitted to withdraw?

You're permitted to withdraw enough to cover tuition for the next 12 months of post-secondary education and related educational fees. The expenses may be for yourself, your spouse or dependents (as defined for Federal income tax purposes) or children who are no longer dependents. The latter permits you to help a married child who may need some continuing help. You may also withdraw the amount needed to cover the additional taxes.

123. I applied to borrow money from my account to buy a new car. This seems like a good idea because the 401(k) loan interest rate is lower and I pay the interest to myself. I was told loans aren't permitted for this reason. Is this right?

This is another of the many areas where the employer is able to establish rules within the legal limits. Your employer has the right to exclude loans for the purpose of buying a car. Employers commonly limit loans to the same list that applies to hardship withdrawals. Since loans are a big administrative headache, employers don't want to allow loans for a long list of purposes.

124. How are the taxes paid when I take a hardship withdrawal?

Unless you elect in writing to waive withholding, your employer is required to withhold 10% of the amount that is withdrawn. This amount is an estimated tax payment to the IRS. The actual taxes are determined when you file your tax return. The 10% that is deducted when you receive the distribution becomes a credit similar to other taxes that are withheld from your pay.

The distribution is added on top of your other income. This amount will be taxed at your top rate, which is determined by the total taxable income you have. You'll also have to pay the 10% early distribution penalty tax. For most people, the total tax paid on the hardship withdrawal amount is in the 25 to 50% range.

125. Why do I have to pay a penalty tax when I take my 401(k) money out for a hardship withdrawal? This seems unfair. It seems severe enough that I have to pay tax on the money that I'm taking out for the hardship.

You're correct that paying the regular income tax on your hardship withdrawal is painful, but the members of Congress decided to impose an additional tax penalty. The 401(k) tax breaks are given to encourage employees to save for retirement. Our government leaders want participants to really think about what they are doing before they withdraw this money and use it for any non-retirement purposes.

126. I'll be able to start contributing to my 401(k) this July following a six-month hardship withdrawal suspension. I want to contribute as much as possible for the rest of the year. How is this amount determined?

You start with the applicable maximum for this year—$11,000. Then you subtract the amount you contributed last year prior to the withdrawal. For example, assume you contributed $4,500 last year. The maximum amount you may contribute this year is $6,500 ($11,000 minus $4,500).

127. My company has a non-qualified stock purchase plan. Do I have to stop making contributions to this plan if I

take a hardship withdrawal?

The answer is yes if your employer uses the deemed hardship method rather than the facts and circumstances method. In this case you're not permitted to make contributions to any employer plan—other than mandatory contributions to a defined benefit plan, or to a health and welfare plan (including one that is part of a cafeteria plan).

128. I've read conflicting opinions about the tax benefits of a loan compared to a hardship withdrawal. What's your opinion?

You're correct that there are varying opinions. I've in fact changed my own opinion as a result of studying this issue more thoroughly. Conventional wisdom has held that loans are better because they aren't taxable. For example, if you need $10,000, you only have to borrow $10,000. With a hardship withdrawal you have to withdraw between $13,000 and $16,000 to cover the taxes for the same $10,000 need.

This appears to be a no-brainer at first glance; however, you really do pay tax with the loan. You just pay it each pay period rather than in one lump sum. The loan is deducted from your pay after you pay taxes. This means it costs much more than $10,000 to repay the loan, because you must pay tax on the loan and the interest as the money is repaid into your account.

Another point to consider is the fact that you must pay both income and Social Security taxes on this loan repayment amount—unless your income is above the Social Security taxable wage limit. The 7.65% Social Security tax bite is close to the 10% penalty tax you pay with a hardship withdrawal. I have reached the conclusion that the net tax effect is about the same for a loan or a hardship withdrawal.

129. Which has a more negative effect on my retirement nest egg—a loan or a

hardship withdrawal?

As you see in Question 128, the tax situation is about the same for either option. But then there's the potential impact on your retirement nest egg. Again, conventional wisdom suggests that a loan is better because the money goes back into your account. This is true, and it's an advantage if you can afford to repay the loan and maintain your contribution level.

But some participants can't afford to do both. The loan is likely to be more disruptive to your retirement savings than a hardship withdrawal in this circumstance because you will lose five years' worth of contributions. This is especially bad if you're also giving up an employer match.

With a hardship withdrawal you'll lose six months of contributions, but you'll be eligible to start making pre-tax contributions again after this period ends. That's a lot better than waiting five years after the loan payments end. With a hardship withdrawal you'll also get four and a half additional years of any employer match.

130. I want to borrow the maximum amount I can from my 401(k) account. I've seen some articles that say I can only borrow 50%, while others say I can borrow more. Which is right? How is this maximum determined?

You're permitted to borrow up to 50% of your vested account balance, but no more than $50,000. There is, however, an exception that has caused confusion. You are permitted to borrow up to 100% of your account balance with a $10,000 maximum. For example, you can borrow 100% if your vested balance is less than $10,000. You can borrow up to $10,000 if your vested balance is between $10,000 and $20,000. Above $20,000, you can borrow 50% of your vested account limited to the $50,000 maximum loan limit.

These different maximums are so confusing that many employers simply let you borrow only 50% subject to the $50,000 maximum. Special rules apply when an additional amount is borrowed whenever there is an existing loan or when a loan existed within 12 months of the new loan.

131. I work for an organization that loans money. We are required to provide full disclosure to borrowers before they take the money. Is similar disclosure required for 401(k) loans?

The loan disclosure laws are established at the state level. Qualified retirement plans are exempt from these state imposed requirements.

132. We are considering adding a loan feature to our 401(k). What are the things we should consider?

Actually there are many things that must be considered. The most significant are the legal requirements for loans and the administrative procedures that are needed for operations. Frankly, I've never met any 401(k) plan sponsor who has anything good to say about loan administration. The best thing you can do is to learn from the experiences of other plan sponsors.

You'll also need a lot of help from the organization that manages your plan. Ask them for a checklist of the decisions you need to make when you set up loans and another checklist of the operating requirements.

One of the most important operating issues you'll have to consider is how many loans a participant may have at one time. It's easy to say you will only permit one at a time, but this can present problems for participants who want to use this money to help with educational expenses. An alternative to multiple loans is to restructure a new loan into one larger combined loan—but there are a few serious compliance issues associated with this solution.

You also have to decide how to handle loan payments for employees who aren't receiving a paycheck during a layoff, strike, extended sickness, etc.

133. I took over the responsibility for the 401(k) at my company several months ago. When I reviewed past hardship withdrawals, I couldn't find anything that proved that employees actually had a hardship. It appears that they simply got their money if they asked for it. Is this okay?

No it isn't. At a minimum, you should have a signed application from the employee that states the reason for the withdrawal request. I would also require the following:

- something that proves the request is valid—such as a copy of the purchase agreement for a home, tuition bill, etc.
- a signed acknowledgement that the employee is aware of all the penalties
- the spouse's consent, if applicable.

By the way, it never hurts to get the spouse's consent—even if your plan doesn't have an annuity payment feature.

134. There's someone we really want to hire who is hesitant to join because of a 401(k) loan situation. She has a large ($20,000) loan from her plan, and she doesn't want to get hit with a taxable distribution plus the penalty tax. What can we do to help?

You could amend your plan to permit her to transfer the loan, but you'll have to permit other employees you hire in the future to do the same thing. Another alternative is for your company to loan her enough money to pay off the loan. This will solve the problem, and you won't have to change the plan.

135. One of our employees has been granted a military leave of absence. He has an unpaid loan balance. What

should we do while he is on leave?

You're permitted to suspend loan payments for a maximum of one year. However, the loan must be paid in full within the original five-year period—unless the loan was for a primary residence. This may be accomplished through either larger loan payments when he returns to work or continued payments at the same level with a balloon at the end for the remaining balance.

Leaving Your Employer

136. I retired last year at age 59. I asked my employer to roll over my money into an IRA. It hasn't happened yet. I've been told this will be done as soon as the year-end work has been completed. Are there any rules on how long employers can take to transfer money?

Amazingly, the only requirement is that your benefit must be paid no later than 60 days after the end of the plan year during which you reach the normal retirement age that has been set in the plan. Age 65 is the normal retirement date that is used in most plans. If this is the case with your plan, your benefit must be paid within 60 days after the end of the plan year during which you reach this age.

Technically, your employer could take quite a long time to process your benefit; however, most employers pay benefits promptly after payment is requested.

The other issue is that employees must be treated in a uniform and non-discriminatory manner. This general rule applies to benefit distributions. Your former employer must handle your benefit distribution the same way it was handled for other employees who terminated before you. But if your employer always takes a long time to process benefit payments, this is no consolation.

Your benefit payment could be delayed because your plan may have a year-end employer contribution that you are entitled to receive. The plan may also limit benefit payments to only once per year after the year-end processing has been completed.

137. I'm looking for a new job. What can I do with the money I have in my 401(k)?

One option is to take it out and spend it however you want. This is permitted, but it's the last thing you should do unless you want to keep working forever. Remember, you don't just lose the amount that you take out and spend. You lose what that money would be worth many years down the road if you kept it invested. This loss can be huge. For example, the $10,000 you withdraw at age 35 would be worth $132,677 at age 65 if you kept it invested and earned 9% per year.

Much better alternatives are to:
- leave the money in your employer's plan, if your vested benefit is more than $5,000
- transfer your money to your next employer's plan when you're eligible
- transfer your money to an IRA.

You should do everything possible to preserve this money for your retirement.

138. Which is better—leaving my money in my former employer's plan or transferring it to an IRA?

I consider transferring your money to an IRA a better option than leaving it in your former employer's plan, because this gives you a lot more investment flexibility. Your investment alternatives are virtually unlimited with an IRA. You are limited to the plan options with your 401(k).

Some people prefer to leave their money in the 401(k) because they don't like having to make new investment decisions. There isn't anything wrong with this decision if you're satisfied with your 401(k) investments. You also have somewhat greater protection from creditors when you leave your money in the 401(k).

A final consideration is the ability to easily get your money out of the plan later. This can be difficult when your former company is sold or when the people who handled the plan are long gone. In any case, ex-employees frequently get a lot less attention.

139. I have over $70,000 in my 401(k) account. Can I transfer this much to an IRA even though it exceeds the IRA limit?

The various limits that apply to personal IRA contributions don't apply to rollovers from employer plans. As a result, you can rollover the entire $70,000 because there isn't any limit on the amount you can roll over from an employer plan into an IRA.

140. What does a direct rollover to an IRA mean?

There are two ways to do an IRA rollover. One is direct and one is indirect. The indirect route is for the employer to distribute the money first to you and then you deposit it into an IRA. The direct route is for the employer to transfer your money directly into the IRA of your choice.

The indirect method is not desirable because the employer is required to withhold 20% for taxes. You'll have to make up this 20% from other sources to avoid a taxable event. For example, $2,000 will be withheld from a $10,000 distribution leaving only $8,000 available to rollover. The $2,000 that was withheld will be taxable unless you make it up using other funds. You must rollover $10,000 to avoid a taxable event. You must also complete the rollover within 60 days after you get the check or the entire amount will be taxable and the $2,000 that was withheld for taxes probably won't be sufficient to cover the taxes you will owe.

This problem can be avoided by having the employer transfer the money directly to the IRA. You frankly also avoid the temptation to spend some or all of the money once you get your hot little hands on it.

141. What's the difference between a regular IRA and an IRA rollover account? Which is better?

A regular IRA is one that you use for personal IRA contributions outside your 401(k) plan. A rollover IRA account is one that you use to deposit money from a former employer-sponsored plan.

Prior to the 2001 tax bill only amounts that were placed into an IRA conduit account could be rolled over into a new employer's 401(k) plan. This was cumbersome because it required maintaining two separate IRAs for the two types of money if you later wanted to transfer your 401(k) account into another 401(k). The good news is that separate IRAs are no longer required to do a rollover from a prior employer plan to an IRA and later to a new employer plan.

Rolling money into another 401(k) plan may increase the amount you can borrow. You may also want to roll this money over to another employer plan if you become a member of a corporate or non-profit board or become involved in some other activity that will increase your liabilty exposure. Money held in a 401(k) gives somewhat greater liability protection than money held in an IRA.

142. I'm about to retire and roll my 401(k) into my IRA. My 401(k) account includes both pre-tax and after-tax contributions. What can I roll over?

The law changed in 2001 to permit the entire amount to be rolled over, including your after-tax contributions. After-tax contributions could not be rolled over prior to this change. There isn't any dollar limit on the amount that may be rolled over.

143. I left my 401(k) money in my former employer's plan, but now I would like to roll it over into an IRA, if possible. I read somewhere that I have to do this within

60 days. I left my former employer over a year ago. Have I missed the boat?

No, the boat is still at the dock waiting for you. The 60-day period is how long you have to complete a rollover after you receive a direct distribution from the plan. You haven't received a direct distribution, so this period hasn't started yet. The best way to complete this rollover is to have your former employer transfer the money directly to your IRA. Otherwise your employer must withhold 20% for taxes, which will make it much more difficult for you to rollover the entire amount.

144. When I left my employer I received a distribution from my 401(k) less the 20% that was withheld for taxes. Does this include the 10% penalty tax due because I left my employer prior to age 55?

The 20% that has been withheld is applied as a credit toward the actual tax you will owe on this money. There is no direct connection between the tax that was withheld and the amount you will ultimately owe. This is similar to taxes that are deducted from your pay. The amount of your actual tax is determined when you file your tax return for the year.

You must add the distribution to your taxable income for the year. The actual tax relative to the distribution will be determined by applying the applicable tax rate plus the 10% early distribution penalty. The total tax due is usually in the 25 to 50% range. Because this is a big tax bill, the 20% withholding tax will probably not cover what you actually owe, unless you have a credit from other taxes you have paid during the year.

145. I have company stock that I own in my 401(k). Since I'm about to retire and request a distribution, I'd like to know more about the special tax breaks I've heard about that apply to company stock. What are they?

Company stock is taxed differently when it is distributed to you from the plan. Any other amount you receive is fully taxable as additional income. With company stock, you pay taxes on the value of the stock at the time you acquired it—not the value at the time that it is distributed to you.

Assume you have $50,000 of company stock that had a value of $20,000 when you received it. At the time of your distribution you'll receive $50,000 worth of stock, but you'll only pay tax on $20,000. Later, when you sell the stock, your investment gain will be taxed as a capital gain, which is better than the regular income tax.

Your heirs will receive an additional tax benefit if you still own the stock at the time of your death. They'll have to pay tax only on the gain that occurs after they receive the stock. They'll never have to pay any income or capital gains tax on the gain that occurred while you had the stock. This is a big tax break, but it's useful only if you don't need the money during your retirement years. You also have to be willing to take a higher risk by having a chunk of money invested in only one stock for a number of years.

146. When I get company stock as part of my 401(k) distribution, how will I know how much tax I have to pay? I don't have any idea how much the stock cost during each of the years it was contributed to my account.

Your employer is responsible for letting you know the total taxable value of the stock when you receive the distribution. Normally, the service provider that maintains participant accounts tracks this information. They usually do this by using average stock prices rather than tracking each participant's actual cost basis for the stock.

147. I intend to keep my company stock after I retire, but I'd like to roll everything else into an IRA. Is this possible—

and if so, how should I do it?

You're permitted to roll over your entire account or to do a partial rollover. You need to do a partial rollover to accomplish your particular goal. Ask your employer to issue the stock directly to you, and then have them transfer the balance directly to your IRA.

By the way, the mandatory 20% tax withholding doesn't apply to company stock, so you'll receive all the shares you own.

148. I recently left my employer and rolled everything—including company stock—into my IRA. I sold the stock after it was rolled over. I recently read there's a tax break that I could get with company stock. Can I still get this benefit if I repurchase the stock?

No, this opportunity is no longer available. You had to keep the stock outside of the IRA to get this tax break. Although you've missed this opportunity, you can achieve a greater level of investment diversification. There are tax breaks associated with company stock, but there are also higher risks when you have a lot of money tied up with one stock.

149. I'm about to leave my employer. I have a 401(k) loan that I won't be able to repay before I leave. I want to roll over the rest of my money to an IRA. I know I will have to pay tax on the unpaid loan balance. Will this tax amount be withheld from my distribution?

You're correct that your unpaid loan balance will be taxable. The 10% early distribution penalty will also be due if you are under age 55. If you roll over the rest of your account, the 20% mandatory tax withholding doesn't apply to loans, so your entire benefit (minus the loan amount) can be transferred to an IRA.

Assume your total account balance is $18,000, you are fully vested and the unpaid loan balance is $5,000. The $5,000 loan balance will be reported as a taxable distribution, but no taxes will be withheld for the loan at this time. The remaining $13,000 can be rolled over into the IRA. You will have to pay the applicable taxes for the unpaid loan when you file your tax return.

150. I'm retiring early next year after I hit age 56. I'll have to dip into my 401(k) money right away. Should I leave my money in the plan or transfer it to an IRA?

The good news is that the 10% penalty tax for early distributions doesn't apply when you leave your employer after age 55, but you must determine how to get the money out you will need. Most 401(k) plans permit only lump sum distributions for administrative reasons. A lump sum distribution will increase the amount of taxes you will have to pay. Monthly payments involve a cost someone has to pay, which is why most employers avoid them.

Your best alternative will be to withdraw the amount you need each year so that only this amount will be taxable. If your plan permits periodic payments, then you have to decide whether you would rather keep the remaining money in your 401(k) or transfer it to an IRA. In either case your money is readily accessible to you. The quality of the investments is the bigger issue. If you're not satisfied with your 401(k) investments, roll the money over into an IRA. Consider leaving your money in the plan if the investments have performed well and the plan permits periodic payments. If your plan requires you to take a lump sum distribution, your only choice is to transfer your money to an IRA. Since you are under age 59½, the 10% early distribution tax will apply to withdrawals from the IRA, unless you take periodic distributions that qualify under Section 72(t). This will require you to take essentially equal annual distributions for at least five years. You'll then be able to increase or decrease your withdrawals after this five-year period ends.

151. I want to get a predictable monthly income when I retire in addition to my monthly Social Security payments. I have $134,000 in my 401(k) account plus some other savings. What's the best way to do this?

One way to accomplish this goal is to invest all your 401(k) money in mutual funds. You can then use an automatic withdrawal plan to get a check each month for a fixed amount. This is accomplished by selling enough shares to cover your monthly check amount.

Assume you split the $134,000 between a bond fund and a large company stock fund. You would instruct the fund company to send you, for example, a $500 monthly check from each fund. Your dividends, interest and realized gains should be reinvested to make it easier for you to receive the same amount each month. You can increase, decrease or suspend your monthly distributions at any time. This is a very flexible arrangement, but there aren't any guarantees. You can outlive your money or your security can be threatened by investment losses.

An annuity is another alternative that guarantees a monthly check for as long as you live—a big plus. The best type of annuity is a variable annuity that gives you the opportunity to select from a wide range of investments. Standard annuities are much less flexible, which is a big negative.

The issuer of the annuity keeps all or a chunk of your money if you die early. You can guarantee payments to a spouse or other beneficiary after your death, but the tradeoff is that you'll receive a smaller payment during your lifetime. With a variable annuity you also continue to assume risks related to your investments, but you don't have to worry about the risk of living too long. You'll still receive a monthly payment even if you live to age 110.

Another possibility is to split your money

between two options. For example, buy a variable annuity with half your money and put the other half into mutual funds. This combination will give you a guaranteed amount of income for life while still retaining some flexibility.

152. I've read about the need to inflation-proof my income during my retirement years. What's the best way to do this?

Unfortunately, inflation won't retire when you do. Prices continue to increase and your buying power weakens after 20 or 30 years of retirement. What you think sounds like a comfortable level of retirement income may in fact provide only the bare necessities.

Professional advisors recommend that you continue to own stocks during your retirement years, because they've historically produced the highest investment return over 20 or 30-year periods. But you still have to deal with the fact that stocks go up and down in value. A 20% drop is much tougher to take at age 70 than at age 29.

The problem is further compounded by the fact that you need to withdraw money to survive. The combination of stock fluctuations and necessary withdrawals will be gut wrenching. That's why it's important to reduce your stock holdings to around 50% and to invest in a stock fund that is much less volatile. You want the old gray mare at this point—not the skittish thoroughbred that may win the Kentucky Derby.

You'll have to periodically increase the amount you withdraw from your retirement investments to offset higher costs due to inflation. You should build an annual increase into your retirement plan. I use 3% for my planning. You can automatically increase the amount you withdraw by 3% each year, or you can hold off for as long as possible and increase your withdrawals only when it's really necessary.

153. I'm trying to determine how much income I'll have when I retire in a couple

of years at age 62. I expect to have about $250,000 in my 401(k) and an IRA plus Social Security. I currently earn $46,000. I've been earning better than 10% a year on my investments. Taking 10% a year from my retirement nest egg plus Social Security should give me more than enough. What do you think?

You've done well and you should be in pretty good shape—but perhaps not quite as well off as you think. A danger for someone in your situation is to not look far enough ahead. You'll be financially comfortable for your first few years of retirement, but you need to plan beyond these years.

It will probably surprise you to learn that $250,000 will provide only about $16,000 per year of inflation-adjusted income, assuming the following:

- a 3% inflation rate
- an investment portfolio of approximately half stocks and half bonds
- the income is needed for 25 years
- nothing will be left at the end of 25 years.

It's important to note that $16,000 is equal to only 6.4% of your $250,000 nest egg—not the 10% or $25,000 you think you'll be able to withdraw annually. The other unfortunate fact is that it's extremely unlikely you'll achieve a 10% average return after you retire. It would be a mistake to include this figure in your planning, because you'd probably have to keep 100% of your money in stocks to have even a chance of hitting such a high return. This level of risk exposure would not be advisable for any retiree. Your investment holdings should be split between stocks and bonds, which will reduce your return, but give you greater security.

You're doing well—but you need to consider other sources of income or save more.

154. I'm trying to decide how to allocate my money after I retire at the end of the

year. I've done well investing in stocks, and I've become used to living with the ups and downs. At age 58 I still consider myself a long-term investor. Since stocks have performed better over the long run, shouldn't I still keep most of my money in stocks?

In prior decades most retirees held only fixed-income investments, and this worked when retirement tended to last for 10 to 15 years. Inflation is somewhat painful after 15 years, but after 30 years your buying power really shrinks.

How you should invest your money after you retire depends upon many factors. This is one time when I strongly recommend using a financial planner or other qualified professional advisor to help you. You may have gotten away with little or no formal planning up to this point, but you really can't afford to just wing it as you move into your retirement years. Going back to work at age 75, if you make a major goof, isn't a very desirable alternative.

Establishing your primary goal is the first thing you need to do. My primary goal for my retirement years is to avoid outliving my financial resources and becoming a financial burden to my children. A secondary concern is leaving something for my children and grandchildren. There are some great resources to help you establish your own priorities and then determine the best way to invest to achieve your goals.

Three finance professors at Trinity University in San Antonio, Texas have conducted extensive studies measuring the probability of running out of retirement money according to different time frames, investment mixes, etc. The following are some of their major conclusions:

- The probability of outliving your nest egg is much greater when 100% is invested in bonds, assuming a 30-year retirement period.
- The probability of having a large amount of money left after 30 years is greatest with 100% invested in stocks—but a 100% stock

allocation isn't recommended for retirees because the potential for a major loss is too high.
- The probability of not outliving your nest egg is the highest with a 50/50 split between stocks and bonds.

You can access this very valuable study at *www.aaii.org* if you're a member of the American Association of Individual Investors. You can also get more information on this subject from Lynn O'Shaughnessy's book, *Retirement Bible,* published by Hungry Minds.

155. I'd like someone to help me decide what to do when I retire next year. I've done some reading and I've come to the conclusion that all the decisions involved are beyond me. How can I find a good advisor?

I totally agree with your assessment that you need help. The combination of tax, estate planning, and investment decisions are mind-boggling. Getting help from someone who is well-versed on these issues is advisable, but finding the right person can be challenging. You can go on the web at *www.napfa.org* to access the site for the National Association of Personal Financial Advisors. Another possibility is to ask friends and co-workers for recommendations in your area.

Once you've found a potential advisor, I recommend an initial meeting to get to know the advisor and have the opportunity to assess this person's skills, personality, integrity, etc. You should also be well prepared for the meeting so that you'll be able to tell if this person really knows what he/she is talking about.

Even if you do consult an advisor, totally placing your future in someone else's hands isn't a good idea. You should have enough knowledge to know whether the advice you're getting makes sense.

You also need to establish early on how the advisor will be paid. I strongly recommend avoiding advisors who are paid solely by selling you products. A good advisor deserves to be paid for financial planning services rendered, but it is best to select an advisor whose advice isn't driven solely by getting paid. An advisor who is paid solely by commissions is forced to sell you products to get paid, some of which may not be in your best interest. In fact, as an additional caution, I'd consider getting a second opinion if an advisor recommends a product that generates a commission.

156. I'm a widow and I have to take care of myself. I want to retire but I don't know if I'll be able to, because I didn't get any retirement benefits from my husband and I haven't been able to save much money. I'll have a modest pension plus Social Security. I own a home. I'm considering what to do with my home and where to live when I retire. What should I do?

Owning your own home is one of the great American dreams, but it's not necessarily a great asset during your retirement years. When you retire you need assets that generate income. A home consumes income, even when there isn't any mortgage. If you haven't tracked how much you spend on your home during an average year, you'll probably be amazed when you do so. Taxes, lawn care, driveway maintenance and the unexpected expenses like a new furnace will take a big chunk of your retirement income. It isn't hard to put between $5,000 and $10,000 per year into an average home without a mortgage.

An alternative is to sell your home and rent a nice property, perhaps in a lower cost area. You can then invest the money into something more productive. When you eliminate the routine house expenses and add in the income from your investments, you'll have more than enough money to cover the rent. You'll also have greater flexibility by having your money in a more liquid investment.

Compliance

157. I'm confused about which employees are considered HCEs in the non-discrimination testing.

Any employee who owned at least 5% of the company during the current or previous plan year must be included in the HCE group. Assume the testing is for the 2002 plan year. Any employee who owned 5% during either 2001 or 2002 must be included in the HCE group. The business interest held by these individuals is also attributed to lineal family members. As a result, the spouse, son, etc. of a 5% owner are also HCEs, regardless of their income levels.

The other factor for determining which employees are HCEs is income. In this instance, you look back to the prior year, which is 2001. Employees who earned more than $85,000 in 2001 are HCEs for the 2002 tests. This compensation limit is increased periodically for inflation. The employer also has the option, when there are many employees who earn over $85,000, to count only those who are among the top 20% highest paid as HCEs. For example, a 100-employee company with 40 employees who earn more than $85,000 could elect to include only the top 20 as HCEs.

158. Is rate of pay or actual pay used to determine which employees are HCEs?

You use the actual pay rather than the rate of pay. This gives highly paid employees who are hired during the year a break if they don't earn enough to exceed the dollar limit. For example, an employee hired on September 12, 2002 at a $200,000 salary will earn approximately $60,000 for the year. This employee will not be considered an HCE in 2002, which will apply to the year 2003 testing.

159. What type of compensation determines whether an employee is an HCE?

All cash compensation is included as reported on the W-2, including pre-tax contributions to a 401(k) and a Section 125 cafeteria plan. However, when you do the non-discrimination test, you don't count any compensation above the compensation limit for the applicable year, which is currently $200,000. This means an HCE who earns much more than $200,000 and who contributes the maximum amount is considered to have contributed 5.5% of pay ($11,000 divided by $200,000).

160. Which employees must be included in the non-discrimination tests for our plan?

This is indeed confusing. You must include all employees who were eligible for any portion of the year that is being tested.

You start by eliminating all employees who were not eligible to contribute at any time during the year. Assume your plan excludes employees who have not completed six months of service. You drop those who were employed for less than six months as of the end of the year.

Then you drop those who have completed six months but will not enter the plan until January 1 of the following year. Suppose your plan permits newly eligible employees to enter the plan on January 1, April 1, July 1 or October 1 after six months of employment. An employee hired on June 3 can't enter the plan until January 1.

Assume the following:
- The total number of employees is 900
- 27 employees will not complete six months of service as of year end
- 10 employees will have completed six months of service by year end, and they'll be permitted to enter the plan on 1/1.

In this example, a total of 863 employees will be included in the non-discrimination tests.

161. How does a plan become top heavy? What has to be done when this occurs?

There's certainly a lot of confusion about this issue. I find that even many professional advisors think that the special nondiscrimination test ties the amount highly compensated employees (HCEs) can contribute to the amount that non-highly compensated employees (non-HCEs) may contribute. These are two completely separate compliance issues.

Simply stated, a plan becomes top heavy whenever more than 60% of the plan assets belong to "key" employees. Previously, one of the many challenges was determining who are key employees. Fortunately, the rules have been simplified to include only:
- 5% owners
- 1% owners whose annual pay is over $150,000
- Officers who make over $130,000, indexed for inflation.

A minimum employer contribution is required whenever a plan is top heavy. This minimum is equal to 3% of each eligible employee's pay—unless all key employees also receive benefits under 3%. For example, even if the plan is top heavy, there would be no required minimum contribution in a year when all key employees receive no benefits. Obviously, all or most key employees want to contribute more than 3% of pay to a 401(k), so the minimum 3% employer contribution for all eligible non-key employees usually kicks in.

Safe Harbor 401(k) plans are exempt from the top heavy requirement due to the mandated employer contribution. Matching contributions made to a standard 401(k) may now be counted toward the 3% required minimum employer contribution. Prior to the 2001 tax bill, matching contributions could be counted only if the key employees didn't receive any matching contributions. Small employers should be sure this issue is addressed in the plan design stage, particularly if they have less than 15 employees.

162. I own a small business and I want to set up a 401(k) for myself and my five employees. My wife is one of the employees. What are the penalties if our plan is top heavy?

The only penalty is the minimum 3% employer contribution you must make for each eligible employee. Assume the four employees who aren't family members earn a total of $120,000. You will have to contribute a total of $3,600 for them as a top heavy contribution. The family members may also receive this 3% contribution in addition the regular employee/employer contributions. Any matching contributions you make may be counted toward the 3% minimum.

163. I've been told my contributions will be limited to 6% of my pay this year because I am now a highly compensated employee. Why can't I contribute the maximum amount?

There are special non-discrimination rules that tie the amount HCEs may contribute to the amount that other eligible employees contribute. HCEs are permitted to contribute the average percentage of pay non-HCEs contribute plus two additional percentage points—but not more than two times the percentage non-HCEs contribute. For example, HCEs may contribute 6% if non-HCEs contribute an average of 4%.

These contribution restrictions are designed to limit the amount of tax benefits that go to the most highly paid employees.

164. When our plan's employee pre-tax contributions fail the non-discrimination test, how is the amount that must be refunded determined?

You first determine the amount of the excess contributions. This excess is computed by reducing the amount of the highest HCE contribution to the next highest HCE percentage. This process continues until the average percentage contributed by the HCEs is at a passable level.

For example, assume there are only three HCEs. One contributed 7%, the second contributed 6% and the third contributed 5.5%. The average of the three contributions is 6.17% (18.5% divided by 3). Note that the tests average the individual percentages rather than the dollar amounts.

Next, assume the non-HCEs contributed an average of 4%. The HCE limit for the year was 6% (4% plus 2). The HCE percentage is .17% above the permitted limit, so it must be reduced by this amount. Since there are three HCEs, the overage must be multiplied by three (.17% x 3 = .51%). The HCE who contributed the most, 7%, must be reduced to 6.49%. Then the sum of the three percentages will be 17.99% with an average of 6%, which is the percentage that is needed to pass.

Finally, assume the HCE who contributed 7% earned $90,000. The excess amount is equal to .51% of $90,000, which is $459. This is the amount of the excess contribution that must be refunded, with applicable investment return.

165. I only contributed 5.5% of my pay to the 401(k) but I was told that due to non-discrimination testing I have to take money out. One of the other HCEs contributed a larger percentage of pay than I did. Why am I the one that has to take money back?

Congress changed the rules the last time they tinkered with the non-discrimination tests. Previously, the HCE who contributed the highest percentage got the refund. Congress changed this so that the HCE or HCEs who contribute the largest amount now must take the refunds. This can produce some rather strange results, however.

Assume in the Question 164 example that the HCE who contributed 5.5% earned $170,000 and contributed $9,350—more than the other two HCEs. This employee will be the one who has to take the $459 refund plus applicable investment income. Obviously, this situation can produce some tension among HCEs because the HCE who caused the plan to fail by contributing the highest percentage may not be the one who has to take money back.

166. I've just been informed that we must refund money from our plan to some of the HCEs for last year. Is the amount refunded taxable? Do we need to file amended W-2s?

The refund is reported as a plan distribution using Form 1099-R, rather than by adjusting the W-2. The refund is to be included in income for the year it was contributed if the refund is made prior to March 15 of the following year. Refunds made after this date are taxable in the year of the refund.

For example, assume that an amount must be refunded to an HCE for the 2002 plan year, but it isn't refunded until April 20, 2003. This amount must be included in the HCE's income for 2003 rather than for 2002. The employer must pay a 10% tax penalty when refunds aren't made prior to March 15 of the applicable year.

Some employers plan to make the refunds after March 15th so they don't have to worry about getting the tests and refunds completed prior to March 15th.

167. My company is having trouble passing the non-discrimination tests. We have to give money back to some of the HCEs every year. How can we better manage this process?

When you do the non-discrimination test for the current year, you're permitted to use the average percentage the non-HCEs contributed during the prior year. As a result, there isn't any reason to fail the test because you know before the year begins exactly how much the HCEs can contribute. You simply need to manage the plan within this limit for the year.

Assume your non-HCEs contributed an average of 5% of pay during 2001. You can use this percentage when you do the year 2002 test. This means that you know that the HCEs can contribute an average of 7% (5% plus 2%) for the current year. You can avoid a failure by limiting all HCEs to a maximum of 7%, or you can permit one or more HCEs to contribute more if one HCE contributes less than 7%. For example, if one HCE decides not to participate, that frees up 7% to be used by other HCEs. Of course, HCEs who decide not to contribute may change their minds later, which will require other HCEs to adjust their contributions downward.

This approach will work if your plan document permits you to use the prior year's results for non-HCEs. If you must use current year non-HCE results, monitor the contributions made by both groups to avoid a failure.

168. We're considering a 401(k) for our company, but we're concerned because not all our lower-paid employees want to contribute. How will this impact the amount our HCEs can contribute?

All employees who are eligible to contribute must be included in the non-discrimination testing. If several employees have a contribution percentage of zero, it brings down the total contribution average for your non-HCEs. Since your HCEs can contribute only two percentage points more than the average non-HCE contribution, non-participation has a big impact. This is why most employers include a match to encourage employees to participate.

169. Are matching contributions subject to non-discrimination tests?

Matching contributions must pass the same non-discrimination tests that apply to employee pre-tax contributions.

Up to this point, I've said that these tests can be passed if the spread between the average contribution for the HCE and the non-HCE isn't more than two percentage points—or more than twice the non-HCE percentage. The non-discrimination tests can also be passed if the HCE percentage isn't more than 1.25 times the non-HCE percentage.

This is actually the primary test rather than the two percentage point spread test. Prior to 2002, 401(k) plans had to pass an aggregate test when neither the pre-tax employee contributions nor the matching contributions passed the 1.25 test. This provision that complicated the testing was included to prevent double usage of the two percentage point spread method. The aggregate test was removed for plan years beginning after December 31, 2001.

170. Our plan doesn't currently have a matching contribution. We're considering adding one to boost participation and make many compliance issues easier. Less than 50% of those who are eligible contribute to the plan now. Which matching rate will produce the best result?

Your participation rate is the norm for plans that don't have an employer match, unless the compensation levels are high. The biggest participation gain comes simply from having a match rather than the match amount.

You should expect your plan participation rate to increase to approximately 70% with a $.25 per $1.00 match, if you do a good job of communicating the change. A somewhat higher participation rate can be expected as you increase the match. Various studies have shown that a $.50 match will only increase the participation rate by 5 to 10%. If you match $1 per $1, your participation rate will most probably exceed 90%. You would think it would be 100% with such a generous match, but some people still don't take advantage of the opportunity for significant savings.

Set the match at whatever level will fit your budget and generate your desired level of participation.

171. We plan to match only part of the amount our employees contribute. What percentage is likely to generate the highest plan participation?

Matching is usually limited to the first 3 to 6% of pay an employee contributes. I am amazed at how much difficulty individuals have understanding how this works—including those at companies who oversee the 401(k). The first problem is that the word "match" suggests that the employer will contribute $1 if the employee contributes $1. This generally isn't the case.

The next point of confusion is that the match—at any level—applies only to a percentage of the employee's contribution. For example, an employee may be permitted to contribute 20% of pay, but the match may apply to only the first 3% of total pay. Some people think that a percentage of the contribution is matched, but this is not the case. A percentage of pay is matched.

Assume your plan matches the first 5% of pay that is contributed. This means that the first $1,500 contributed by an employee who earns $30,000 will be matched. The employee will be permitted to contribute more, but only the first 5% of total pay is matched. Some people mistakenly think that only 5% of the $1,500 contribution is matched.

As you decide on the amount of the match, there are two major factors to consider: the cost and the level that will produce the best participation and contribution results. Employees are typically encouraged to contribute the maximum amount that is matched. As a result, this percentage becomes the target contribution level for many employees. Setting this percentage at 6% instead of 4% is likely to generate a somewhat higher level of contributions. You could survey your employees to see what level is likely to produce the results you want.

172. How do employees who leave during the year impact the employee pretax contribution test? Can we exclude them?

Employees who leave during the year must be included if they were eligible to contribute during any portion of the year when you test the employee pre-tax contribution. However, you can exclude employees who were eligible but left before their plan entry date.

Assume your plan allows employees to start contributing on January 1, April 1, July 1 or October 1 after three months of employment. Next assume an employee hired on January 7 leaves on May 28. This employee completed 3 months of employment on April 7 but didn't stay around until the July 1 entry date. As a result, the employee would not be included in the test. However, it would have been necessary to include the employee if he stayed beyond July 1.

173. How is the average for the non-HCEs and HCEs actually determined? Do you get the average by adding the total amount contributed and then dividing this by total pay for each group?

You actually compute the average of the individual contribution percentages rather than the dollars involved. First you get an actual contribution percentage for each eligible employee. You do this by dividing the employee's contributions for the year by total pay. For example, the applicable percentage for an employee who earned $78,650 and contributed $3,560 is 4.53% ($3,560 divided by $78,650). To get the average you add the individual percentages for each group and then divide this total by the number of employees in the group.

The following is an example for a plan that has three eligible HCEs:

Employee	Compensation	Contribution	Contribution Percentage
A	$98,390	$ 6,535	6.64%
B	83,050	11,000	13.24
C	78,650	3,560	4.53

The sum of the individual percentages is 24.41, which for three employees generates an average of 8.14%.

174. My husband and I both own a business that has 15 other employees. None of the other employees are highly compensated and I don't draw any salary. My husband normally earns approximately $100,000, but he can only contribute 6% of his pay to our 401(k) plan due to the non-discrimination tests. Should I draw a salary and contribute to the plan?

Your idea is a good one, but there's a better alternative. I recommend drawing a modest salary since you're actively involved in the business. You should not, however, make any contributions to the plan. Amazingly, this will enable your husband to contribute 12% of his $100,000 pay ($11,000 plus $1,000 catch-up if age 50) instead of only 6%. I'm making this recommendation on the assumption that your goal is to contribute the highest possible combined amount, regardless of who makes the contribution.

Here's how it works. Any employee who owns at least 5% of the business is considered an HCE, regardless of the income that is earned. Both you and your husband are HCEs even if he owns all the stock, because this is how the law is written. You could in fact be considered an employee even though you aren't paid a salary if you provide services to the business. But I recommend that you receive a salary to eliminate any possible doubt that you are in fact an employee. The amount could be as little as $5,000.

Assuming you're an eligible employee, you'll be counted as an HCE when the plan tests are done, even though you don't contribute to the plan. The plan will now have two HCEs instead of only one. Your contribution percentage will be 0% because you aren't contributing. The HCE average will still be only 6% if your husband contributes 12% because the sum of the HCE percentages is 12% divided by two HCEs.

If you follow this advice, you may have to adjust the plan's eligibility provisions so you will be eligible to join the plan—regardless of how many hours you work per year.

175. I own a small business and I want to contribute as much as possible to our 401(k). My son and daughter work for me but they don't own any stock. How do they affect my contribution level? They earn around $35,000, so they aren't high-paid employees.

Your son and daughter's compensation isn't high, but they must be included in the HCE group despite this fact. Your stock is attributed to them, which means they are considered 5% owners. This fact will greatly restrict how much they can contribute. HCEs are typically able to contribute only 5 to 8% of their pay. If 6% is the limit for your plan, for example, your son and daughter will be able to contribute only about $2,100, much less than other employees with similiar earnings.

The amount you're permitted to contribute will be limited to the same percentage. However, the three of you can split the total percentage among you as you wish. For example, if your son and daughter decide to contribute only 4% each, you may use the 2% available from each of them to increase your percentage from 6% to 10%.

176. We're starting a new 401(k) at our company. I handle the payroll and I'm confused about how to handle the taxes when I deduct this money from employee pay.

This is very confusing because pre-tax con-tributions aren't totally pre-tax. Employee contri-butions aren't subject to Federal income tax, but they're still subject to Social Security tax. So the employee and the employer must still pay the FICA taxes on gross income. This is different than Federal income taxes that are withheld only from the net pay after the employee contributions are made.

Then there are state and local income/wage taxes that must be considered. We Pennsylvanians must pay the state income tax on gross pay, even though the guy who designed the first 401(k) savings plan is a native of this state. My local municipality also taxes the gross pay earned prior to employee contributions. These variances sure do complicate things, particularly for employers that have employees spread throughout the country. Either your payroll system or your pay-roll processor must cope with these variances.

177. How are the net and gross pay amounts reported on the W-2s we prepare for our employees at year end?

You report the employee's net pay after deducting pre-tax contributions for the year in the box that is used to report compensation sub-ject to Federal income tax. Then you report the employee's gross pay in the block where Social Security compensation is reported. You record whichever compensation amount is subject to tax in the blocks where compensation for state and local taxes are reported (based upon the tax laws for each state and local municipality).

Assume an employee's gross pay prior to any pre-tax contributions was $37,500, and the employee contributed $3,000 to the plan. You should report $34,500 as the amount subject to Federal income tax and $37,500 as the amount subject to Social Security tax. Then report what-ever amount is applicable for state and local tax purposes. (I have assumed there are no pre-tax contributions to any other plan.)

178. We're thinking about changing our 401(k) to a safe harbor plan so we don't have to worry about failing the non-discrimination tests. What do we need to do?

The primary requirement is to modify the plan to include a fully vested employer contribution that satisfies the minimum requirements. There are two types of permissible employer contributions—a match and an automatic contribution. With the match, the contribution must be equal to at least 4% of pay, which may be structured in a number of ways. For example, you could match $1 per $1 limited to 4% of pay or you could match $1 per $1 for the first 3% of pay that is contributed and then drop down to only $.50 for the next 2% of pay.

I'll use an employee earning $30,000 to illustrate the difference. When the match is $1 per $1 limited to 4% of pay and the employee contributes $1,200, the employer match would also be $1,200. With the split match, the first 3% contributed—$900—would be matched in full. The next 2% of pay contributed— $600—would get a 50% match or another $300. Only employees who contribute get the employer match. The maximum cost would be equal to 4% of eligible pay if all employees contributed enough to get the full match.

With the automatic contribution, each employee receives a 3% of pay contribution without having to make any contribution. The total cost will be equal to 3% of eligible pay, regardless of how much employees contribute. The company may contribute more with either approach, but a lower contribution isn't permitted.

179. With a Safe Harbor 401(k), which type of employer contribution is best?

It's primarily a matter of your plan goals. Do you want to give the employer contribution to all employees or just to those who contribute? Is the company willing to contribute 4% of pay if all eligible employees contribute enough to get a full

match? The automatic contribution is obviously better if you want to cap the employer contribution at the lowest possible level—3% instead of 4%.

180. I keep reading about the plan document. What is it and who has it?

This is a legal instrument that establishes the major terms of the plan. It covers things like eligibility, types of contributions, vesting, benefit payment options and procedures, investment structure and compliance requirements. This is one of the things that is required to start a plan. The plan must be operated in accordance with its plan document provisions. The person who oversees the plan at your company usually holds the document and participants have the right to see it.

181. How are distributions reported to the IRS and who is responsible?

All distributions must be reported to the IRS on Form 1099-R. The employer is responsible for doing so, but most employers have a service provider handle this function. There are codes on the Form 1099-R to select for the various types of distributions such as hardship withdrawal, refund of excess contributions, etc.

182. What reports must be filed for the plan and who is responsible for filing them?

In addition to reporting all distributions, a Form 5500 must be filed for the plan each year. The filing deadline is 7 months after the end of the plan year unless the employer obtains a filing extension. The employer is responsible for filing the 5500, but this form is usually completed by a service provider. It's then sent to the employer for signing and filing.

183. Our plan has both a matching employer contribution and a profit-sharing contribution. My matching contributions are fully vested after three

years, but the profit-sharing contributions aren't fully vested until after seven years. Is this legal?

Your employer is permitted to use two different vesting arrangements even though both types of contributions are made to the same plan. This is permissible if each arrangement satisfies the applicable legal requirements. The year 2001 tax changes require more liberal vesting of matching contributions than for other types of employer contributions. This may be the reason why your plan has two different vesting arrangements.

Matching contributions must be 100% vested after three years of service, or they must vest at the rate of 20% per year starting with the second year. Other employer contributions must vest 100% after five years or 20% per year starting after three years—reaching 100% after seven years.

184. We're considering terminating our plan. Are there any special requirements?

All contributions become fully vested whenever a plan is terminated, regardless of years of service, etc. Although the trust that holds the plan assets can be continued indefinitely, the plan is usually completely shut down. The plan trustee(s) and the plan administrator must continue to operate the plan with the frozen assets solely for the benefit of participants and their beneficiaries until all assets are distributed. Typically, benefits are paid to the participants shortly after the plan is terminated or the assets are transferred to another plan.

185. Our company has a plan administrator who seems to have a lot of responsibility for the plan. Is this the organization that is managing the plan?

It's an ERISA requirement that each plan has a plan administrator. The employer that sponsors the plan is usually named the plan administrator, but a specific corporate officer or a committee is usually appointed by the company to carry out these duties. The organization that manages the plan normally isn't the plan administrator because they don't want this responsibility.

The plan administrator has certain functions that are difficult for anyone outside the company to perform. One is distribution of the Summary Plan Description to all participants. The service provider usually prepares the SPD for distribution, but this organization isn't able to control the distribution to all eligible employees. The plan administrator can be fined for failing to perform duties such as this.

186. Who must receive minimum distributions from the plan and when?

The law was changed several years ago so that active employees (other than 5% owners) don't have to take any money out of the plan until after they leave the company—regardless of how old they are. An active 75-year-old employee can continue to contribute without any requirement to take money out. Of course, minimum distributions must begin when employment ceases.

Employees who are 5% owners must take minimum distributions beginning by the April 1st following the year they reach age 70½—even if they are still employed.

187. One of our employees works part-time for another company. What are the implications?

As long as the two businesses aren't commonly owned, the only issue is the employee pre-tax contribution dollar limit. The $11,000 limit is a calendar year limit that can't be exceeded—regardless of how many employers someone works for during the year. This is the only instance where there is a connection between the two employers.

188. We operate our plan on an April 1 through March 31 fiscal year. Does this fiscal year pose any challenges?

Fiscal year plans present a number of special challenges. One of them is keeping track of the various contribution limits and compliance deadlines. Changes in limits, the laws governing plans, etc., are commonly effective as of a specific date and after the first day of the plan year.

For example, a specific change may be effective for the first plan year beginning after December 31, 2001. With non-calendar plan years, it's difficult to keep the years straight to know which limit applies. To compound matters, the dollar limit is always based upon the calendar year—whereas most other limits are based on the plan year.

I've always recommended running the 401(k) on the calendar year rather than the company's fiscal year, unless there is a strong reason to do otherwise. Running the plan on the calendar year is also easier for participants.

Spousal Benefits

189. The last time I saw my spouse was over two years ago. I have no idea where he is. When I tried to change my beneficiary to my children, I was told I needed his approval. Is this right? Why can't I name whomever I want as my beneficiary?

There is a provision in the laws that requires spousal consent in order to name someone else as your primary beneficiary. This provision was added to the law years ago to protect the rights of females, but it works both ways. This creates a serious problem in situations like yours until you are able to get a divorce or find your spouse to get his consent.

190. I'm planning to get married again. I have three children from an earlier marriage who I have named as my beneficiaries. I don't want my husband to get the money. Will my children still get my 401(k) money if I get married?

Your new spouse will automatically become your primary beneficiary as soon as the wedding vows are exchanged. You must file a new beneficiary form as soon as possible after you're married. The spousal waiver must be signed by your husband and it must be witnessed by a notary or plan representative.

191. I read that my spouse will automatically become my primary beneficiary if I get married. Is this correct? Should I get a pre-nuptial agreement so I can keep my children as my primary beneficiary?

It is correct that your spouse will automatically become your primary beneficiary as soon as you are married—regardless of the form you have filed with your employer. The law requires the spousal waiver must be signed by your spouse. The person you intend to marry isn't your spouse until the marriage occurs. As a result, a pre-nuptial agreement may not work.

You may want to wait until after the ceremony to get the spousal waiver signed. This is the only way you can be sure the beneficiaries you name will get this money. You'll be taking a chance that your spouse won't sign the waiver after you are married. If so, you'll have much bigger problems than beneficiary arrangements to worry about.

192. One of the participants in our 401(k) recently died. He named his children as the beneficiaries but he had recently remarried. His new spouse did not sign a spousal waiver. What should we do?

You are caught in a tough situation where you could be sued no matter what you do. The spouse has a legal right to the benefit regardless of the fact that the participant didn't name her as the primary beneficiary. You are legally required to pay this benefit to the spouse unless she waives her right to get it. However, the children may sue if you pay the benefit to the wife. And of course, the spouse may sue you if you pay the benefit to the children.

This problem can be resolved in a friendly manner if the spouse is willing to waive the benefit. I recommend asking her to sign such a waiver. If she isn't willing to do so, you should ask an ERISA attorney for help before making any payments.

193. One of our single employees died recently. She named her mother as her primary beneficiary when she joined the plan, but her mother died a couple of years ago. What should we do?

Your plan document should contain a provision that will cover this situation. Look for a provision in the document that establishes a beneficiary priority that applies whenever a participant dies and there isn't any living beneficiary who has been named by the employee.

194. What is a QDRO and how will it impact me if I get a divorce?

QDRO stands for Qualified Domestic Relations Order. This is a provision of the law that gives the non-employee spouse a right to get a portion of the employee's retirement benefits in the event of a divorce. A QDRO works both ways—a wife can claim all or a portion of a husband's benefit and vice versa. The splitting of 401(k) and other retirement benefits is resolved during the divorce proceedings.

Your best protection would be to use a good attorney to represent you during the divorce.

195. We received a QDRO for our plan requiring us to give half an employee's

benefit to his ex-spouse. How should this be done?

Split the account in accordance with the terms of the QDRO, if possible. Generally, you should split the participant's account into two accounts—one for the employee and one for the ex-spouse. The ex-spouse will have the same rights as the employee, unless the QDRO provides otherwise. The QDRO should provide for the spouse to get half of the account as of a specific date or to get a specific dollar amount.

You'll have to seek clarification if the language in the QDRO isn't workable or if it's inadequate. This is common because the attorneys who handle divorce work aren't familiar with how 401(k)s operate.

196. My husband and I are getting a divorce. He wants half my 401(k) account. This is bad enough, but I don't want his girlfriend to get the money if he dies. Can this money go to my children instead?

Your spouse has a legal right to claim a portion of your 401(k) account; however, the exact details should be resolved during the divorce proceedings and become part of the final agreement. If he is willing, the agreement could give you the right to control who will get this money in the event of his death. However this right may only be workable while the money remains in the 401(k) because it will be virtually impossible to track after he takes the money out of the plan and mixes it with other money.

197. My soon-to-be ex-spouse is pushing to get half my 401(k) money. Will I have to pay taxes on the money he gets?

Your soon-to-be ex-spouse will have to pay taxes on his share of the benefit. Make sure this is included in the divorce settlement.

198. I was recently given half my ex-

spouse's 401(k) money. When can I get it?

The divorce agreement should specify when you can take the money out of the plan. The agreement may not permit you to take your benefit until your ex-spouse takes his/her benefit. If this point isn't covered by the divorce agreement, you're able to take the benefit on the earliest retirement date provided under your ex-spouse's plan. You'll have to get this date from the employer.

199. We have a couple of participants in our plan who may be getting divorced. I've heard that handling QDROs is tough. I don't want to wait to find out. Where can I get help now?

Properly handling a QDRO is difficult. The potential for trouble is increased by the fact that the parties involved in the divorce usually aren't on good terms. The situation can become even more difficult when the divorce involves a senior executive. One former client, the president of a company, forbid us from providing any information to his wife's attorney, even though we were served a court order requiring us to provide the requested information. We chose to follow the court order.

It's best to establish policies and procedures for your plan in advance. Some employers have a QDRO kit that they give to both parties to help them deal with this issue. This can be very useful because divorce attorneys usually aren't familiar with retirement plans. As a result, it's often impossible for employers to comply with some of the specific terms of QDROs they receive. I recommend getting professional help from an ERISA attorney who has had experience with QDROs. Your service provider should also be able to help. QDRO Consultants Company is one firm that specializes in this field. (Their phone number is 800-527-8481.)

200. I've read that our company can be sued if we pay a benefit to a beneficiary other than a spouse who has been named by a participant. With constant marital changes, how can we be expected to keep track?

It is difficult to keep track of employees' personal lives. For this reason, it's important to remind employees to keep their beneficiary designations up to date. Your company could indeed be sued if it pays benefits to someone other than the employee's spouse without the spouse's consent. The following are some things you can do to reduce your risk:

- require a notary to witness the spousal waiver rather than a company employee
- watch for changes in marital status that may show up elsewhere, such as medical coverage and group life insurance beneficiary changes
- inform all participants about the spousal waiver requirements and remind them to keep their named beneficiaries current at least annually.

I also recommend taking reasonable steps to make certain a deceased employee didn't have a spouse before you pay benefits from the 401(k) or another retirement plan to someone else.

Notes

Reorder Information

ADDITIONAL COPIES (25 OR LESS)
$14.99 plus $5 shipping and handling

Please mail $19.99 payment per book to:

401(k) Association
2150 Dutch Hollow Road
Jersey Shore, PA 17740

BULK PURCHASES
Please contact the Publisher: 401(k) Association

www.401association.com
Email: *tedbenna@penn.com*